DATE DUE

APR 1 0 2008	

Reference Guides in Literature

Jack Salzman, *Editor*

Jacob A. Riis:
A Reference Guide

Lewis Fried
John Fierst

G. K. HALL & CO., 70 LINCOLN STREET, BOSTON, MASS.

Library of Congress Cataloging in Publication Data

Fried, Lewis.
    Jacob A. Riis: a reference guide.

    (Reference guides in literature)
    Includes index.
    1. Riis, Jacob August, 1849-1914--Bibliography.
I.   Fierst, John, joint author.
Z8745.8.F75   (HV28.R54)   016.36250924   76-56804
ISBN 0-8161-7862-3

This publication is printed on permanent/durable acid-free paper
MANUFACTURED IN THE UNITED STATES OF AMERICA

Contents

Introduction vii

Bibliographic Note xix

Writings about Jacob A. Riis, 1899-1975 1

Index 145

Introduction

Perhaps no other figure in American urban history can be more credited with exposing and dramatizing tenement life than Jacob A. Riis. His impact and the popularity of his works are not hard to define. For Riis was an ideologue, extolling his own version of Christian athleticism to an audience at once unfamiliar with pragmatic social theory and somewhat fearful of a seemingly idle, unconstrained lower class. Possessing a Dickensian talent for quickly vivifying a milieu, a character, an event, Riis was able to place the wretched life of the poor in a political context. No longer were the inhabitants of tenements to be seen as a completely shiftless, dangerous class, a teeming refuse that lived, to paraphrase Henry James, at the bottom of a fish-bowl. Riis viewed "the other half" as would-be Americans marking the partial failure of a Christian, democratic process.

The judgments about self and society that informed his first major work, How the Other Half Lives; Studies Among the Tenements of New York (1890), underwent little change in his later writings. This condition not only reflected his growing discomfort with the absorption of an energetic social work by an increasingly theoretical social science but also was consonant with the visible conditions of East Side tenement life; in the two decades that followed How the Other Half Lives, the East Side was not radically transformed. Riis's program could not stop the massive, and successive, waves of immigrants from breaking upon this area; it could not cope with the immigrant's desire, now that he was in the promised city, to desperately cling to the mores and language of a distant country. However, it could spiritually take the child out of the slum; it could aid--in fact, shape--the future American citizen. As a result, Riis's works are all of a piece and based upon four theses:

I. Disorder in social life, the chaos and crime the tenements bred, reflected political injustice. Contractors, builders, and landlords, all eager for high profits; Tammany Hall ward bosses promoting graft, police corruption, and the saloon; and an uninformed citizenry not caring about reform were responsible for the slum.

II. Environment shaped character. A child's will would be de-
formed by local conditions that forced him either into the
back alleys or the sweatshops.

III. The family was the most powerful unit that could promote the
values of concern, love, and community. However, the family
was crumbling under the blows of tenement life: grueling
work, exorbitant rents, unsanitary and often deadly dwellings,
the lure of the dive, the lack of parks and playgrounds.

IV. The school was the best agent to rescue the child. Through
encouragement and development of cooperation, honesty, and
learning, a citizenry could be created that was uninfected by
tenement life.

Each point entails the others, and all demand vigorous personal com-
mitment. In broad outline, this plan reminds us of social philoso-
phies evolved from a radically different heritage, but more
academically known today--those of Mead, Dewey, and Mumford. Yet the
novels of a rapidly urbanized North and mid-West, works such as Studs
Lonigan, An American Tragedy, Never Come Morning, and Knock on Any
Door, recall Riis's early argument that the shaping of selves and the
culture of cities are congruent.

Riis devoted much of his life to the exposition and application
of this program. At times, he lost sight of the differences between
his own struggles and those of the people whom he so passionately
wished to help. Coming from Ribe, Denmark, to New York in 1870, Riis,
at twenty-one, had a trade (carpentry), a knowledge of English (as a
boy he had read Cooper and Dickens), some education (his father was a
school-master), and, most importantly, had not fled his homeland (he
left, in part, because of ill-requited love). His parlous days,
sleeping in police lodging houses, working in New York and Pennsylvania, often strapped for cash and food, were marked by unceasing
energy and determination. His gradual progress from laborer, to
editor of a small Brooklyn paper, to a major police reporter confirmed
his belief that given an indomitable will, a man could rise in America.

The question remains whether Riis could only describe the impov-
erished immigrants with a humane sympathy or understandingly empathize
with them. He despised the Chinese (in his early days of fame, he
cried that they "must go"), had grudging praise of Russian Jews
("Money is their God"), claimed that the Negro accepted menial positions willingly ("his past traditions and natural love of ease perhaps as yet fit him best"), and argued that the Italian not only
adapted to, but also created, the lowest of ways in the slum ("if
allowed to follow his natural bent"). Unfortunate as these state-
ments are, no reformer would so willingly battle for the children of
the tenements: there is no such thing, Riis declaimed, as a bad
boy.

INTRODUCTION

How the Other Half Lives redeemed Riis's vow to consecrate his
pen to the service of his fellow man and God. As a police reporter
with a thorough knowledge of the polyglot East Side (an area that
had the highest population density in the world), Riis had long prac-
tice in writing "human interest" stories, in developing the affective
content of a piece. In this sense, his journalism resembled that of
his colleagues, most notably Lincoln Steffens (who would amusedly
"create" crime waves) and Abraham Cahan, future editor of the Forward
(who would exploit and refine shund reporting).

By no means the first study of New York's urban poor, How the
Other Half Lives achieved its compelling effects through moral exhor-
tation, by direct addresses to the reader, by translating the statistics of poverty into dramatic vignettes, and by pointing out the
urgency of reform. The "Introduction" raised the spectre of future
upheaval; "The Man with the Knife" portrayed a violent, slashing
attack upon the leisured classes; "How the Case Stands" argued that
our government had no defense against the "sea of a mighty population
held in galling fetters," a mass that "heaves uneasily in the
tenements."

No less importantly, the book plays upon the literal and meta-
phorical aspects of darkness. While following Riis on a tour of the
slums, the reader is trapped in blackness, unable to distinguish the
human figures from the landscape of the tenements. He is engulfed by
the chaos of back alleys, rear tenements, and hidden pitfalls when he
turns, with the narrator, the corner from prosperity to poverty.

For Riis's book, true to Dickens' spirit, uncovered an unknown,
exotic world that harbored an almost mysterious, intriguing population that the well-to-do would have heard about but not have seen.
The lower East Side's contiguity with a familiar neighborhood of
property and commerce, its financial and political relationship with
Tammany, its claim upon "Christian" action marked the border between
superstition and enlightenment, corruption and reform.

How, Riis asked, are these people to become Americans? How, and
in what manner, would they adopt the virtues of honesty and redemp-
tion? Under what conditions would their boundless energy become
refined and orderly? Perhaps belying his optimism, Riis claimed that
the "first tenement New York knew bore the mark of Cain from its
birth...."

The book's influence was immense; Riis became an international
figure. James Russell Lowell said that after reading the work "I
felt as Dante must have when he looked over the edge of the abyss."[1]
Ernest Poole remembered how he "hungrily" studied the book, for tenement life struck him "as a tremendous new field, scarcely touched by
American writers...."[2] Theodore Roosevelt, then a Police Commissioner
of New York City, left his calling card on Riis's desk, marking the
beginning of Riis's most important friendship. B. O. Flower, editor

of the Arena, cited Riis's findings in his own study of the tenements, Civilization's Inferno. Stephen Crane heard Riis lecture in New Jersey.

A reviewer for the Christian Union compared How the Other Half Lives to Booth's In Darkest England[3]; the Brooklyn Eagle did the same.[4] The London Morning Post praised Riis's study.[5] The London Saturday Review proclaimed that "We know of no single book, in the enormous and official independent literature on the subject of over-crowding in English cities, that is at all comparable with the vivid, and thorough chronicle of Mr. Riis."[6] The Chicago Times called the work one "of immense shuddering interest."[7] The New York Evening Sun observed that How the Other Half Lives "makes one of the most unique and valuable volumes which has appeared on the dangerous classes of New York."[8] The Silver Cross pointed out that save for Helen Campbell's "'Prisoners of Poverty,' our literature has nothing like" Riis's book.[9] "No book of the year," the Dial stated, "has aroused a deeper interest or wider discussion than Mr. Riis's earnest study of the poor and outcast."[10]

However, Riis's cry for the abolition of the tenement system and his championing of the humanity of "the other half" did not go un-challenged. Amidst wide-spread praise for his book, several writers contested his ideology and hope. A reviewer for the Critic complained that How the Other Half Lives demonstrated "a lack of broad and pene-trative vision, a singularly warped sense of justice at times, and a roughness amounting almost to brutality."[11] A journalist for the Nation argued that "Mr. Riis is not always discreet; he seems to give his assent to the extraordinary proposition that American women who reside in the country ought not to sew upon cheap clothing, because they come into contact with a degraded class of immigrants that choose to herd like pigs in the slums of the Tenth Ward of New York."[12] The Sunday School Times stated that the problem of the poor hinged on their own intransigence, and that congestion in New York was due to its narrow length.[13] While such adverse commentary defined a minor-ity position, it lent strength to anti-immigration efforts. In the North American Review of January, 1891, Henry Cabot Lodge, attacking a liberal American immigration policy, asked his readers to turn to How the Other Half Lives for a "vivid picture" of the "degrading effect of this constant importation of the lowest forms of labor."[14]

The Children of the Poor (1892), Riis's sequel to How the Other Half Lives, underlined the desire to educate (and thereby Americanize) the progeny of the urban, immigrant poor. Through school reform, the establishment of playgrounds, and contact with the countryside and its mores, the tenement child's character would reflect an ordered environment. Riis's praise of pastoral virtues, more powerfully stated in his autobiography, The Making of an American (1901), and in his homage to Ribe, The Old Town (1909), revealed an aesthetic of order consonant with moral experience. His study of children in tene-ments argued that education would eliminate juvenile crime in the city,

and the playgrounds would help the children of the slums perceive,
as he put it in a lecture, "moral relations."[15] In fact, his pas-
sionate advocacy of small parks, recreation areas, fresh air funds,
the kindergarten, and social experiments such as the George Junior
Republic were, in part, responsible for changing the shape and re-
sources of neighborhoods and transforming the concepts of normal
urban childhood.

Riis's later accounts of his war against the tenements, A Ten
Years' War (1900) and The Battle with the Slum (1902)--this last a
somewhat expanded version of the former work--were received by an
audience no longer ignorant of tenement problems. The Tenement House
Committee of 1894, the Small Parks Committee, the Lexow Committee,
the Good Government Clubs, and the rise of a critical realism took a
prophetic timbre from Riis's volumes. He was now a major reformer,
but one in the company of major reformers, and, somewhat sadly, out
of place with more modern theorists such as Lawrence Veiller.

If Riis, now a veteran of lecture tours that spanned the country,
was no longer in the vanguard of contemporary social theory and discovery, he remained a figure that symbolized the humane philanthropy
and spirit of reform characteristic of the 'nineties. The Outlook,
in a review of The Battle with the Slum, credited him with presenting
a vitalized sociology,[16] and DeForest and Veiller pointed out that he
had done "more to educate the general public about tenement-house
reform than any other individual."[17] In The National Cyclopaedia of
American Biography, Riis's life was described as the "greatest moral
lesson in recent years...."[18] In an account of the opening of Roosevelt Gymnasium, Riis's spirit, claimed a journalist, motivated the
Settlement workers.[19] A. E. Winship, writing for the Journal of Education in 1913, the penultimate year of Riis's life, observed that
"behind all the later movements in which Jane Addams, William R.
George, Judge Lindsey, and John E. Gunckel have won international
renown, stands Jacob Riis in his first attack on vicious child labor
conditions in the Hester St. district."[20] Roosevelt had earlier
called him "my ideal" of decent citizenship.[21]

In the year of his death, Riis was eulogized as a tireless,
humane, and pioneering reformer to whom America would be deeply indebted. "No man," the Outlook mourned, "has ever more vitally and
faithfully expressed and interpreted the American Spirit than Jacob
Riis...."[22] The Craftsman lamented that Riis "was a man whom America
could ill have spared in the story of her spiritual progress."[23]
Riis's real service to the public, the New York Times pointed out,
was his "calling the attention of many with more power than himself
to 'the other half' and the way it lived."[24] Jane E. Robbins, in the
Survey, remembered Riis as "the finest immigrant that we have ever
known."[25]

With the passage of time, Riis's life and achievements were
viewed with more critical objectivity. Attention turned to three

broad facets: his relationship with Roosevelt, his ideology, and his contributions to photographic journalism. Moreover, Riis remained an attractive enough figure, representative of the complexities of a unique epoch, to serve as the subject for three biographies.

Riis's adulation of Roosevelt can only be described as hero worship, involving the consequences of apparent naivete, and, perhaps, self-deception. Riis had always been fascinated by large, almost epic characters who possessed a robust courage, honor, and righteous pride. His Theodore Roosevelt the Citizen (1904), a campaign biography, was a rose-colored study; its sentiments, in our own day, appear mawkish, for Riis was not only trapped by the Roosevelt legend but also could be numbered among its creators. The key to Roosevelt's character, as Riis saw it, was a Christian vigor. "In life," Riis quoted, "as in a football game, the principle to follow is: Hit the line hard; don't foul and don't shirk, but hit the line hard." The metaphor and spirit are revealing in themselves. A reviewer for the Bookman (1904) bemusedly wrote that Riis, in this biography, "gives us a frankly enthusiastic appreciation of the god of his idolatry."[26] A writer for the Nation protested that the book "may mark the beginning of a new politico-literary era."[27] Riis's volume "is strenuous, it is loud, it is fervid, it is unmeasured, it is not logical."[28] However, George Gladden saw some merit in Riis's portrait of Roosevelt. "Cold criticism," he pointed out, "has never been a characteristic of the best biographies of living men."[29]

Riis's sustained friendship with Roosevelt, cemented by nighttime excursions in which the reporter led the Police Commissioner through the unsavory districts of New York, should have provided ample opportunities for the growth of dispassionate judgment. It is, perhaps, a credit to Riis's overwhelming good faith that Roosevelt's temporizing, his awareness for concession in the hope of a national career, appeared as moral evenhandedness, or better, a just stand. Roosevelt's refusal to appoint Florence Kelley as Factory Inspector, his failure to understand fully the plight of the laborer, and his reluctance to wage war on trusts might have caused another man to look more guardedly upon his cynosure. Riis never did. As Filler has succinctly put it, it was enough for Riis "who hated politics and did not care to acquaint himself with its realities that Roosevelt spoke vigorous words and got things done."[30]

Riis's uncritical acceptance of the virtues of his youth, and his assumed superiority to the wretched immigrants he encountered, have received the examination they deserve. Francesco Cordasco has argued that Riis was a victim of the prejudices of his time. We cannot understand the Danish reformer if we focus solely on his crude caricature of the immigrant poor and on his concept of Americanization.[31] Yet Riis, as Charles Madison observed, often overlooked the "healthier shoots" in the tenements, and was not able to overcome his racial prejudices.[32] Donald Bigelow has persuasively suggested that Riis's "concern for red-blooded people of 'American stock' was endemic and

to Riis important. Only when the immigrant was thoroughly assimi-
lated could he begin to live properly."[33]

It is not well known that Riis was a pioneering figure in the
history of documentary photography. In his early days as a reporter,
his use of the camera to expose the degrading conditions of tenement
life was limited by available light. With the development of flash-
powder, Riis had a technological edge in his service, and he used it
well. Yet his portraits of slum life, often shocking the reader,
were not thought of as subjects in their own right.

In 1947, at the Museum of the City of New York, Alexander Alland
exhibited prints made from Riis's original glass plates; Alland's
essay, "The Battle with the Slum," was the first to fully explore
Riis's photographic achievements.[34] In a review of the exhibition, a
writer for Hobbies observed that Riis "found the lens, which could
not lie or understate, a mightier weapon than the spoken word, a living proof to supplement the pen."[35] Beaumont Newhall, in The History
of Photography from 1839 to the Present Day, claimed that Riis "choose
unerringly" the camera positions that would best "tell the story."[36]
The Gernsheims, in A Concise History of Photography, spoke of Riis's
"poignant" photographs and compared him to Hine and others who "used
the camera instinctively as an objective commentator on life."[37] In
his recent work, Jacob A. Riis; Photographer & Citizen, Alland points
out that Riis used the camera to record, not create.[38]

Few historians disagree about the nature of Riis's work; fewer
see him as he did not see himself. This may be traced to the success
of his autobiography in which he depicted himself in terms not unlike
those found in his biography of Roosevelt--energetic, dedicated, and
committed to the humane side of an issue. There is a great deal of
truth in this presentation of self, and no one who knew Riis ques-
tioned it. Yet we should remember that The Making of an American,
like Antin's The Promised Land and Bok's The Americanization of
Edward Bok, is in the tradition of affirmative American autobiography,
a genre that interprets the travails of immigrant life as confirma-
tion of American idealism, promises of equality and upward mobility.
Such works are popular and appealing precisely because they reduce
disenchantment, failure, and sorrow to symbolic, unambiguous issues
and events. Analysis of self becomes confused with formulae for
success. As a result, for all the recounting of personal struggle, a
facelessness, a loss of characteristic style occurs. For as these
authors intimate, Americanization demands the eradication of a unique
past that does not comport well with the present.

The first full-length biography of Riis was Louise Ware's Jacob A.
Riis; Police Reporter, Reformer, Useful Citizen (1938). Ware's reli-
ance upon the face value of The Making of an American, "an amazingly
revealing document [that] gives us the best study of his career to
1901,"[39] provided the frame for his portrait. She saw him as a "plain
man" with an exuberant, zestful spirit. His humanity and concern for

the poor, in fact, found an eloquent spokeswoman. If not for her research, the sheer empirical data and surface of Riis's life would have remained partially hidden.

James Lane's Jacob A. Riis and the American City (1974), based on an earlier doctoral dissertation,[40] provided a deeper, and shrewder, analysis of Riis's character. While Lane emphasized Riis's humane philanthropy, his thinking in terms of the individual, his bridging the gap between two Americas, Lane aptly portrayed the difficulties of a man who stressed patriarchal strength in the face of familial rebelliousness. With a bold touch, Lane's picture of Riis uncovers a stubbornness and rigidity of thought underneath a consuming moral purpose.

Edith Meyer's "Not Charity but Justice"; The Story of Jacob A. Riis (1974) takes much of its detail from Riis's own writings. Retelling Riis's struggles, she rightly stresses that he was but one reformer amongst many, but that his voice was probably the most powerful and audible in the demand for change.

In our own time, we take Riis's desire for continued, commonsensical urban reform that satisfies man's rational needs and rights as a "given." We take for granted (though we are often wrong) that urban planning has as its raison d'etre the restoration of the human subject to its rightful place in city history. For Riis's concerns--the creation of an informed, committed public, the growth of free men within a city that reflects its human potential--are contemporary chords in an old score: it is shameful for men to deprive others of dignity.

We are deeply indebted to Professors Jane Benson and Clara Jackson of Kent State University's School of Library Science and to Ms. Ilona Kovacs, Assistant Chief of Technical Services, of the National Széchénye Library in Budapest for providing us with immeasurable assistance. Hazel Young and Susan Rosenberger of Kent State University's library gave us unflagging help. This project could not have succeeded without a grant-in-aid from the Graduate Research Council of Kent State University, and the encouragement of Deans Allan Coogan and Melvyn Feinberg. In our travels from Kent to Washington and New York, we were invaluably aided by Mr. and Mrs. Walter Oliven, Mr. and Mrs. Thomas Magnani, and Mr. and Mrs. Peter J. Valaer. No less importantly, Cornell Capa of the International Center of Photography, Henry J. Alderman of the Institute of Human Relations, the staff at the Cohen Library, the Forty-Second Street Library, and the Library of Congress provided us with needed documentation and information. Mr. and Mrs. E. Halldorsson translated Danish material for us. Very special thanks must be given to Mrs. Sarah Fierst who spent considerable time typing our early draft. Ms. Dana Duzinski and Mr. William Perry put volumes of notes in order; Mr. Thomas Maze, Mr. Gary Bossin, Ms. Najwa Hashem and Ms. Donna Marsel double-checked

INTRODUCTION

our work. Finally, Ms. Wilma Crawford, with patience and grace, typed the manuscript and helped us revise it.

------

[1] James Russell Lowell, quoted in Anon., "Jacob A. Riis, Roosevelt's Ideal Citizen," American Review of Reviews, 50 (July 1914), 97-98 (1914.B14).

[2] Ernest Poole, The Bridge; My Own Story (New York: Macmillan Company, 1940), p. 66 (1940.B4).

[3] Anon., "Darkest New York," Christian Union (approx. November 1890), Scrpbk. p. 4 (1890.B3).

[4] Anon., "Booth and Riis," Brooklyn Eagle (21 November 1890), Scrpbk. p. 5 (1890.B2).

[5] Anon., "How the Other Half Lives," London Morning Post (3 June 1891), Scrpbk. pp. [16-20] (1891.B17).

[6] Anon., "New York Tenements," London Saturday Review (12 December 1891), Scrpbk. pp. [16-20] (1891.B29).

[7] Anon., "Literary Brevities," Chicago Times (20 December 1890), Scrpbk. p. 5 (1890.B15).

[8] Anon., "How the Other Half Lives," New York Evening Sun (18 November 1890), Scrpbk. p. 5 (1890.B10).

[9] Anon., "Book Notices," Silver Cross (approx. February 1891), Scrpbk. p. 22 (1891.B2).

[10] Anon., "Charles Scribner's Son's New Books," Dial, 11 (April 1891), 364 (1891.B4).

[11] Anon., "Literature," Critic, 17 (27 December 1890), 332 (1890.B16).

[12] Anon., "How the Other Half Lives," Nation, 52 (5 February 1891), 121 (1891.B18).

[13] Anon., No heading found, Sunday School Times (17 January 1891), Scrpbk. p. 15 (1891.B49).

[14] Henry Cabot Lodge, "The Restriction of Immigration," North American Review, 152 (January 1891), 27-36 (1891.B72).

[15] Anon., "Children of the Tenements," New York Mail and Express (29 March 1895), Scrpbk. p. 85 (1895.B4).

[16] Anon., "Books of the Week," Outlook, 73 (3 January 1903), 89-90 (1903.B5).

[17] Robert W. DeForest and Lawrence Veiller, eds., The Tenement House Problem, 2 vols. (New York: Macmillan Company, 1903), Vol. 1, p. 105 (1903.B24).

[18] Anon., "Riis, Jacob August," National Cyclopaedia of American Biography, 13 (New York: James T. White & Company, 1906), 114-15 (1906.B5).

[19] Paul U. Kellogg, "What Jacob Riis and a Thousand Boys Are Up To: The Opening of the Roosevelt Gymnasium on Henry Street This Week," Charities and the Commons, 17 (No date given, 1907), 167-70 (1907.B4).

[20] A. E. Winship, "Roxy and Timon of Hester St.," Journal of Education, 77 (12 June 1913), 652-54 (1913.B4).

[21] Anon., "Riis Is Called 'My Ideal Man' by Roosevelt," New York News (8 September 1903), Scrpbk. pp. [197-end] (1903.B18).

[22] Anon., "A Great Hearted American," Outlook, 107 (6 June 1914), 267 (1914.B5).

[23] Anon., "Jacob A. Riis: Friend of the American People," Craftsman, 26 (July 1914), 459-61 (1914.B14).

[24] Anon., "Jacob Riis and His Work," New York Times (28 May 1914), p. 12 (1914.B17).

[25] Jane E. Robbins, "A Maker of Americans," Survey, 32 (6 June 1914), 285-86 (1914.B41).

[26] Anon., "President Roosevelt," Bookman, 26 (June 1904), 100-101 (1904.B10).

[27] Anon., "Theodore Roosevelt the Citizen," Nation, 79 (8 September 1904), 204-5 (1904.B15).

[28] Op. cit. (1904.B15).

[29] George Gladden, "Theodore Roosevelt. Two New Books," Current Literature, 36 (April 1904), 390-97 (1904.B17).

[30] Louis Filler, Crusaders for American Liberalism; The Story of the Muckrakers (New York: Harcourt, Brace & Company, 1939), pp. 45-46 (1939.B3).

[31] Francesco Cordasco, "Introduction," Jacob Riis Revisited; Poverty and the Slum in Another Era (New York: Doubleday and Company, 1968), p. xxi (1968.B2).

[32] Charles A. Madison, "Preface," How the Other Half Lives, by Jacob A. Riis (New York: Dover, 1971), p. vii (1971.B7).

[33] Donald Bigelow, "Introduction," How the Other Half Lives, by Jacob A. Riis (New York: Hill & Wang, 1957), p. xiii (1957.B1).

[34] Alexander Alland et al., "'The Battle with the Slum' 1887-1897." U. S. Camera 1948, ed. Tom Maloney (New York: U. S. Camera Publishers, 1947), pp. 11-18, 345, 346 (1947.B1).

[35] Anon., "The Battle with the Slum," Hobbies, 52 (September 1947), 21 (1947.B2).

INTRODUCTION

[36] Beaumont Newhall, The History of Photography, from 1839 to the Present Day (New York: Museum of Modern Art, 1964), pp. 139–40 (1964.B2).

[37] Helmut Gernsheim and Alison Gernsheim, A Concise History of Photography (New York: Grosset & Dunlap, 1965), pp. 148, 190 (1965.B6).

[38] See Alexander Alland, Jacob A. Riis; Photographer & Citizen (Millerton, New York: Aperture, 1974) (1974.A1).

[39] Louise Ware, "Author's Note," Jacob A. Riis; Police Reporter, Reformer, Useful Citizen (New York: D. Appleton-Century Company, 1938), p. xvii (1938.A1).

[40] James B. Lane, "Bridge to the Other Half: The Life and Urban Reform Work of Jacob A. Riis" (Ph.D. diss., University of Maryland, 1970) (1970.A1).

Bibliographic Note

All Riis scholars are deeply indebted to the Library of Congress,
which, in twelve manuscript boxes, houses the bulk of Riis's papers.
We have worked from the catalogued, identifiable, and ordered bulk
of this collection. A number of entries for this reference guide
have been selected from the scrapbooks placed in boxes 9 and 10.
Magazine and newspaper articles, probably gathered by a press clipping service, fill the scrapbook placed in box 10 and make it the
most comprehensive secondary source treating Riis's life. It is
likely Riis provided the titles, sources, and dates written at the
top of each clipping mounted in the scrapbooks. Because most entries
are taken from the scrapbook placed in box 10, it is referred to as
Scrpbk. in the reference guide. The scrapbook in box 9 is Scrpbk. 2.
Because some of the scrapbook pages are unnumbered, entries selected
from unnumbered pages are identified by the page numbers, enclosed in
brackets, of the last numbered scrapbook page previous to the entry
and the first numbered page following the entry. Riis sometimes made
notes in the margins of the scrapbooks. Where pertinent, these notes
have been transcribed in the reference guide. All books are entered
under year of copyright in conformity with Library of Congress
specifications.

Writings about Jacob A. Riis, 1889-1975

1889 A BOOKS - NONE

1889 B SHORTER WRITINGS

1 ANON. "Flowers for Poor Children," New York Times
       (14 January), p. 9.
          Riis appeals to public for flowers to be given to poor
       children.

2 ANON. "How the Other Half Lives," Waterbury Daily Republican
       (30 November). Scrpbk. 2, p. 102.
          Riis's "How the Other Half Lives," in Scribner's Maga-
       zine, "alarmingly set[s] forth" the horrors of New York's
       tenements.

3 ANON. No heading found, Evangelist (5 December). Scrpbk. 2,
       p. 102.
          Riis's paper for Scribner's Magazine, "How the Other Half
       Lives," is a "sadly truthful account."

4 ANON. No heading found, London Morning Advertiser
       (13 December). Scrpbk. 2, p. 107.
          Riis's descriptions of the New York slums are recounted.
       The writer of this report "on poor quarters" is "Mr. Jacob
       Rus, of the principal police court in that city...."
       Riis's photographs confirm the veracity of his account.

5 ANON. No heading found, New York Evening Post (6 December).
       Scrpbk. 2, p. 102.
          Announcement that Scribner's has an interesting paper
       [by Riis] "on the poor of this city, with illustrations
       that recall the aspects of European poverty."

1890 A BOOKS - NONE

1890

1890 B SHORTER WRITINGS

1   ANON.   "Ambitious King's Daughters," New York Herald
    (22 November). Scrpbk. p. 9.
       Report on the annual public meeting of the King's
    Daughters and Sons held November twenty-first.
    Mrs. Margaret Bottoms, Mrs. Isabella Davis, "Y. A. Riis,
    and several others" made addresses.

2   ANON.   "Booth and Riis," Brooklyn Eagle (21 November).
    Scrpbk. p. 5.
       Riis's How the Other Half Lives "does for darkest New
    York" what Gen. Booth's In Darkest England "does for
    London slums."

3   ANON.   "Darkest New York," Christian Union (approx. November).
    Scrpbk. p. 4.
       Darkest England as described by Booth, and darkest New
    York as described by Riis portend disaster. The "future
    safety" of this nation "depends on our ability to drain
    the morasses of poverty and crime which are to be found
    in almost all our great cities."

4   ANON.   "Dr. Adler on Poverty," New York Tribune
    (22 December). Scrpbk. p. 7.
       Adler spoke at Chickering Hall on "What Should Be Done
    for the Poor." That people are "awaiting light" upon the
    problem of the poor has created interest in books like
    "Riis's 'How the Other Half Lives,'" he suggested.

5   ANON.   "How the Other Half Lives," Boston Post (26 December).
    Scrpbk. p. 15.
       How the Other Half Lives deserves to be studied and Riis
    "deserves the thanks of Christendom for his services in
    the cause of humanity."

6   ANON.   "How the Other Half Lives," Boston Times (30 November).
    Scrpbk. p. 15.
       How the Other Half Lives is "a commanding invitation to
    the thick of the battle against social injustice."

7   ANON.   "How the Other Half Lives," Christian Intelligencer
    (24 December). Scrpbk. p. 8.
       Reproves those who allow to exist "within a stone's cast
    of the chief business thoroughfares...such masses of for-
    lorn humanity, housed and huddled together after the manner
    described by Mr. Riis." Books like How the Other Half
    Lives not only "lift the curtains, and expose to public

gaze the great evils of the [tenement house] system" but "hasten the day of reform."

8   ANON.   "How the Other Half Lives. A Glimpse at Darkest New York," Christian Union (27 November), pp. 706-7. Scrpbk. pp. 2-3.
        Commends Riis's book to all Christian Union readers. Also quotes Riis as saying he learned English by reading Dickens and that he admired James Fenimore Cooper.

9   ANON.   "How the Other Half Lives," Mail and Express (approx. December). Scrpbk. p. 15.
        Quick examination of Riis's life in the United States. Relates such incidents as the time Riis slept in a grave-yard and the time he was forced to go hungry for three days. Includes a drawing of Riis.

10 ANON.   "How the Other Half Lives," New York Evening Sun (18 November). Scrpbk. p. 5.
        How the Other Half Lives "makes one of the most unique and valuable volumes which has appeared on the dangerous classes of New York."

11 ANON.   "How the Other Half Lives," New York Evening Sun (13 December). Scrpbk. p. 13.
        Announcement of Riis's essay on tenement poor in Evening Sun. After reading the article, if a man does not desire to help the poor at this season, he will be "very unusual... and also a human hog."

12 ANON.   "How the Other Half Lives," San Francisco Chronicle (7 December). Scrpbk. p. 14.
        How the Other Half Lives "ought to do much good in arousing public sentiment against the worst evil of the chief American city."

13 ANON.   "'How the Other Half Lives,'" Zion's Herald (24 December). Scrpbk. p. 10.
        Works like How the Other Half Lives are "necessary in order to awaken Christendom to an intelligent apprehension of actual [slum] conditions."

14 ANON.   "In the World of Literature," New York Press (23 November). Scrpbk. p. 4.
        How the Other Half Lives describes "the exact status of the wretched inhabitants of our tenement houses."

1890

15   ANON.   "Literary Brevities," Chicago Times (20 December).
        Scrpbk. p. 5.
            How the Other Half Lives, "a book of immense shuddering
        interest," outlines "what organized society--that is,
        about one fourth or less of the whole--has to expect from
        the other three fourths...."

16   ANON.   "Literature," Critic, 17 (27 December), 332.
            How the Other Half Lives demonstrates "a lack of broad
        and penetrative vision, a singularly warped sense of jus-
        tice at times, and a roughness amounting almost to
        brutality."

17   ANON.   "New Literature," Brooklyn Times (29 November).
        Scrpbk. pp. 6-7.
            How the Other Half Lives is "simply offering, in
        rigorous, humane, and fascinating narrative, the plain
        lineaments of truth" about the slums.

18   ANON.   No heading found, Argonaut (30 March). Scrpbk. p. 13.
            In How the Other Half Lives Riis "writes of the pitiful
        sights he sees...with the feeling of one who is deeply
        moved by compassion...."

*19   ANON.   No heading found, Boston Budget and Beacon
        (23 November). Scrpbk. p. 13.

20   ANON.   No heading found, Boston Gazette (22 November).
        Scrpbk. p. 13.
            How the Other Half Lives tells "the sad story of the
        poorest of the poor."

21   ANON.   No heading found, Boston Journal (29 November).
        Scrpbk. p. 6.
            How the other Half Lives will "convince and awaken the
        reader to anxious attention."

22   ANON.   No heading found, Buffalo Express (7 December).
        Scrpbk. p. 15.
            Riis seen as a sympathetic observer of tenement life,
        and "all who read his book" as "better equipped for the
        advocacy of practical reforms, intelligent legislation,
        and a just enforcement of the law."

23   ANON.   No heading found, Cambridge Tribune (20 December).
        Scrpbk. p. 15.
            How the Other Half Lives reveals "that our boastful
        Western civilization, on its own fresh, broad continent,

has not been able to grow without the festering sores that
corrupt older communities."

24   ANON.   No heading found, Chicago Inter-Ocean (13 December).
     Scrpbk. p. 22.
        Interest manifested by the public in How the Other Half
     Lives is a good sign of the time. Picture Riis draws of
     New York is "truthful," and his suggestions are "wise and
     practical."

25   ANON.   No heading found, Christian at Work (25 December).
     Scrpbk. p. 13.
        How the Other Half Lives "is dark enough to send a chill
     to any heart."

26   ANON.   No heading found, Christian Inquirer (4 December).
     Scrpbk. p. 8.
        Early years Riis spent in America summarized. Riis's
     "upward course has proved the possibilities open [in this
     country] to a young man with an earnest purpose." Readers
     of How the Other Half Lives "will certainly find out how
     to dispense their charities more discriminately and
     usefully."

27   ANON.   No heading found, Cleveland Leader (21 December).
     Scrpbk. p. 10.
        How the Other Half Lives will cause the public "to hold
     before its mind as a companion picture [to the luxury and
     grandeur of metropolitan life] 'the other half.'"

28   ANON.   No heading found, Detroit Journal (31 January).
     Scrpbk. p. 14.
        Views given of tenements [in How the Other Half Lives]
     are appalling, though the author's style is "diffuse and
     at times overflowing."

29   ANON.   No heading found, Hartford Courant (16 December).
     Scrpbk. p. 15.
        How the Other Half Lives presents "facts to be faced and
     fought against, else is our Christianity a pretext and a
     lie...."

30   ANON.   No heading found, Home Journal (24 December).
     Scrpbk. p. 7.
        Facts of tenement life presented in How the Other Half
     Lives should be looked at "dispassionately, and from an
     unprejudiced standpoint." Property owners, because they
     are only partly responsible for the tenement house evil,
     should not be denounced.

1890

31   ANON. No heading found, Indianapolis News (24 December).
      Scrpbk. pp. [16-20].
         Riis "has gone systematically to work; not 'slumming it,'
      or with mere curiosity, but with kindly heart, and pencil,
      and 'kodak.'" How the Other Half Lives is "one of the
      sociological studies which characterize this age and time."

32   ANON. No heading found, Mail and Express (20 December).
      Scrpbk. p. 6.
         How the Other Half Lives, a "valuable and suggestive
      book," commended "heartily" to all Mail and Express
      readers.

33   ANON. No heading found, Morning News (22 November).
      Scrpbk. p. 7.
         Riis shows in How the Other Half Lives "how closely
      connected this system [the tenement system] is with the
      vice, crime and poverty of the metropolis."

34   ANON. No heading found, New York Herald (23 November).
      Scrpbk. p. 5.
         How the Other Half Lives warns that "the influence, as
      a whole, of living without sufficient room, light, air,
      water, and privacy...is dangerous to the society of today
      and the future."

35   ANON. No heading found, New York Sun (December). Scrpbk.
      p. 7.
         How the Other Half Lives is "a mine of information
      regarding the ways of life of the very poor in this city."

36   ANON. No heading found, Newark Daily Advertiser
      (27 December). Scrpbk. p. 14.
         How the Other Half Lives "awakens thoughts of surprise
      and horror."

37   ANON. No heading found, Pittsburgh Chronicle Telegraph
      (26 November). Scrpbk. p. 15.
         A short, complimentary review of How the Other Half
      Lives.

38   ANON. No heading found, Pittsburgh Times (27 December).
      Scrpbk. p. 15.
         Riis's book is "a big step...to make known how it [the
      other half] lives."

39   ANON. No heading found, Portland Advertiser (20 November).
      Scrpbk. p. 13.

How the Other Half Lives recommends itself to those interested "in the reformation of the criminal classes" and to the general reader interested in facts, incidents and illustrations of the life of the poor.

40   ANON.   No heading found, Presbyterian (approx. December). Scrpbk. p. 14.
     Riis in How the Other Half Lives takes "a serious and intelligent look into the condition of the degraded and poverty stricken masses of our own land."

41   ANON.   No heading found, Public Opinion (13 December). Scrpbk. p. 7.
     How the Other Half Lives "is a powerful book. The thinking world had best heed the warning it sounds." It demonstrates the causes of the tenement problem are three: the mere pittance paid to working people, avarice of the wealthy class, and the apathy of the poor.

42   ANON.   No heading found, Silver Cross (January). Scrpbk. 2, p. 104.
     Report of Riis's address to the King's Daughters on November 25. Riis spoke about the importance of a "Flower Mission."

43   ANON.   No heading found, Springfield Daily Union (31 December). Scrpbk. p. 15.
     Review of How the Other Half Lives. Blames the tenement system for crimes in the city. "It is to this pernicious system that at least 80 per cent of the crimes of a great city may be credited."

44   ANON.   No heading found, St. Louis Republic (22 November). Scrpbk. p. 14.
     How the Other Half Lives shows Riis is a defeatist who feels "the tenements will exist in New York forever."

45   ANON.   No heading found, Time Nationalist (29 November). Scrpbk. p. 6.
     "All honor is due [Riis] a man who [in How the Other Half Lives] dares strike such sturdy blows for our honest poor."

46   ANON.   "The Poor and Their Homes," Congregationalist (25 December). Scrpbk. p. 22.
     The success of How the Other Half Lives demonstrates that "attention already has been directed sucessfully to the condition and needs of the poor" and that the public "now chiefly requires to be shown the best manner of reforming what is amiss."

1890

47   ANON. "The Problem of Destitution," New York <u>Sun</u>
       (22 December). Scrpbk. p. 7.
         <u>Sun</u>'s coverage of Adler's speech at Chickering Hall.
       Points out how Adler made use of Riis's statistics.

48   ANON. "The Seamy Side," <u>New York Tribune</u> (25 November), p. 8.
       Scrpbk. p. 4.
         "Only a cynic can lay it [<u>How the Other Half Lives</u>]
       down without falling into serious reflection upon the
       grave questions it raises...." The troubles of the poor
       are many, from the exploitation of women laborers to prof-
       iteering landlords. Tenements as they stand destroy the
       family. The New York tenement should be improved, its
       bad features amended.

49   ANON. "The Two Halves of Society," <u>Chicago Tribune</u>
       (13 December). Scrpbk. p. 14.
         <u>How the Other Half Lives</u> proves drink more than eco-
       nomics underlies the misery of the slums.

50   ANON. "A Wicked Four Hundred," <u>Brooklyn Times</u> (15 December).
       Scrpbk. p. 9.
         Rev. J. Coleman Adams in a lecture entitled "The Four
       Hundred and the Other Half" compared two books, <u>Society
       As I Have Found It</u> and <u>How the Other Half Lives</u>. The
       first, about the "best society" in America, he found
       bombastic, snobbish, and pernicious. Riis's book he
       called "remarkable."

51   F., J. "Darkest New York," <u>Churchman</u> (18 December).
       Scrpbk. pp. 20-21.
         An account of Riis's early life in America that argues,
       "After such experience, personal and professional, he
       ought to know, and undoubtedly does know, as much about
       the dark spots of New York as any man in the city." Sum-
       marizes Riis's thoughts on the tenements as he expressed
       them in <u>How the Other Half Lives</u>.

<u>1891 A BOOKS - NONE</u>

<u>1891 B SHORTER WRITINGS</u>

1   ANON. "Book Notices," <u>Silver Cross</u> (January). Scrpbk. p. 22.
       <u>How the Other Half Lives</u> "is one long story, full of
       pathos, and yet so terse, and strong, and sensible, that
       it is like a living, pitying soul going forth to make it-
       self felt in behalf of all suffering souls everywhere."

2   ANON.   "Book Notices," <u>Silver Cross</u> (approx. February).
        Scrpbk. p. 22.
        "Leaving out Helen Campbell's 'Prisoners of Poverty,'
        our literature has nothing like it [<u>How the Other Half
        Lives</u>]."

3   ANON.   "Books about Four Great Cities," <u>Cosmopolitan Maga-
        zine</u> (November), p. 510. Scrpbk. p. 24.
        <u>How the Other Half Lives</u> should be read at once by
        "every dweller in New York, not to say every inhabitant
        of any great city," since it presents facts enabling
        "those of us who have ten dollars in our pockets to under-
        stand better the lives of the poor devils to whom ten
        cents is a mighty sum."

4   ANON.   "Charles Scribner's Son's New Books," <u>Dial</u>, 11 (April),
        364.
        <u>How the Other Half Lives</u>, "Mr. Riis's earnest study of
        the poor and outcast," has aroused as much interest and
        wide discussion as any book this year.

5   ANON.   "The Chautauqua Press Club," <u>Chautauqua Assembly
        Herald</u> (22 July). Scrpbk. p. 27.
        Riis spoke at a "delightful reception," given by the
        Press Club, "which was attended by many of the best
        Chautauquans."

6   ANON.   "Christian at Work," no journal given (August).
        Scrpbk. 2, p. 129.
        Riis is commended for focusing public attention on the
        failure of city authorities to provide parks for the poor.

7   ANON.   "Discussing Some Social Problems," <u>New York Tribune</u>
        (19 January). Scrpbk. p. 31.
        Before the Union Seminary Alumni Club, Riis "arraigned
        the Church for its neglect of the poor, many of whom live
        in filthy tenement-houses owned by rich church corpora-
        tions or by wealthy church members."

8   ANON.   "Editorial Notes," <u>Arena</u>, 3 (February), 375-84.
        Terms <u>How the Other Half Lives</u> a "valuable work" and
        says, "The pathos of some of these simple narrations
        eclipses the finest touches of the masters in fiction."

9   ANON.   "Feeding Her Audience," <u>New York Tribune</u> (23 July).
        Scrpbk. p. 27.
        "Jacob A. Riis surprised Chautauquans last night by tel-
        ling them 'How the Other Half Lives' in the metropolis."

1891

Mrs. Emma Ewing afterwards told them how badly both sides of society cook and eat.

10   ANON.   "Filled with Misery," New Haven Palladium (20 July). Scrpbk. p. 28.
       Riis lectured at Calvary Baptist Church, making "a most profound impression upon those present."

11   ANON.   "Fruit of the Slums," Jamestown Journal (23 July). Scrpbk. p. 27.
       Speaking at Chautauqua, Riis expressed his wish that more of the money spent on foreign missions be spent "in uplifting our home heathen."

12 . ANON.   "Horrors of the Sweat Shop," Boston Herald (8 May). Scrpbk. p. 30.
       Riis "described the manufacture of clothing in Gotham's tenement houses," in his Huntington Hall address.

13   ANON.   "How the Other Half Live," Boston Herald (9 April). Scrpbk. p. 29.
       Speaking of alcoholism, Riis told the Unitarian Club of Boston that destitution was its cause, not alcoholism the cause of destitution.

14   ANON.   "How the Other Half Lives," Boston Advertiser (9 April). Scrpbk. p. 29.
       Coverage of Riis's lecture at the Vendome. Lists topics-- East Side tenements, Bottle Alley, etc.--on which Riis spoke.

15   ANON.   "How the Other Half Lives," Boston Post (10 April). Scrpbk. p. 29.
       Answers to the problems Riis outlined in his April 18 lecture on the slums are not easy to find; the problems "cannot be met off-hand by blaming those who own or manage the houses which are so overcrowded, nor by having such houses torn down or forced to receive fewer occupants."

16   ANON.   "How the Other Half Lives," Chautauqua Assembly Herald (22 July). Scrpbk. p. 27.
       Another review of the illustrated lecture on the slums Riis delivered in the Chautauqua Amphitheater: "Mr. Riis is master of his subject and held it up in many lights, frequently making keen thrusts toward high places in revealing the causes of the evils he described."

17   ANON.   "How the Other Half Lives," London Morning Post
       (3 June). Scrpbk. pp. [16-20].
         In How the Other Half Lives Riis "speaks out, and is to
       be congratulated" for his large share of "moral courage."

18   ANON.   "How the Other Half Lives," Nation, 52 (5 February),
       121.
         How the Other Half Lives exhibits two tendencies of the
       age: "the disposition to study the pathology of society"
       and "the propensity to regard social therapeutics as con-
       sisting in a change of material conditions." The reviewer
       argues Riis is not "always discreet; he seems to give his
       assent to the extraordinary proposition that American wo-
       men who reside in the country ought not to sew upon cheap
       clothing, because they come into contact with a degraded
       class of immigrants that choose to herd like pigs in the
       slums of the Tenth Ward of New York." [Same review
       appears in the New York Evening Post, February 14, 1891.
       See 1891.B43.]

19   ANON.   "How the Other Half Lives," New Haven Journal-Courier
       (20 July). Scrpbk. p. 28.
         Riis delivered his "How the Other Half Lives" lecture
       in the Calvary Baptist Church. At one point he "spoke in
       praise of the late Mrs. Astor's habit of sending every
       Christmas 100 boys, taken from the street, to comfortable
       homes in the west."

20   ANON.   "How the Other Half Lives," illegible source
       (21 February). Scrpbk. p. 24.
         "The camera of Mr. Jacob A. Riis, of this city...has
       been put to a noble use" in How the Other Half Lives. All
       Riis's "descriptive powers" are not so meaningful as his
       photographs.

21   ANON.   "How the Other Half Lives," War-Cry (3 January),
       pp. 1-3. Scrpbk. pp. 11-13.
         Riis's story "What the December Sun Saw in New York on
       One Day's Brief Journey" describes the slum districts
       where the Salvation Army labors, and is reprinted here in
       the Army's official paper.

22   ANON.   "Its Horrors Revealed," Boston Daily Globe (8 May).
       Scrpbk. p. 30.
         Riis argued at the General Conference of Charities that
       the "sweaters" were destroying the clothing business.

1891

23   ANON.   "Jacob A. Riis," Book Buyer, 7 (January), 658–59.
         Riis gave this account of his first years in America to
     a representative of the Christian Union. He tells how
     his dog had a fit one night in front of a police station
     and how a policeman clubbed it out of its misery. Later,
     in The Making of an American, he changes this story,
     claiming the policeman maliciously slammed the dog against
     the front steps of the station.

24   ANON.   "Literature Today," Chicago Herald (10 January).
     Scrpbk. p. 9.
         How the Other Half Lives "is a thoughtful and timely
     book, to be alike studied by philanthropists and
     landlords."

25   ANON.   "The Lounger," Critic (17 January), pp. 31-32.
         A short description of Riis who had won popularity
     recently for his How the Other Half Lives. Quotes Riis
     on the pronunciation of his name: "'it is as if written
     Rees. I am the last of that name, of a dozen brothers,
     and I will never change the spelling of it as has been
     suggested, for it is an honorable name.'"

26   ANON.   "Matters We Ought to Know," New York Times
     (4 January), p. 19.
         Review of How the Other Half Lives. Poses the question:
     "Does it [the upper half] care?" Follows with an histor-
     ical sketch of the growth of tenements in the U.S. Closes
     with these suggestions to help the other half: improve
     their morals and permit them in time to save money.

27   ANON.   "Mr. Riis Tells the Other Half," Chautauqua Assembly
     Herald (23 July). Scrpbk. p. 27.
         Under this heading are arranged five separate articles:
     one lists Riis as one of the "many lecturers new to the
     Chautauqua platform"; two are questions directed to the
     readers about the effectiveness of Riis's lecture and
     about "his arguments in favor of restricted immigration";
     a fourth reviews Riis's life, and a fifth reviews his
     lecture, calling it a "scathing and blistering criticism
     on our civilization."

28   ANON.   "New York and London Contrasted," New York Evening
     Sun (30 March). Scrpbk. p. 21.
         Reprint of London Daily News review of How the Other
     Half Lives. States social evils which generate slums are
     the same in London, New York, Paris, and Berlin.

29   ANON.   "New York Tenements," London <u>Saturday Review</u>
         (12 December). Scrpbk. pp. [16-20].
         A comparison of London slums to New York slums, touched
         off by the publication in England of <u>How the Other Half</u>
         <u>Lives</u>: "We know of no single book, in the enormous offi-
         cial and independent literature on the subject of over-
         crowding in English cities, that is at all comparable with
         the vivid and thorough chronicle of Mr. Riis."

30   ANON.   No heading found, <u>Boston Evening Record</u> (13 April).
         Scrpbk. p. 29.
         A reply to Gen. Booth's statement that New York is on
         the same dark road as London: "Mr. Booth is a little
         late," since "The word and pen pictures of Jacob Riis of
         the New York Sun have said this in stronger language."

31   ANON.   No heading found, <u>Boston Evening Transcript</u>
         (10 April). Scrpbk. p. 29.
         Having presented a lecture, illustrated with stere-
         optican slides, to the Unitarian Club of Boston, Riis
         concluded: "these scenes in a so-called Christian land
         are calling for a new Martin Luther."

32   ANON.   No heading found, <u>Brooklyn Times</u> (9 May). Scrpbk.
         p. 13.
         Asked if he planned to write another book after the
         success of <u>How the Other Half Lives</u>, Riis replied he did
         not believe in following his book with another on the basis
         of assumed demand.

33   ANON.   No heading found, <u>Chicago Tribune</u> (24 January).
         Scrpbk. p. 10.
         Short biographical sketch of Riis.

34   ANON.   No heading found, <u>Christian at Work</u> (approx. January).
         Scrpbk. p. 21.
         <u>How the Other Half Lives</u> was written "with the distinct
         view of stirring up Christian men and women to greater
         activity in the work of rescuing the fallen and lifting up
         poor and degraded humanity."

35   ANON.   No heading found, Coventry, England <u>Mercury</u>
         (13 January). Scrpbk. p. 14.
         Of all the facts about the seamy side of New York given
         in <u>How the Other Half Lives</u> the worst is that ten percent
         of New York's population go to a "pauper's grave."

1891

36   ANON.   No heading found, <u>Evangelist</u> (15 January).
      Scrpbk. p. 21.
         "Such study has never before been made with anything at
      all approaching to the thoroughness and insight" of <u>How</u>
      <u>the Other Half Lives</u>. This book shows how the tenement
      homes of the poor breed the misery found in the slums.

37   ANON.   No heading found, <u>London Daily News</u> (approx. February).
      Scrpbk. p. 24.
         Sees great danger for the United States in "the positive
      lust of the good things of life that prevails among all
      classes, 'since' nobody accepts poverty as a condition."
      States Riis dreads the thought of what might happen when
      the population of immigrant poor in the U.S. doubles.

38   ANON.   No heading found, <u>Milwaukee Sentinel</u> (4 January).
      Scrpbk. p. 14.
         The story of Riis's life, followed by a short review of
      <u>How the Other Half Lives</u>. Feels the book should be read
      by those who have the power to change the situation in the
      tenements.

39   ANON.   No heading found, <u>Minneapolis Tribune</u> (4 January).
      Scrpbk. p. 15.
         <u>How the Other Half Lives</u> not only portrays "the New York
      underworld," but is "a helpful and critical consideration
      of the forces therein at work, and the best means of coun-
      teracting them."

40   ANON.   No heading found, <u>New England Magazine</u> (June).
      Scrpbk. p. 24.
         <u>How the Other Half Lives</u> is "one of the strongest
      arraignments of our so-called civilization in the New
      World, which has yet appeared...." It proves that "Human
      nature adjusts itself to its environment, and we are all
      responsible when we permit that environment to be that of
      the Five Points and the Bowery."

41   ANON.   No heading found, New York <u>Commercial Advertiser</u>
      (28 January). Scrpbk. p. 15.
         A response to a statement the White Cross societies
      issued about the indifference of women wage earners toward
      virtue. Editor agrees with Riis's statement: "to the
      everlasting credit of New York's working girl let it be
      said that, rough though her road may be, all but hopeless
      her battle with life, only in the rarest instances does
      she go astray."

42   ANON.   No heading found, <u>New York Critic</u> (7 March).
        Scrpbk. pp. [16-20].
          Riis's description of New York's slums in <u>How the Other</u>
    <u>Half Lives</u> "takes everybody by surprise" in London.

43   ANON.   No heading found, New York <u>Evening Post</u> (14 February).
        Scrpbk. p. 22.
          <u>How the Other Half Lives</u> exhibits two tendencies of the
    age: "the disposition to study the pathology of society,"
    and "the propensity to regard social therapeutics as con-
    sisting in a change of material conditions." [Same review
    appears in the February 15, 1891, issue of <u>The Nation</u>.
    See 1891.B18.]

44   ANON.   No heading found, New York <u>World</u> (5 May).
        Scrpbk. p. 22.
          "'How the Other Half Live' has suggested the title for
    a series of papers in the English Illustrated Magazine."

45   ANON.   No heading found, <u>Silver Cross</u> (February).
        Scrpbk. p. 22.
          <u>How the Other Half Lives</u> is an "awakener of thought and
    a disseminator of light."

46   ANON.   No heading found, <u>Silver Cross</u> (February).
        Scrpbk. p. 22.
          The King's Daughters request aid from all those who,
    "like Jacob Riis," wish to promote the work of their
    Tenement-House Committee.

47   ANON.   No heading found, <u>Silver Cross</u> (August or September).
        Scrpbk. 2, p. 133.
          Riis's speech at Ocean Grove is reported. Riis's book
    ought to be read by every member of the Order [the King's
    Daughters].

48   ANON.   No heading found, <u>Spirit</u> (February). Scrpbk. p. 13.
        <u>How the Other Half Lives</u>, which should remind New York
    Christians of the Sermon on the Mount, has had an enormous
    sale.

49   ANON.   No heading found, <u>Sunday School Times</u> (17 January).
        Scrpbk. p. 15.
          Unfavorable review of <u>How the Other Half Lives</u>. Contends
    that much of the problem of the poor hinges on their own
    intransigence and that congestion in New York is due to the
    narrow length of the city.

1891

50   ANON.   No heading found, <u>Times-Democrat</u> (1 November).
      Scrpbk. pp. [16-20].
         "If some fiction writer of genius had gathered the
      material contained in Jacob Riis' remarkable book, 'How
      the Other Half Lives,' he might have made a wonderful
      novel out of it."

51   ANON.   No heading found, <u>Working Woman</u> (5 January).
      Scrpbk. p. 10.
         All thinking men and women in this country should have
      in their libraries a copy of <u>How the Other Half Lives</u>,
      which shows "how the tenement house system creates mil-
      lionaire landlords."

52   ANON.   "The 'Other Half's' Champion," <u>Brooklyn Times</u>
      (14 March). Scrpbk. p. 9.
         Riis is "one of the quietest and unassuming men in New
      York," and <u>How the Other Half Lives</u> is one of the best
      books of the season "not only in manner but in matter."

53   ANON.   "Remedies for 'Sweating,'" <u>Boston Traveller</u> (8 May).
      Scrpbk. p. 30.
         Riis, at Huntington Hall, said he considers the sanitary
      aspects of the sweating system before he considers its
      industrial aspects.

54   ANON.   "Reporter J. A. Riis," <u>Boston Daily Advertiser</u>
      (8 May). Scrpbk. p. 30.
         Riis's address at the General Conference of Charities is
      printed here verbatim. Riis called the sweating system "a
      slavery far worse than that of the blacks ever was."

55   ANON.   "A Reporter's Experience," Washington <u>Evening Star</u>
      (10 November). Scrpbk. p. 28.
         Along with details of the lecture Riis gave at the
      Christians at Work convention, Riis's popularity in
      England is mentioned. Hugh Price Hughes and Dr. Stephenson,
      "the president of English Methodism," asked to see Riis
      during their visits to the United States.

56   ANON.   "Shadows of a Great City," <u>Jamestown Journal</u>
      (22 July). Scrpbk. p. 27.
         During his talk at the Chautauquan Amphitheater about
      the poor in the slums of New York, Riis dwelled upon the
      "'utter debasement and degradation of the yellow Mongo-
      lians'" and won applause for his remark "'The Chinese must
      go.'"

57 ANON. "Slums of a Great City," Washington Post
(10 November). Scrpbk. p. 28.
Riis spoke before the Christians at Work convention
about Five Points, Blind Man's Alley, slum children, beer
dives, and other themes typical of his lectures.

58 ANON. "Small Parks for the Poor," New York Tribune
(10 August). Scrpbk. 2, p. 129.
Riis's articles in The Christian Union call "forcible
attention" to the "gross" conduct of city authorities who
have failed to provide parks for the poor.

59 ANON. "Something to Think About," Boston Post (9 April).
Scrpbk. p. 29.
Riis lectured and showed slides before the Unitarian
Club at the Hotel Vendome. He suggested two solutions
to the slum problem: education of the children of the
slums and improvement of the environment and tenement
houses.

60 ANON. "Squalid Abodes," Boston Traveller (9 April).
Scrpbk. p. 29.
Riis's talk at the Vendome was "a realistic picture of
life in the New York slums," but Riis's "admirable wit"
relieved the loathsome tale.

61 ANON. "Study Hours by the Lake," New York Tribune
(22 July). Scrpbk. p. 27.
Short notice stating that Riis in Chautauqua delivered
a lecture entitled, after his book, "How the Other Half
Lives."

62 ANON. "The Sweating System," Boston Morning Journal (8 May).
Scrpbk. p. 30.
The most worthy part of Riis's lecture before the
Associated Charities was "his explanation of how the sys-
tem [sweating system] results in the spread of contagious
diseases."

63 ANON. "Talk about New Books," Catholic World, 52 (February),
766, 769.
How the Other Half Lives "will, we hope, arrest the
attention of those who are responsible by either omission
or commission for the actual state of things [in the tenement districts]."

64 ANON. "Tenement House Laror," Boston Post (8 May).
Scrpbk. p. 30.

1891

> Riis, at Huntington Hall, took time "to call attention
> to the dangers from immigration." He was applauded for
> saying "'Immigration should be stopped in some manner.
> Fifty thousand people a year is enough to come into the
> country.'"

65   ANON.   "Treason," Christian Union (8 August). Scrpbk. 2,
>   p. 129.
>   Riis's plea for parks is "little less than a story of
>   treason" for the "Board of Street Opening and Improvement"
>   has the power to "secure for the poor the parks which the
>   unenforced law provides."

66   ANON.   "The Unitarian Club," Boston Journal (9 April).
>   Scrpbk. p. 29.
>   Besides stories of his own experiences in the slums,
>   Riis presented to the Unitarians slides and statistics.
>   He complained of "the apathy of those who did not know,
>   and when they knew, did not care, about the squalor and
>   vice and wretchedness."

67   CAMPBELL, HELEN; KNOX, THOMAS W., and BYRNES, THOMAS.
>   Darkness and Daylight; or, Lights and Shadows of New York
>   Life. Hartford: A. D. Worthington & Co., p. xii.
>   Riis, along with E. Warrin, Jr., and Frederick Vilmar,
>   is thanked for placing at the publisher's disposal photo-
>   graphs "from which very interesting selections have been
>   made."

68   F., H.   "Talk and Alarm in Europe," New York Times (1 March),
>   p. 1.
>   How the Other Half Lives was republished in London "and
>   attracted an unusual amount of attention." Riis's descrip-
>   tion of New York's slums took "everybody by surprise."

69   GREER, REV. DR.   "Sermons of the Day," New York Tribune
>   (approx. June). Scrpbk. p. 25.
>   In his sermon on "Christianity and the Cripple,"
>   Dr. Greer comments on Riis's discussion of the tenements
>   in How the Other Half Lives.

70   HUGHES, REV. HUGH PRICE.   "Evangelization of Great Cities,"
>   Christian Advocate (5 November), pp. 4, 745. Scrpbk. p. 26.
>   "On both sides of the Atlantic" urbanization has brought
>   about a new "separation of the classes." New York, like
>   London, has, as Riis's How the Other Half Lives demon-
>   strates, outrageous slums, and, at the same time, million-
>   aires on the other end of town.

71   KINKEAD, ALEXANDER L. No heading found, <u>Epoch</u> (16 January).
        Scrpbk. p. 9.
           Tenement dwellers will reap the rewards of <u>How the Other</u>
        <u>Half Lives</u>, a book which "will certainly set on foot addi-
        tional movements of the amelioration of the poor."

72   LODGE, HENRY CABOT. "The Restriction of Immigration," <u>North</u>
        <u>American Review</u>, 152 (January), 27-36.
           Lodge first presents his arguments against the liberal
        immigration policy of the U.S., then directs his readers
        to <u>How the Other Half Lives</u> for a "vivid picture" of "the
        degrading effect of this constant importation of the low-
        est forms of labor."

73   P., H. O. No heading found, <u>Twentieth Century</u> (8 January).
        Scrpbk. p. 8.
           Poverty, "the unspeakable horror of this world," begot
        the evils which pervade New York's tenement districts.
        Riis's exposure of poverty in <u>How the Other Half Lives</u> "is
        a very necessary and useful work."

1892 A BOOKS - NONE

1892 B SHORTER WRITINGS

1   ANON. "The Children of the Poor," <u>Buffalo Christian Advocate</u>
        (1 December). Scrpbk. p. 67.
           <u>The Children of the Poor</u> is "a most valuable contribu-
        tion to the fundamental literature of applied sociology."
        In Riis's book "the life of the poor pleads its own un-
        happy cause most eloquently."

2   ANON. "The Children of the Poor," <u>Christian Register</u>
        (1 December). Scrpbk. p. 67.
           <u>The Children of the Poor</u>, "is not the work of a <u>dilet-</u>
        <u>tante</u> 'slummer' who holds a vinaigrette under his nose
        while he inspects the dwellings of the poor." Riis's
        message is "prevention" not sympathy.

3   ANON. "The Children of the Poor," <u>Christian Union</u>
        (10 December). Scrpbk. pp. 76-77.
           Review of--plus excerpts from--<u>The Children of the Poor</u>.
        Riis viewed as natural expert on the problems of the city:
        "Problems of life for the masses in the great cities are
        becoming so vast and complex that they are producing by
        natural law experts who are competent to deal with them."

1892

4   ANON.   "'The Children of the Poor,'" <u>Critic</u>, 18 (17 December), 340-41.
     "He [Riis] has gone down into the depths of humanity, and into the homes where sunlight is but little known, and has come back, to call out the rest of humanity, and to tell them how their brothers and sisters live." Reading <u>The Children of the Poor</u> "warms the heart" and "strengthens faith in God."

5   ANON.   "The Children of the Poor," <u>Monthly Bulletin of St. John's Guild</u>, 1 (November). Scrpbk. p. 71.
     Riis's <u>The Children of the Poor</u> is "a valuable contribution to the data upon which all systematic, humane and charitable efforts should be based...."

6   ANON.   "Children of the Poor," <u>New York Evening Sun</u> (8 November). Scrpbk. p. 65.
     The reform work begun in <u>How the Other Half Lives</u> has been furthered in Riis's second book, <u>The Children of the Poor</u>. Riis's promotion of industrial schools, Fresh Air Funds, kindergartens, and other reforms beneficial to the children, as well as his discussion of child labor, education, and crime, will interest the public, the philanthropists, and the legislators alike.

7   ANON.   "Children of the Poor," <u>San Francisco Chronicle</u> (20 November). Scrpbk. p. 66.
     The sum of Riis's observations in <u>The Children of the Poor</u> is that "in child rescue lies the hope of cutting down pauperism and crime."

8   ANON.   "'The Children of the Poor,'" <u>Zion's Herald</u> (14 December). Scrpbk. pp. 68-69.
     A review of <u>The Children of the Poor</u>, with illustrations and "generous excerpts." Riis's second book "will accomplish great good in turning the thought of the philanthropic and benevolent...to do better work for the children of the poor."

9   ANON.   "Heredity and Poverty," <u>New York Tribune</u> (20 November). Scrpbk. p. 65.
     Riis's investigations into New York's slums, his contact with men of different races, and his findings, published in <u>The Children of the Poor</u>, indicate "the moral quality of the individual has nothing to do with the race from which he sprang, but is wholly a personal tendency due to training, good or bad, as the case may be, from childhood."

10   ANON. "How the Other Half Lives," Asbury Park Spray
        (21 July). Scrpbk. p. 33.
          Riis lectured July 20 and raised a "considerable sum of
money" for the King's Daughters. Who sponsored his lecture and where it was delivered are undisclosed.

11   ANON. "In the Slums of New York," New York Daily News
        (24 January). Scrpbk. p. 32.
          "The annals of the poor have seldom been brought to pub-
lic view with the force and degree of careful study that
characterizes" How the Other Half Lives. Three "bald
facts" confront New Yorkers: "a tremendous, ever-swelling
crowd of wage earners," which needs proper housing; a
deficiency of homes; and the unconscionable rents demanded
of the poor.

12   ANON. "The King's Daughters in a Great City," no journal
        given (8 April). Scrpbk. p. 33.
          Riis's lecture sponsored by the Lend a Hand Band of
King's Sons in Easton, Pennsylvania, was "a truthful
portrayal of the dark picture of the life of the
Metropolis...."

13   ANON. "Last Words," Boston Journal (17 November).
        Scrpbk. p. 31.
          On the last day of the Christian Workers' conference,
Riis talked about the King's Daughters: how the order
started, how it was operating, and what its future plans
were.

14   ANON. "Misery in the Slums," Washington Post (30 January).
        Scrpbk. p. 31.
          At the Unitarian Church in Washington Riis lectured for
the benefit of the Newsboys' and Children's Aid Society.
The ignorance and vice of European immigrants should not
be feared, he suggested, because generally their children
prove to be good Americans.

15   ANON. "Mr. Riis' Lecture," Washington Evening Star
        (30 January). Scrpbk. p. 33.
          Another review of Riis's benefit lecture for the News-
boys' and Children's Aid Society. Riis is called "an
earnest Christian worker."

16   ANON. "New Books," New London Telegraph (16 December).
        Scrpbk. p. 72.
          "The pathos and power" of The Children of the Poor "lie
in its truth." Riis proves again he can command "the deep

and increasing interest of many" in "the woe that is within an arrow flight of wealth and...luxury."

17 ANON. No heading found, Boston Literary World (19 October). Scrpbk. p. 66.
Field report on Riis's activities: "Mr. Riis has for the past few months been devoting himself heart and soul to the study of the children in the poverty-stricken districts here, and the results of his investigations are embodied in his second book, The Children of the Poor."

18 ANON. No heading found, Brooklyn Times (12 November). Scrpbk. p. 65.
The children in The Children of the Poor are presented "not in the sentimental outlines of the goody story book, but as they actually are."

19 ANON. No heading found, Farm, Field, and Fireside (17 December). Scrpbk. p. 66.
In The Children of the Poor Riis, "a kind of Christopher Columbus in the world of poverty," has answered "The question 'Who and where are the slum children of New York to-day'?"

20 ANON. No heading found, Independent (24 November). Scrpbk. 67.
"To well-informed readers much of this matter [The Children of the Poor] will not be new." Riis's complaints about "The inhuman action of the 'Trade Unions' in shutting out apprentices" show "bold good sense," however.

21 ANON. No heading found, New York Evening Post (5 May). Scrpbk. p. 64.
Review of Riis's article, "The Children of the Poor," which appeared in Scribner's. Applauds Riis for his "realism" and "natural comedy."

22 ANON. No heading found, New York Sun (19 November). Scrpbk. p. 65.
Riis, "a most patient and painstaking investigator," knows the slums of New York better than any other reporter. His The Children of the Poor is another "story of the slums."

23 ANON. No heading found, New York Sun (26 April). Scrpbk. p. 64.
Announces that "Children of the Poor" will be one of the four principle articles to make up Scribner's Magazine for May.

24   ANON.   "The Other Half," Baltimore Sun (30 March).
        Scrpbk. p. 33.
         Review of Harris Concert Hall lecture. Riis spoke
        about tenements, slum children, alcohol, the King's
        Daughters.

25   ANON.   "Ousted the Trustees," Brooklyn Times (22 December).
        Scrpbk. 2, p. 148.
         Riis argued that there ought to be a union free school
        at Richmond Hill. The present Board of Trustees ought to
        be replaced, and the school refurbished.

26   ANON.   "Phases of Modern Life," illegible source (17 November).
        Scrpbk. p. 31.
         A short biographical sketch of Riis. Riis has penned
        long, illegible comment in margin.

27   ANON.   "Poverty in New York," Brooklyn Citizen (11 December).
        Scrpbk. pp. [34-52].
         Riis, according to this article, felt New York's task in
        dealing with poverty was exceptionally difficult, since it
        was the city where most immigrants landed, and where con-
        sequently, the helpless and unambitious of their number
        remained.

28   ANON.   "Silver Lake Assembly," Buffalo Express (29 July).
        Scrpbk. p. 33.
         Riis's lecture gave "great satisfaction." Riis related
        incident in which he nearly forgot his lecture.

29   ANON.   "A Study of Darkest New York," Christian at Work
        (3 March). Scrpbk. p. 32.
         Notice that Scribner's has published "a new and cheaper
        edition" of How the Other Half Lives. Quotes Riis as
        having said of the first edition: "I wrote the book be-
        cause I could not help it. It seemed to come together of
        itself."

30   ANON.   "Sunday at Lakeside," Toledo Blade (1 August).
        Scrpbk. p. 33.
         During a July and August tour Riis lectured at Silver
        Lake, New York, Lakeside, Ohio, and Bayview, Michigan
        assemblies. His lecture at Lakeside is listed among other
        activities at the assembly. Riis penned in the margin his
        itinerary, and mentioned he traveled "some 2300 miles...
        and got $300 for the trip."

1892

31   ANON.   "That Wretched Other Half," illegible source
         (30 March). Scrpbk. p. 32.
             Riis gave a lecture entitled "The Other Half--How it
         Lives and Dies" at the Concert Hall of the Academy of
         Music.

32   ARLAND, WIRT.   "Little Children of the Poor," St. Louis
         Chronicle (23 December). Scrpbk. p. 70.
             The Children of the Poor is mentioned along with the
         Society for the Prevention of Cruelty to Children, Charles
         Loring Brace, and the new children's industrial schools,
         in this brief history of the Children's Aid Society.

33   CRANE, STEPHEN.   "On the Jersey Coast," New York Tribune
         (24 July), p. 22.
             In this unsigned article, Crane reports that Riis "gave
         an illustrated lecture" about the poor in tenements. The
         talk was given at the Beach Auditorium in Asbury Park.

34   McLOUGHLIN, WILLIAM P.   "Evictions in New York's Tenement
         Houses," Arena, 37 (December), 48-57.
             McLoughlin argues that each year too many poor but
         honorable persons are turned out of their homes in New
         York. The number of poor trapped in the East End is
         greater than that of "Old London." He cites Riis's How
         the Other Half Lives as his source of information.

1893 A BOOKS - NONE

1893 B SHORTER WRITINGS

1   ANON.   "Abandoned Farms," Silver Cross (April). Scrpbk. p. 58.
             Presents pictures and stories of the New York slums--a
         mother who commits suicide, abandoning her family of nine;
         a woman at work in an attic, with her two small children.
         Asks reader: "Shall they have a chance in the Summer hay-
         fields and paradise glens of New England...?"

2   ANON.   "Abandoned Farms," Silver Cross (February), p. 174.
         Scrpbk. p. 56.
             The King's Daughters printed this series of articles in
         the Silver Cross. Quoting Riis often, the editor argues
         that since tenements make for evil, why not relocate slum
         residents on the deserted farms of the beautiful Connec-
         ticut Valley.

3 ANON. "Abandoned Farms," Silver Cross (March). Scrpbk. p. 57.
       Additional arguments for the relocation of slum residents.
       Crowded homes and streets and the sale of liquor to chil-
       dren, part and parcel of life in the slums, are reasons
       enough to move children out of the foul air of the tene-
       ment districts and into the fresh air of the country.

4 ANON. "Book Notices," New York Evening Sun (23 November).
       Scrpbk. pp. [106-113].
       A review of Nibsy's Christmas; Riis is commended for
       writing "out of fulness of knowledge in his acquaintance
       with the burdened side of New York life...."

5 ANON. "Books of Today," illegible source (25 January).
       Scrpbk. p. 66.
       If the principle of education, the foundation of our
       American democracy, is to prevail, attention must be paid
       to Riis's book The Children of the Poor, which "presents
       a connected view of the social conditions to be met, the
       agencies employed and the results obtained" in the effort
       to rescue the slum children from their environment.

6 ANON. "'The Children of the Poor,'" Five Points House of
       Industry Report (February). Scrpbk. p. 77.
       The Children of the Poor is "a most entertaining book."
       Riis merits the title "Columbus of poverty facts."

7 ANON. "'The Children of the Poor,'" Humanity and Health
       (February). Scrpbk. p. 77.
       The mission of The Children of the Poor is "to show that
       we had better educate and direct aright; had better pre-
       vent crime and criminals by proper environment and
       education."

8 ANON. "Children of the Poor," London Public Opinion
       (13 October). Scrpbk. p. 77.
       The Children of the Poor shows that "the honest tax-
       payers of New York and California...allow themselves to be
       robbed wholesale" by the well-to-do-parents of pauper
       children.

9 ANON. "'Children of the Poor,'" New Bedford Evening Standard
       (5 December). Scrpbk. p. 83.
       Though "not an eloquent speaker," Riis "held the closest
       attention of his audience" at Grace House as he told of
       "the misery, filth, and degradation that is to be found in
       the tenement house districts of large cities."

1893

10   ANON.   "The Children of the Poor," New York Evening World
         (25 February). Scrpbk. p. 53.
            Riis gave his first lecture of a series of lectures for
         women sponsored by the alumnae of the New York Normal
         School. He talked of the children who were victims of
         the slum, and appealed to young teachers in the audience
         to found more kindergartens.

11   ANON.   "The Factor of Character," no journal given (approx.
         March). Scrpbk. pp. [139-41].
            Introduced by the Rev. Fred B. Allen at Association Hall,
         Riis pointed out that "the solution of all great social
         problems depended largely on the factor of character." He
         stressed the need to develop the "moral sense" and the
         desire for "self-help" in the character of the slum
         dweller.

12   ANON.   "Facts about the Poor," Newark Evening News (4 May).
         Scrpbk. p. 83.
            Speaking before the King's Daughters' Circle of the
         Silver Cross, Riis lamented the fact that 50,000 school-
         age children in New York do not attend school. He attri-
         buted a recent increase in crime "to the lack of a
         proportionate increase in educational advantages," and he
         harshly criticized, moreover, the sending of children "to
         truant homes and reform schools."

13   ANON.   "The Fresh Air Work," Newark Daily Advertiser (4 May).
         Scrpbk. p. 82.
            Women of Newark "thronged" to the lecture-room of the
         Park Presbyterian Church to listen to Riis talk about the
         fresh air work of the King's Daughters. Riis also spoke
         about poor children, crime, and the lack of educational
         facilities in New York.

14   ANON.   "Hearing a Lecture by Jacob A. Riis," New York Tribune
         (12 April). Scrpbk. p. 83.
            Riis, "the well-known writer on social problems and an
         earnest worker to alleviate the sufferings of the poor,"
         addressed the King's Daughters on the tenement house
         problem and the means for its alleviation.

15   ANON.   "'How the Other Half Lives,'" Coup d'Etat (April).
         Scrpbk. p. 81.
            Comment on the realism of Riis's Galesburg, Illinois,
         lecture. "To us who are unfamiliar with life in a large
         city, it was a revelation." Riis's stereopticon views
         "were certainly more realistic than any words could be."

16   ANON.   "How the Other Half Lives," no journal given
          (21 March).   Scrpbk. p. 81.
          After having listened to Riis speak about crowded tene-
       ments, growler gangs, the Children's Aid Society, the
       editor of this Galesburg, Illinois, paper wishes him "God-
       speed in his work."

17   ANON.   "How the Other Half Lives," Rockford Morning Repub-
          lican (22 March).   Scrpbk. p. 80.
          The problem of "poverty and the relation of capital and
       labor" must be solved, declared Riis in his lecture at the
       Second Congregational Church.

18   ANON.   "Illustrated Lectures," New Bedford Evening Journal
          (5 December).   Scrpbk. p. 83.
          Riis delivered a free lecture at Grace House in which he
       described tenements "let out to sleepers at 5 cents a
       spot," Italian rag pickers, and gangs of "toughs," as part
       of "the natural product of...life among the poor classes
       of great cities."

19   ANON.   "Interesting Indeed," Highland Democrat (6 May).
          Scrpbk. p. 83.
          Several hundred listeners well appreciated Riis's lec-
       ture on 'How the Other Half Lives' delivered Thursday
       evening in the Depew Opera House.

20   ANON.   "Jacob A. Riis Before the Church Club," New York
          Tribune (4 March).   Scrpbk. p. 53.
          In his address to members of the Church Club Riis urged
       them to take an interest in kindergartens and industrial
       schools for the sake of the tenement children.

21   ANON.   "Jacob Riis Talks of the Poor," Rockford Star
          (22 March).   Scrpbk. p. 80.
          After giving his lecture on the New York slum, Riis com-
       plimented the citizens of Rockford for "the condition of
       affairs" in their city, saying that "the greatest evidence
       of the city's prosperity was the fact that the majority of
       laborers owned their own homes."

22   ANON.   "Life in the Slums," Wisconsin State Journal
          (20 March).   Scrpbk. p. 82.
          In the Madison Congressional Church, March 19, Riis gave
       a "discourse upon slumming."   Dr. Richard T. Ely introduced
       him to the audience.

1893

23   ANON.   "Low Life In London," no journal given (approx.
        March). Scrpbk. pp. [139-41].
        A review of Arthur Morison's Tales of Mean Streets.
        Reviewer believes that the humor of the story "That Brute
        Simmons" points to "comic elements" in "squalor," and
        guesses that "our own Mr. Riis in his studies of New York,
        must have taken cognizance of many things which were gro-
        tesquely humorous."

24   ANON.   "Made Trouble for College Women," Chicago Tribune
        (approx. April). Scrpbk. p. 64.
        Riis's articles for Scribner's Magazine "threatened to
        demoralize the College Settlement in Rivington Street."
        Patrons of the settlement's reading room recognized them-
        selves as the wretched poor of whom Riis wrote. Editor
        suggests reformers too easily forget that "Poverty has its
        sensibilities."

25   ANON.   "New Publications," New Orleans Times Democrat
        (February). Scrpbk. p. 77.
        The Children of the Poor is "a very clear and intel-
        ligible statement of the proportions to which the evil
        [child destruction in the slums] has grown."

26   ANON.   "New Publications," New York Times (10 December), p. 23.
        Review of Nibsy's Christmas. "There is truth--hard, de-
        pressing truth--in all these stories, for there is no man
        who can come nearer to the dread facts of the slums than
        Mr. Riis."

27   ANON.   "New York's Criminals," Providence Journal
        (6 December). Scrpbk. p. 83.
        Riis "painted a vivid picture of the evil effects of the
        crowded tenement-house life of New York...and showed how
        it was partly responsible for a great portion of the
        crimes committed," in his speech at Sayles Hall. He also
        denounced the speculators who built the tenements, and he
        warned that it was "a matter of business and of justice"
        to provide the workingman "with the opportunity to secure
        a home."

28   ANON.   "Nibsy's Christmas," Boston Times (3 December).
        Scrpbk. pp. [106-13].
        The book "is a most appropriate reminder at this holiday
        season of just what Christmas ought to mean to people who
        live in those parts of a big city where the sun shines and
        in its shining reveals no trace of filth and wretchedness."

29   ANON.   "Nibsy's Christmas," New York Evangelist
         (21 December). Scrpbk. pp. [106-13].
         A review of Riis's melodramatic Christmas tales; Riis
         writes "not to give an hour's amusement...but to make men
         and women see what actually exists...."

30   ANON.   No heading found, Boston Gazette (2 December).
         Scrpbk. pp. [106-13].
         Nibsy's Christmas is commended for its power to "inspire
         gentle and charitable thoughts for the poor and the suf-
         fering during the festive season."

31   ANON.   No heading found, Chicago Herald (19 March).
         Scrpbk. p. 80.
         Notice in the society column. "Mrs. John C. Coonley...
         entertained about a hundred guests on Friday evening, who
         listened to Jacob Rice of New York."

32   ANON.   No heading found, London Spectator (17 June).
         Scrpbk. p. 72.
         The problem of the children, which perplexes Londoners,
         is similar to the problem that perplexes New Yorkers.
         That The Children of the Poor will be highly interesting
         to an English audience "need hardly be said."

33   ANON.   No heading found, New York Evangelist (6 April).
         Scrpbk. p. 53.
         On April 11 the first annual meeting of the Tenement
         House Chapter of the Order of the King's Daughters and
         Sons will be held. Riis will deliver his stereopticon
         address.

34   ANON.   No heading found, Normal School Echo (March).
         Scrpbk. p. 53.
         Girls in training at the school, upon Riis's advice,
         have taken a new interest in kindergarten work.

35   ANON.   No heading found, University Review (January).
         Scrpbk. p. 33.
         Riis, in The Children of the Poor, "takes the position
         and sustains it conclusively that a child's environment
         is more responsible than heredity for the way he turns
         out."

36   ANON.   No heading found, Wellesley Magazine (May).
         Scrpbk. p. 84.
         Telling about "'The Children of the Poor'" Riis made
         the hearts of his audience "burn within," during his
         speech at Wellesley College.

1893

37   ANON.   "On Tenement-House Life," Chicago <u>Inter-Ocean</u>
         (19 March). Scrpbk. p. 80.
            At Hull House, Riis, on his first western trip, talked
         briefly about the improved conditions of tenement-house
         life in New York.

38   ANON.   "The Other Half," no journal given (21 March).
         Scrpbk. p. 81.
            Riis spoke about the "other half" in Galesburg, Illinois,
         March 20, stressing the importance of police station im-
         provement and rent control.

39   ANON.   "Our Boys and Girls," <u>Boston Pilot</u> (December).
         Scrpbk. pp. [106-13].
            A review of <u>Nibsy's Christmas</u>. Explaining the plot of
         the conventional Christmas story, the reviewer turns to
         Riis's book and points out that its "merit is that it
         reminds one that there are thousands of lives, and young
         lives too, into which not the smallest sparkle of the
         Christmas gaiety and jollity ever enters...."

40   ANON.   "Our Filthy Thoroughfares," <u>Chicago Tribune</u> (21 March).
         Scrpbk. pp. 80-81.
            Disputes the "caustic references" Riis made in his lec-
         ture at Hull House "to the (un)sanitary conditions of
         Chicago." A severe winter accounts for the filth on the
         streets, and the danger of cholera is not, contrary to
         Riis's claim, as great in Chicago as it is in New York.

41   ANON.   "A Sad Exhibit," <u>Rockford Register-Gazette</u>
         (22 March). Scrpbk. p. 80.
            Riis delivered a lecture at the Second Congregational
         Church that was "full of interest and appealing to the
         sober reflection of every listener." Riis spoke about
         tenement life.

42   ANON.   "Says the Streets Need Cleaning," <u>Chicago Tribune</u>
         (19 March). Scrpbk. p. 80.
            Riis told a Chicago audience at Hull House to get their
         streets and alleys cleaned up: "If cholera should come
         this summer...you never would be able to stamp it out in
         certain districts through which I passed today."

43   ANON.   "The Slums of New York," <u>Churchman</u> (11 March).
         Scrpbk. p. 53.
            Riis spoke before the Church Club, March 3. His descrip-
         tions of New York's slums were "terse, humorous, enter-
         taining, and touching."

30

44   ANON.   "Spoke of the Slums," Madison Democrat (21 March).
         Scrpbk. p. 82.
            At the Congressional Church in Madison, Wisconsin, Riis
         spoke of tenements and tenement children. A handsome
         collection was taken up for the Children's Aid Society.

45   ANON.   "A Study of Immigrant Children," Springfield Repub-
         lican (1 March). Scrpbk. p. 78.
            The Children of the Poor is "a careful and thorough
         survey "of the slum child's life at home, in the street,
         in the factory, at school, and in the industrial estab-
         lishment. The ambition of the Italian and Jewish "elders"
         to have their children "rise above their surroundings"
         deserves praise.

46   ANON.   "Tenement House Evil," New Bedford Mercury
         (5 December). Scrpbk. p. 83.
            The tenement house problem could be solved, said Riis
         at Grace House, "by reaching the children."

47   ANON.   "Woes of the Poor," New York Recorder (24 January).
         Scrpbk. p. 53.
            Riis called this report--in which his name is misspelled
         "Jacob I. Riisi"--of a speech he delivered to the Charity
         Organization of Castleton "rot." Riis spoke in Castleton
         on the work of the Charity Organization in and near New
         York City.

48   ANON.   "The Writer of the Poor," New Orleans Times Democrat
         (5 November). Scrpbk. p. 77.
            Riis carries out "a distinctive mission"; prior to him
         "no writer had been chosen the instrument of doing so much
         good."

49   DEVINS, REV. JOHN B. "The Children of the Poor," Charities
         Review (January). Scrpbk. pp. 74-76.
            Riis aimed in The Children of the Poor "to gather facts
         for other men to build upon." He states a "vital truth"
         when he says, "'the problem of the children is a problem
         of the state.'"

*50   FLOWER, B. O. Civilization's Inferno; or, Studies in the
         Social Cellar. Boston: Arena Publishing Company, 1893.
            Flower mentions Riis's data about New York tenements and
         quotes him concerning "the special needs of the poor"
         there.

1893

51 REYNOLDS, MARCUS T. The Housing of the Poor in American
        Cities. Baltimore: American Economy Association, p. 58.
        Quotes Riis's argument in How the Other Half Lives
    about having the state regulate tenement house rents, and
    contends that this is a "questionable" scheme.

1894 A BOOKS - NONE

1894 B SHORTER WRITINGS

1   ANON.   "Arraigned by a Universalist," New York Tribune
        (18 December). Scrpbk. p. 84.
        At a dinner given by the members of the Universalist
    Society, Riis spoke in behalf of "the little waifs of the
    slum." At the same dinner Dr. Edwin C. Bolles reprehended
    Trinity Church for its ownership of unsanitary tenement
    houses.

2   ANON.   "Children of the Poor," Boston Transcript
        (22 March). Scrpbk. p. 84.
        On March 21, the Unitarian Club listened to what Riis,
    with the aid of stereopticon slides, had to say about New
    York's "lower strata of life."

3   ANON.   "Discussion before the Nineteenth Century Club," New
        York Evening Post (December). Scrpbk. p. 84.
        At the Club's December meeting, Riis spoke about "the
    conditions and needs of the poor of the East Side, dwelling
    especially upon the inadequate school accommodations,
    afforded in that district below Fourteenth Street." [At
    top, Riis wrote "The great success."]

4   ANON.   "A Free Employment Bureau," Boston Herald (September).
        Scrpbk. p. 104.
        The Parker Memorial will establish an employment bureau
    based on the principles of Riis's Forum essay, "How to
    Bring Work and Workers Together."

5   ANON.   "Good Work for Charity," New York Tribune (11 April).
        Scrpbk. p. 84.
        "Charity can be extended without encouraging professional
    pauperism, and...work among the children will sooner erad-
    icate the evils in the tenement house districts than any-
    thing else," Riis told the New York Tenement-House Chapter
    of the King's Daughters and Sons at its second annual
    meeting April 10.

6   ANON.   Illegible title, St. George's Chronicle (June).
Scrpbk. p. 83.
     Riis's "interesting talk on 'The Children of the Poor'"
touched in its hearers "every faculty of mind and heart."

7   ANON.   "Lecture by Jacob A. Riis," Wilkes-Barre Literary
News-Letter (April). Scrpbk. p. 84.
     Riis is scheduled to give a lecture entitled "Tenement
Life in New York City" in the Wilkes-Barre Y.M.C.A. Hall
on May 4. Proceeds go to the poor of the city.

8   ANON.   "Making Thieves in the Metropolis," Review of Reviews
(December). Scrpbk. p. 104.
     Riis argues that truant boys "who won't go to school
should be put in the hands of the Children's Aid Society."

9   ANON.   No heading found, New York Sun (September).
Scrpbk. p. 104.
     Comments upon Riis's "plain statement of existing condi-
tions in New York," a plea for school playgrounds which
caught public attention in the September issue of Century.

10   ANON.   No heading found, Union Signal (13 September).
Scrpbk. p. 104.
     Examines Riis's "How to Bring Work and Workers Together";
Riis pointed out the success of the "Ohio experiment"
which, in 1890, established free employment offices. Riis
"hints at possible weaknesses and their remedy, and points
out what he believes would be most desirable and satisfac-
tory results on all sides if this experiment were repeated
in other states."

11   ANON.   "Notes," Nation, 59 (15 November), 104.
     Looks at Riis's "The Making of Thieves in New York," and
observes that it "does not expose abuses without showing
ways of correcting them. The only missing link is between
men and money."

12   ANON.   "Poor Children," Boston Journal (22 March).
Scrpbk. p. 84.
     The account of "'Child Life in New York City'" Riis gave
to the Unitarian Club was "lucidly and succinctly rendered."
In manner Riis reminded one of Hans Christian Anderson.

13   ANON.   "The Riis Lecture," Wilkes-Barre Record (6 May).
Scrpbk. p. 84.
     Riis's lecture May sixth at the Y.M.C.A. "was an aston-
ishing revelation of a vast field in the great city [New
York] for 'Christian Endeavor' and missionary work."

1894

14   ANON.   "School Reform Discussed," <u>New York Times</u>
        (7 June), p. 5. Scrpbk. p. 84.
            Riis attended a meeting of Good Government Club E held
        to discuss changes in the city's school system.

15   ANON.   "What if Tony Does Play Hookey," <u>New York Herald</u>
        (7 December). Scrpbk. p. 85.
            Riis outlined for the New York Kindergarten Association
        "the different phases of the kindergarten problem." That
        the children of the streets "have powers for good, as well
        as evil" was his theme.

16   FLOWER, B. O. "Some Sidelights of the Tenement House Evil,"
        <u>Arena</u>, 9 (April), 673-83.
            Flower sees the enlightenment of earnest men to the
        evils of the tenement as a way of changing the conditions
        of the oppressed. He quotes from Riis's <u>How the Other</u>
        <u>Half Lives</u> and refers to a speech Riis gave: "Mr. Riis in
        speaking of New York, says: 'The worst tenements in New
        York do not, as a rule, look bad....'"

17   TOLMAN, WILLIAM HOWE and HULL, WILLIAM I. <u>Handbook of Socio-</u>
        <u>logical Information with Especial Reference to New York</u>
        <u>City</u>. New York: The Knickerbocker Press, 1894, pp. 37,
        66, 79, 95, 251.
            Riis's <u>The Children of the Poor</u>, "based on a storehouse
        of facts," is suggested reading for "The Child Problem"
        and "Child Labor." <u>How the Other Half Lives</u> affords
        "valuable premises from which to draw conclusions," and
        is suggested reading for the "Tenement House Problem."

<u>1895 A BOOKS - NONE</u>

<u>1895 B SHORTER WRITINGS</u>

1   ANON.   "Aid to State Charities," <u>New York Tribune</u> (19 April).
        Scrpbk. p. 88.
            A special meeting of the State Charities Aid Association
        was called April 18 and was attended by "well-known and
        influential men and women" of New York--among them was
        Riis, who gave a talk about the Association's work with
        children.

2   ANON.   "Americanism in Municipal Politics," <u>Buffalo Express</u>
        (15 September). Scrpbk. p. 93.
            Speaking before the Liberal Club, Roosevelt argued that
        questions of creed are irrelevant in "our politics" so

long as our candidates "are honest and in good faith
Americans." Riis is praised for help given to Roosevelt;
and How the Other Half Lives is cited as the "best study
of American tenement-house life...."

3   ANON.   "Children as Workers," New York Sun (20 April).
    Scrpbk. p. 106.
        Recounts Riis's testimony about the success of the
    Factory Inspection law on the East Side's child labor.
    Riis argued that "the law had done some good...but the
    law was frequently evaded by the father of the child giv-
    ing a higher age on the certificate allowing the child to
    enter a workshop."

4   ANON.   "Children of the Tenements," New York Mail and Express
    (29 March). Scrpbk. p. 85.
        Education will eliminate juvenile depravity in the city,
    and more playgrounds will help slum children to perceive
    "moral relations," Riis reasoned in his lecture for the
    New York Kindergarten Association.

5   ANON.   "Congregational Association," Brooklyn Eagle
    (23 October). Scrpbk. p. 83.
        Riis told members of the New York and Brooklyn Associa-
    tion of Congregational Churches that he wished to see more
    small parks, cooking schools established in every church,
    and an end to the dime novel.

6   ANON.   "A Golden Opportunity," Brooklyn Eagle (30 April).
    Scrpbk. p. 86.
        The Rembrandt Club invited Riis to speak at its recep-
    tion held for the benefit of the kindergarten cause.
    Riis's enthusiasm, "the result of knowledge and imagina-
    tion surcharged with feeling...makes him one of the most
    convincing and uplifting platform forces within or around
    the metropolis."

7   ANON.   "He Intends to Appoint Women," New York Herald
    (25 January). Scrpbk. p. 87.
        Speaking before the Women's Association for the Improve-
    ment of the Public Schools, Riis said that Mayor Strong
    told him that women would be appointed to the Board of
    Education.

8   ANON.   "Lecture at New Century Club," Wilmington Morning News
    (6 April). Scrpbk. p. 89.
        Riis was "frequently applauded" April 5 for his "'How
    the Other Half Lives'" lecture, "a narrative of [his]
    experiences...in the slums of New York, beginning with the

1895

exploration of the old tenement houses, continuing through the courts and alleys of the city and ending with visits to its newsboys' lodging-houses, public kindergartens and foundling hospitals."

9   ANON.   "A Lecture by Jacob A. Riis," New York Tribune (24 May). Scrpbk. p. 86.
    At All Souls' Unitarian Church, in a benefit speech for the Working Women's Society, Riis "made an appeal for the education and reclamation of the children now growing up in evil ways in the alleys and rookeries of the city."

10 ANON.   "Live Among the Poor," New York Herald (10 April). Scrpbk. p. 87.
    On April 9 the King's Daughters and Sons held their annual meeting. "The principal features of the meeting were the addresses by Jacob A. Riis...and Mrs. Charles Russell Lowell." Riis strongly urged "the extension of libraries among the poor."

11 ANON.   "Magazine Articles," Annals of the American Academy of Political and Social Sciences, 6 (September), 341-42.
    Mentions "Clearing of Mulberry Bend" article in August Review of Reviews.

12 ANON.   "A Message from the Slums," Hartford Courant (22 May). Scrpbk. p. 85.
    No matter how hardened, every boy has "a spark of good-ness," Riis told the Connecticut Congregational Club. Boys like the fictitious "Tony" will never become good citizens unless churches and Christian people come to their rescue.

13 ANON.   "Mr. Riis Injures His Eyes," New York Sun (1 February). Scrpbk. p. 88.
    Riis could not speak to the City Vigilance League January 31 because he hurt his eye in taking off his glasses.

14 ANON.   "Mr. Riis to Lecture on Tenements--Matinee at Abbey's Theatre," New York Times (24 March), p. 11.
    Another announcement of the lecture Riis scheduled to deliver at Sherry's for the benefit of the New York Tene-ment Association.

15 ANON.   "Mr. Riis's Complaint," New York Tribune (21 December). Scrpbk. p. 113.
    Mentions Riis's complaint to the Health Board; Riis protested that the condition of Mulberry Bend, now cleared

of tenements for the purpose of making a park, had not
been improved. The lot was "detrimental to health and
dangerous to life."

16   ANON.   "Mr. Riis's Figures Were Close," New York Tribune
(8 June). Scrpbk. p. 87.
     Riis estimated that "50,000 children of school age" in
New York "did not attend any school," whereas "City Super-
intendent Jasper...estimated the number to be between 5,000
and 8,000." The school census proved Riis's figures
accurate.

17   ANON.   "Mr. Riis's Lecture," New York Times (29 March), p. 8.
     Review of the lecture Riis delivered at Sherry's:
"there are few, if any, who can so eloquently and truth-
fully bring the scenes of the tenement districts before
the eyes of the rich."

18   ANON.   "Need of More Schools," New York Times (10 January),
p. 7. Scrpbk. p. 86.
     Members of Good Government Club G held a meeting
January 9 at which Riis "delivered an exhaustive address."
Riis contended that the city's school buildings "could
not be in worse condition," and that "it would be cheaper
to pay $10,000,000 to provide proper accommodation for the
school children...than to have them trained up as criminals
in the streets to fill the jails and reformatories."

19   ANON.   No heading found, illegible source (February).
Scrpbk. p. 87.
     Riis told "'The Story of Little Nibsy'" to those gathered
in the rectory of the Church of the Resurrection, February
12.

20   ANON.   No heading found, New York Sun (25 March).
Scrpbk. p. 85.
     Riis to speak at Sherry's. Benefits go to the Kinder-
garten Association.

21   ANON.   No heading found, New York Tribune (21 December).
Scrpbk. p. 113.
     Riis has grounds for complaining about the site of what
was Mulberry Bend. The area remains a desolate lot.

22   ANON.   No heading found, New York World (5 May).
Scrpbk. p. 22.
     Announcement: "Mr. Jacob Riis's well-known book, 'How
the Other Half Lives' has suggested the title for a series
of papers in the English Illustrated Magazine."

1895

23   ANON.   "Playgrounds for City Poor," <u>Philadelphia Methodist</u>
         (1895). Scrpbk. p. 79.
         A call "to every good citizen and Christian" to agitate
         for the playground movement. Simultaneously in New York
         under the leadership of Riis and others and in Philadel-
         phia under the Cultural Extension League, the movement for
         children's playgrounds rapidly gains ground.

24   ANON.   "Social Leaders Arrange Benefits for Several Worthy
         Institutions," <u>New York Times</u> (17 March), p. 11.
         Announces Riis "will deliver a lecture, illustrated with
         stereopticon views, at Sherry's on the evening of March
         28." States Riis "believes that kindergarten training is
         necessary for the salvation and education of the children
         of the poor."

25   ANON.   "The Tenement Children," <u>New York Tribune</u> (9 June).
         Scrpbk. p. 106.
         Describes the problem of child labor in the East Side
         and says that Riis "recently surprised Mayor Strong by
         making an application to be appointed a factory inspector
         without pay. He also has interested the City Vigilance
         League in the subject..." Riis strongly suggested that
         there should be not one, but twenty, unpaid factory
         inspectors.

26   ANON.   "Tenement-House Children," <u>New York Evening Post</u>
         (approx. March). Scrpbk. p. 85.
         For the benefit of the Kindergarten Association Riis,
         who "believes that kindergarten training is necessary for
         the salvation and education of the children of the poor,"
         is to speak at Sherry's.

27   ANON.   "'Twas Woman's Club Day," <u>Brooklyn Eagle</u> (May).
         Scrpbk. p. 86.
         Before the Brooklyn Woman's Club Riis expounded his
         belief that "kindergarten is the right beginning of all
         education." Though "no cure all," kindergarten is "the
         earliest and most important barrier that blocks the way
         to the jail for such as are going there now in droves,"
         he argued.

28   ANON.   "Useful Mission Work," <u>Philadelphia Times</u> (26 March).
         Scrpbk. p. 87.
         Riis was one of the speakers at the Convention of
         Christian Workers in Philadelphia. "Although he took no
         text his discourse was evidently founded upon the well-
         known biblical maxim that cleanliness is next to godliness."

29   ANON.   "Work Among the Poor," New York Times (10 April),
        p. 8.   Scrpbk. p. 87.
        "It is one of the greatest of offenses to take all the
        beauty out of a child's life," Riis told his audience at
        the sixth annual meeting of the King's Daughters and Sons'
        Tenement House Chapter. He shared the platform with
        Mrs. Josephine S. Lowell.

30   BRISBANE, ARTHUR.   "Some Good Accomplished," New York World
        (22 May). Scrpbk. p. 89.
        Editorial comment on legislation recently passed "for
        the betterment of New York and the benefit of its chil-
        dren." Brisbane recognizes Riis's efforts to get the
        playground bill passed: "The bill providing for chil-
        dren's playgrounds is mainly the work of Mr. Jacob A. Riis."

31   CRAIG, OSCAR.   "Agencies for the Prevention of Pauperism,"
        in The Poor in Great Cities, by Robert Woods et al. New
        York: Charles Scribner's Son's, 1895, pp. 339-69.
        Riis is cited, with Charles Loring Brace, for enforcing
        the public conscience with the need for poor relief.

*32 Tenement-House Committee of 1894. Report of the Tenement-
        House Committee of 1894. Albany: James B. Lyon, State
        Printer, 1895. Scattered references to Riis. R. Fulton
        Cutting mentions that before the passage of the latest
        amendments to the Tenement-House Act, Riis pointed out
        "these buildings...as notable examples of flagrant dere-
        liction." The houses "were all that Mr. Riis had pictured
        them...."

1896 A BOOKS - NONE

1896 B SHORTER WRITINGS

1   ANON.   "Cheer of St. Nicholas," New York Times (8 December),
        p. 2. Scrpbk. pp. [127-28].
        At the annual banquet of the St. Nicholas Society, Police
        Commissioner Roosevelt commended Riis for his "most stal-
        wart assistance," and said "...I am almost tempted to call
        [him] the most useful citizen in New York...."

2   ANON.   "Corruption Not the Trouble," New York Times
        (16 December), p. 3.
        Riis reports to the Good Government Club on improvements
        the Club has wrought in way of tenements, schools, and
        prisons; he laments the fact that city officials place

obstacles in the path of reformers: "'The trouble with this city,' said Mr. Riis, 'is not unadulterated corruption. It is stupidity, with incidental corruption.'"

3   ANON.   "The Day of Little Things," Brooklyn Eagle
         (19 October). Scrpbk. p. 127.
            Report of Riis's speech in Plymouth Church. Riis
         addressed himself to the strengths and weaknesses of the
         Good Government Clubs, and on the need for citizens to
         become involved in local affairs.

4   ANON.   "Edward Atkinson's Figures," New York Evening Sun
         (15 February). Scrpbk. p. 126.
            Describes the debate between Riis and Atkinson at the
         Century Club in Boston. Atkinson argued that the slum-
         dweller, not the conscience of the reformer, created the
         tenement house problem. Riis pointed out that "the whole
         question of the tenements was one of public conscience..."
         and observed that "in the case of those persons who had
         lived in Mulberry Bend...when they were turned out they
         were absorbed into other parts of the city without
         difficulty."

5   ANON.   "Good Government Club Plans," no journal given (1896).
         Scrpbk. pp. [127-28].
            Describes Riis's speech to Club A of the Good Government
         Clubs on February 20. Riis "spoke in a way which attracted
         the members..." and was elected General Secretary. Riis's
         job is assigning tasks to the various clubs.

6   ANON.   "Jacob Riis Doesn't Know Passaic," no journal given
         (20 November). Scrpbk. p. 135.
            Riis's observation--that Passaic had no places that
         rivalled the New York slums--is disputed. Passaic has
         tenements which "easily rank with the worst of his
         pictures."

7   ANON.   "King's Daughters' Day," New York Sun (10 April).
         Scrpbk. p. 127.
            In this report of the celebration, Mrs. Louis Seymour
         pointed out that the New York Tenement House Chapter was
         organized "because the summer corps of physicians found
         that there was no one to aid them in carrying out their
         attempts at relief. The doctors went to Jacob Riis...and
         Mr. Riis promptly went to the King's Daughters and put
         the case before them."

8   ANON.   "Millions of Babies," New York Tribune (18 December).
        Scrpbk. pp. [127-28].
            At the home of Mrs. Parsons, Riis spoke "in the interests
        of the Bryson Day Nursery." Riis "urged the need of caring
        for the poor, and gave graphic pictures, both pathetic and
        amusing, of his experiences with the waifs and wanderers
        of all ages and sizes in this great city."

9   ANON.   "Mr. Riis's Hen Roost," New York Sun (30 January).
        Scrpbk. p. 126.
            Story tells of Riis's efforts to raise chickens at his
        Richmond Hill home only to have most of the brood stolen
        by a "hungry Richmond Hiller." Article goes on to say
        that "It is a part of Mr. Riis's nature to be hopeful.
        He has hopes even that some day the tenement houses will
        go and that all poor people will live in houses with per-
        fect sanitary arrangements and that happiness will take
        the place of misery."

10   ANON.   "Plenty of Work Ahead," New York Tribune (18 October).
        Scrpbk. p. 128.
            Quotes Riis's speech, "The Day of Little Things,"
        delivered at Plymouth Church in Brooklyn.

11   ANON.   "Result of Mr. Riis' Lecture," Passaic Daily News
        (23 November). Scrpbk. p. 127.
            Mentions an earlier speech by Riis and its effect:
        "Last evening the Y.M.C.A. parlor was filled to overflow-
        ing with an audience gathered to discuss plans for prac-
        tical work along the lines indicated by Jacob Riis in his
        recent lecture."

12   ANON.   "Talked on the Tenement House Problem," Boston
        Transcript (13 February). Scrpbk. p. 126.
            Riis spoke of the effects of the slum upon the tenement
        house dweller. He pointed out that "conscience was what
        was needed to solve the tenement-house problem. Not more
        law, but enforcement of existing law, was required."

13   ANON.   "They Work in the Tenements," New York Sun (15 April).
        Scrpbk. p. 126.
            Article about the sixth anniversary of the New York
        Tenement House Chapter of the King's Daughters and Sons.
        Miss Sophia Brewster observed that the Chapter "really had
        its birth in the heart and brain of Jacob A. Riis...."

14   ANON.   "To Have a New Party," New York Times (27 May), p. 8.
            At a meeting of the Good Government Club, Riis spoke of
        the movement to improve the sanitary conditions of
        tenements.

1896

15 ANON. "Truant Schools Discussed," New York Tribune
(22 February). Scrpbk. p. 126.
Reports Riis's address to the Public Education Association. Riis pointed out that the war against truants could
be won by constructing more schools, and more attractive
schools.

16 PRYOR, JAMES W. "Notes on Municipal Government," Annals of
the American Academy of Political and Social Science, 8
(November), 573-86.
States Riis was appointed general agent of the Good
Government Club. Riis's success in enlisting the support
of the authorities in his "strenuous efforts to improve
the condition under which the great body of New York's
citizens live" is noted, as also the fact that "nearly a
hundred rear tenements have now been condemned"--the
result of a special investigation conducted by Riis since
the time of his appointment.

17 ROOSEVELT, THEODORE. "Police Department," New York Journal
(22 July). Scrpbk. p. 116.
In a "Report to the Board of Police Commissioners,"
Roosevelt proposes Riis for an appointment to the Commission, and of the candidate says that "No man knows more
about the details of the Police Department and would be a
better advisor than Mr. Jacob Riis."

1897 A BOOKS - NONE

1897 B SHORTER WRITINGS

1 ANON. "The Church Club of New York," Churchman (10 April),
pp. 567-68. Scrpbk. p. 131.
At a meeting of the Club on March 31, Riis spoke about
"Social Discontent, Its Causes and Remedies." Riis emphasized that "the Church ought to furnish a solution for
the present discontent...." He pointed out that "there
is too little flexibility in the present social structure.... This century has given us popular government,
which has in a measure failed to attain to anything like
the success that its proposers believed it would reach."

2 ANON. "Citizenship in the Tenements," Century Magazine, 33
n.s. (December), 313.
Riis's books--How the Other Lives, The Children of the
Poor--"are brimming as well with the drama of lowly life
as with facts and practical suggestions--suggestions

which...have born fruit even beyond the hopes of this
cheerful and persistent philanthropist."

3   ANON.   "Conlin Disobedient," New York Evening Sun (16 April).
Scrpbk. p. 130.
      Riis called upon to testify in a news leak case regarding
the apparently confidential handling of the arrest of men
charged with stealing Civil Service papers.

4   ANON.   "Evils of the Tenements," no journal given
(4 January). Scrpbk. p. 129.
      At a dinner of the Reform Club, Riis spoke about the
moral aspects of the tenement-house system. The system
was "an invention of Satan," and Riis argued that it "is
entirely unnatural and fosters immorality. It destroys
the home and home instincts. Hence the tenement question
is a social as well as a moral question."

5   ANON.   "For Little Orphans," Plainfield Daily (6 October).
Scrpbk. p. 133.
      Speaking at a Presbyterian Church, Riis's "subject was
the typical city 'tough' whom he called Tony." Riis
described the lack of opportunity that faced the child in
the slum. He asked, "Bad boy? Bosh! He is only normal;
give him a chance to amuse himself in a natural way, and
you won't see so much crime."

6   ANON.   "Fresh-Air Charity," Baltimore News (18 May).
Scrpbk. p. 132.
      Riis, in an interview, describes the benefits of the
Fresh-Air Fund, and the need for city playgrounds.

7   ANON.   "The Fresh-Air Fund," Baltimore News (18 May).
Scrpbk. pp. [131-32].
      The article lauds Riis's efforts in promoting the Fresh-
Air Fund, and mentions the latter's successes.

8   ANON.   "The Genesis of the Gang," Chautauqua Assembly Herald
(6 August). Scrpbk. p. 133.
      A description of Riis's speech which dealt with the life
of "a typical street-arab...." Riis described his early
struggles in Jamestown where he worked for a furniture
factory, and mentioned his newspaper days in New York.

9   ANON.   "Graveyard; Playground," New York Sun (2 March).
Scrpbk. p. 130.
      At a meeting of the East Side Good Government Club, Riis
reported on the progress made in securing necessary consent

from officials of the city and the corporation of a ceme-
tery to transform a forgotten graveyard into a playground.

10 ANON. "How Criminals Are Made," Newark Evening News
(18 March). Scrpbk. p. 129.
Riis, in the Association Hall of Newark, spoke of the
reform work in New York that was coping with vagrants and
tenement children. He commended Newark for barring from
its library "two of New York's sensational papers."

11 ANON. "International Convention of the Brotherhood of
St. Andrew," Churchman (23 October), pp. 501, 525.
Scrpbk. pp. [133-35].
Discussing the question "What are the conditions of
social progress," Riis asserted "that men can be helped
toward reformation, regeneration, by the reformation of
their environment...." He observed that the "demand of
society to-day was for justice, and that justice was a
condition of true social progress." Riis argued that the
poor, "in their ignorant groping for relief...are wont at
times to wander off on wild theories, such as Socialism,
and even anarchy."

12 ANON. "A Miracle and a Miracle Worker," Christian Work
(21 October). Scrpbk. pp. [133-35].
A tribute to Riis for being responsible for the creation
of Mulberry Bend Park. Riis "originated the 'small parks'
scheme" and he "pushed it in the press and Legislature...."
He has "lived to see his plans well on their way to full
fruition."

13 ANON. "Moss and Parker in a Row," no journal given (26 May).
Scrpbk. p. 116.
Reports Riis's interpretation of the Clarendon Hall
incident; Riis attested to Roosevelt's unblemished
character.

14 ANON. "Mulberry Bend's Park," New York Sun (16 June).
Scrpbk. p. 132.
A report of the opening of the park, formerly the site
of Mulberry Bend. Commissioner Waring called "for three
cheers for Jacob A. Riis, to whom, he declared, the chief
credit for getting the park was due."

15 ANON. "New York Tenements," Brooklyn Eagle (14 October).
Scrpbk. pp. [133-35].
A report of Riis's lecture at the Vassar Institute.
After speaking of the need to reclaim tenement children,
Riis praised Theodore Roosevelt as Police Commissioner.

16 ANON.   No heading found, New York <u>Sun</u> (21 March).
        Scrpbk. p. 130.
        Short blurb about Riis's "discourse upon tenement house
        life" at the home of Judge Henry Howland.

17 ANON.   "Parks and Play-Grounds," <u>Harper's Weekly</u>, 41
        (18 September), 919.
        The thoughts expressed in Riis's "Small Parks and
        Public-School Play-Grounds" pertain not only to the condi-
        tions of New York, but also to those of large American
        cities.

18 ANON.   "Play as Part of an Education," <u>Pathfinder</u> (29 May).
        Scrpbk. pp. [131-32].
        A brief mention of Riis's address to the Civic Club of
        Philadelphia. Riis stressed the element of play in the
        cultivation of a boy's moral nature.

19 ANON.   "Playground for City Children," <u>New York Tribune</u>
        (1 May), p. 14.
        Review of Riis's lecture delivered before the Physical
        Education Society of New York. Riis "pointed out the
        moral as well as the physical value of playgrounds," and
        provided suggestions for their establishment and
        regulation.

20 ANON.   "Scenes in the Big Tenements," <u>Poughkeepsie News-Press</u>
        (14 October). Scrpbk. p. 133.
        At a speech delivered in the Vassar Institute, Riis--
        after describing his association with the King's Daughters--
        depicted the plight of slum children who succumb to their
        environment. At one point he argued that "Love one another
        is the solution of all the difficulties."

21 ANON.   "Schoolrooms for Clubs," New York <u>Sun</u> (6 January).
        Scrpbk. p. 129.
        In a report to the council of confederated Good Govern-
        ment Clubs, Riis detailed his investigations of "the where-
        abouts of the boys and girls of the poorer districts at
        night before bed time." Riis "conceived the idea of open-
        ing the schoolhouses for them, as has been done in London
        for some years."

22 ANON.   "Will It Bear Good Fruit," no journal given (no date
        given). Scrpbk. p. 142.
        Riis's lecture to the Christian Endeavorers of Passaic
        "is simply an old story rehashed in new colors and with
        new features." Riis spoke of the work of charitable

1897

organizations "to uplift the poor and lonely." Riis has "a marked German accent" and he "is a native of Hamburg, Germany."

23 ANON. "Work for Athletes," New York Evening Post (4 December). Scrpbk. pp. [133–35].
    Praises Riis--in an article examining the athlete's virtues--for "persistence and endurance, physical and moral...."

24 DEVINE, EDWARD T. "The Shiftless and Floating City Population," Annals of the American Academy of Political and Social Science, 10 (September), 149–64.
    A discussion of poverty and its correction. Devine dismisses the attitudes of the social revolutionist and the ineffective conservative in favor of the reformer who "looks for radical change in the long run." He refers to Riis in a discussion of the stale-beer dives: "The Stale-beer dives, of which Mr. Riis has given the best description, have disappeared within a very short time."

25 HULL, WILLIAM I. "The Children of the Other Half," Arena, 17 (June), 1039–51.
    The children are forced to live in the midst of poverty, drunkenness, and squalor, argues Hull, who derived the title of this article, it seems, from Riis's How the Other Half Lives.

26 ROOSEVELT, THEODORE. "Administering the New York Police Force," in American Ideals and Other Essays, Social and Political. New York: G. P. Putnam's Sons, pp. 160–88.
    Cites Riis's valuable advice in helping the force. Riis "helped us most by advice and counsel, by stalwart, loyal friendship, and by ardent championship of all that was good against all that was evil...."

27 _____. "Municipal Administration: The New York Police Force," Atlantic Monthly, 80 (September), 289–300.
    Same article as "Administering the New York Police Force (1897.B26)."

1898 A BOOKS - NONE

1898 B SHORTER WRITINGS

1 ANON. "Children of the Poor," Providence Journal (26 October). Scrpbk. p. 139.

Speaking in Sayles Hall, Riis described conditions that
existed at the beginning of his work in New York, and
showed slides of New York's slums.

2   ANON.   "The City Child's Case," Fall River Evening News
    (1 April). Scrpbk. p. 136.
        Winning a "ready hearing," Riis spoke about "The Boy and
    His Sister," a subject that dealt with "the condition of
    and moving influences surrounding the boy and the girl in
    tenement-house districts of New York and other American
    cities...." Riis is described as a "first class speaker"
    who "has mastery of the art of public deliverance...."

3   ANON.   "The Federation of Churches and Christian Workers in
    New York City," Annals of the American Academy of Political
    and Social Science, 11 (March), 296-98.
        Riis listed as a member of the Investigation Committee,
    sponsored by The Federation of Churches and Christian
    Workers in New York City, which reported on conditions in
    the Nineteenth Assembly District, "a tenement-house sec-
    tion lying between Sixtieth and Sixty-eighth streets."

4   ANON.   "Good Side of the Slums," Brooklyn Eagle (18 February).
    Scrpbk. p. 136.
        Riis asserted that the young men who were products of
    the lower East Side were not altogether to blame for the
    flaws in their character. In fact, a large number of these
    youths "made better men than could be expected when condi-
    tions surrounding their home life were taken into consider-
    ation." Riis spoke of the need for recreational facilities
    for slum children.

5   ANON.   "Good Work," Buffalo Commercial (18 November).
    Scrpbk. p. 135.
        At the Independent Club, Riis spoke about "Tony's Hard-
    ships," the story of a slum-dweller's education and
    career. Riis is lauded for his interesting talk and for
    helping to bring about one of the most successful meetings
    the Club has had.

6   ANON.   "Home, School, Play," no journal given (18 November).
    Scrpbk. p. 138.
        Riis spoke of "Tony's Hardships" to 125 members of the
    Independent Club. The article quotes Riis observing that
    the three "supports"--home, school, and play--"have been
    torn away from the New York child of the slums...and
    greed, grief and selfishness have taken their place."

1898

7   ANON.   "In Memory of Waring," New York Times (23 November),
       pp. 6-7.
          Riis, the last speaker at a public eulogy of Waring,
       said that he "not only swept our streets, but swept the
       cobwebs out of our civic conscience as well."

8   ANON.   "It Must and Shall Prevail," Buffalo Commercial
       (18 November). Scrpbk. p. 136.
          Riis's praise of Roosevelt is quoted, and the article
       points out that Roosevelt's tactics vindicated the career
       of Col. Waring.

9   ANON.   "J. A. Riis on Slum Life," Chicago Times-Herald
       (1 August). Scrpbk. p. 137.
          Called a "high authority on the rescue work of city
       slums," Riis was asked to "give some account of his ex-
       perience in the slums in New York and elsewhere...." Riis
       is quoted at length about the ambition of upward mobility
       that marks many inhabitants of the slums. Riis observed
       that the demolition of tenements is "a destructive remedy"
       and pointed to the constructive work of R. Fulton Cutting.

10   ANON.   "Jacob A. Riis Before Holyoke Audiences," Springfield
       Republican (19 December). Scrpbk. p. 136.
          Mentions two of Riis's speeches, and Riis's stereopticon
       slides of buildings torn down by the New York Board of
       Health.

11   ANON.   "Literature," New York Evening Post (no date given).
       Scrpbk. p. 135.
          A short piece commenting upon Riis's Century article,
       "Light in Dark Places." Only workers in the Tenement
       House Commission, the Health Department, or the Associated
       Charity "can read between the lines of this noble showing
       of results."

12   ANON.   "Miscellaneous," Outlook, 60 (10 December), 923.
          Review of Out of Mulberry Street: "Every story in the
       book is inspiring because it recognizes that love is the
       greatest gift in life," and "hope, not hopelessness, is
       the result of reading these photographic pictures of life
       in lower New York."

13   ANON.   "Mr. Riis's Lay Sermon," Century, n.s. (November 1898-
       April 1899), p. 315.
          A New England pastor invited Riis, who was vacationing
       in the Berkshire area, to speak to the youth of his church
       about the virtues of country life and the false allurements
       of the city. Riis outlined the misfortunes of slum life
       and prophesied a future prosperity for the farm.

14   ANON.   No heading found, <u>Boston Evening Transcript</u>
         (30 November). Scrpbk. p. 136.
         Speaking about "The Battle with the Slum" Riis described
     what had been done in New York to destroy impoverished
     areas.

15   ANON.   "Regeneration of Our 'Tony,'" <u>Buffalo Evening News</u>
         (18 November). Scrpbk. p. 138.
         Another report of Riis's address to the Independent
     Club. Of Riis, the article states that "he speaks right
     from the heart--the heart of a true philanthropist--and
     tells you just what he knows and not what he or someone
     else has worked out in theory." Talking for two hours,
     Riis described Tony "in all his phases of degraded develop-
     ment, from the ragged infant to the old tout in the prison
     cell."

16   ANON.   "Slum Boys of New York," <u>Buffalo Evening Times</u>
         (18 November). Scrpbk. p. 137.
         In a speech to the Independent Club, Riis dwelt on
     "Tony's Hardships." Tony has been made what he is "not
     through his own fault, but through ours, for we have robbed
     him of home, school and play."

17   ANON.   "Their Salvation," <u>Philadelphia Ledger</u> (16 February).
         Scrpbk. p. 136.
         Under the auspices of the City Parks Association, the
     Horticultural Society, and the Civic Club, Riis talked
     about "The Children of the Poor and the Need of Playgrounds,
     Open Spaces, and Recreation Piers in Large Cities." Riis
     spoke of the difficulties in molding good citizens out of
     slum children, and argued that "given opportunities for
     play, the perversion of a lad's nature is practically
     stopped."

18   ANON.   "They Cheered Roosevelt," no journal given (18 October).
         Scrpbk. p. 117.
         The report of a speech by Riis at the New Haven Congrega-
     tional Club; Riis is labeled "Reis." His talk was "really
     fragments of thoughts" from <u>How the Other Half Lives</u>. "In
     speaking of boys' clubs Mr. Reis said that the boys' club
     is beter than the policeman's and it costs less. He also
     said that a cooking school was worth 50,000 sermons...."

19   ANON.   "Tony's Hardships," <u>Buffalo Courier</u> (18 November).
         Scrpbk. p. 137.
         Riis tells of his first encounter with "Tony," a street
     urchin, and describes the tenement system that worked

1898

against Tony's moral character. "The champion outrage against Tony," Riis declaimed, "is in robbing the boy of play." The tenement environment was responsible for Tony's plight.

20 ANON. "Wiping Out the New York Slums," Toronto Mail-Express (19 September). Scrpbk. p. 117.
A lengthy interview with Riis in which he speaks of his writings, his activities, and their effects.

21 ANON. "World Has Killed the Sweatshops," New York World (October). Scrpbk. p. 139.
Riis, appointed to investigate the evils of sweatshops, declared that "exposures in The World already had resulted in the greatest improvement in the sweatshop conditions...." Riis is quoted about the O'Leary controversy, and the battle against the sweatshop.

22 AYRES, PHILLIP W. "Summer School in Philanthropy," Annals of the American Academy of Political and Social Science, 12 (September), 319-23.
Riis lectured on "the gathering and study of statistics" to a class training in philanthropic work during the six weeks between June 20 and July 30, 1898. This summer course was sponsored by the New York Charity Organization.

23 PAULDING, J. K. "The Public School as a Center of Community Life," Educational Journal, 15 (February), 147-54.
Argues that public schools are agencies that "work in behalf of the common life," and that "They furnish on the whole, the strongest social force available in furtherance of the establishment of a common or national ideal." Commends Riis's proposal to make playgrounds of new school houses public playgrounds for the children of the neighborhood.

1899 A BOOKS - NONE

1899 B SHORTER WRITINGS

1 ANON. "About the Slums," Richmond [illegible] Times (7 November). Scrpbk. pp. [154-59].
Riis is called a "famous New York newspaper man, whose special assignment is police reporting." Riis's address was entitled "The Slums of New York."

2   ANON.   "Citizens Dine Roosevelt," New York Times (25 March),
        p. 7.
            In an address to the "Citizens' Union Club of the
        Twenty-seventh and Twenty-ninth Assembly districts,"
        Roosevelt proclaimed that Riis was one of "the two men we
        could least afford to lose in New York...." The other was
        Arthur Von Briesen.

3   ANON.   "Jacob Riis an 'Easy Mark,'" no journal given (no date
        given). Scrpbk. pp. [154-59].
            In a brief vignette, Riis is described as a man who
        "can't resist sentiment of the wholesome kind" even though
        he is a veteran police reporter.

4   ANON.   "King's Daughters' Settlement," Charities 2 (13 May),
        10.
            Riis, introduced as "the most useful man in the city,"
        spoke about the great value of the settlement's work.

5   ANON.   "Move for Slum Parks," Chicago Times-Herald
        (11 November). Scrpbk. pp. [154-159].
            Addressing the Merchants' Club, Riis pointed out that
        the real victim of the slum is the home, and that the "way
        to fight back" is to build playgrounds. "It is a wicked
        city," he said, "where the boy is denied a chance to play
        and to go to school. Build your parks and playgrounds,
        and the boy gets a chance at once, and when he gets it he
        will go to work and back you up."

6   ANON.   No heading found, Charities, 2 (13 May), 14.
            Riis's series of articles, beginning with the May number
        of the Atlantic Monthly, deals with the life of the poor,
        and the changes "that have come in their condition in the
        ten years" since How the Other Half Lives was published.

7   ANON.   No heading found, New York Evening Post (16 November).
        Scrpbk. p. [unnumbered loose page].
            Credits Riis for his part in school reform: "There is
        improvement in the schools...all due in a measure to the
        efforts of enthusiasts in whose work Mr. Riis must be held
        to have had a great share."

8   ANON.   "Rewards of Study Given to Graduates," Brooklyn Eagle
        (23 June). Scrpbk. pp. [154-59].
            At the graduation ceremony held by Pratt Institute,
        Riis instructed the graduates to set before them "two men
        as examples"--Theodore Roosevelt and George E. Waring.
        Waring "did not weigh expediency" and Roosevelt "never had

any other standard than the right, with a strong mind and a strong body...." Riis's speech drew long applause.

9   ANON. "Riis, Jacob August," in Who's Who in America; A Biographical Dictionary of Living Men and Women of the United States, 1899-1900, edited by John W. Leonard. Chicago: A. N. Marquis and Company, p. 607.
      Brief sketch of Riis's life and American career.

10   ANON. "The Slums of New York," Tribune Republican (28 January). Scrpbk. p. 141.
      Describes Riis's address at the Academy of Music and his previous appearance at the "Theological school" and Allegheny College. Riis spoke of "the misery of the poor in the centres of population and the ensuing vice and crime...."

11   ANON. "Want Sunlight in Slums," Chicago Tribune (12 November). Scrpbk. pp. [154-59].
      In an account of Riis's speech to the Merchants' Club, the play movement is stressed. Riis observed that "It was in the minds of the men who wrote the constitution that our boys should play. If that is not in your minds and in mine then the constitution is not worth the paper it is written on." He added that a boy "robbed of his chance to play will not be an honest and effective man--you can't depend on him at the polls."

12   FITCH, illegible. No heading found, San Francisco Chronicle (January). Scrpbk. p. 141.
      A review of Out of Mulberry Street; most of these stories have come from the New York Sun and are "one of the features of the great newspaper." These stories are crafted and "finely wrought...." The book will "stimulate genuine charitable work among the poor...."

13   GROSZMANN, MAXIMILIAN P. E. "Criminality in Children. II. As to Cures," Arena, 22 (November), 644-52.
      Riis's "Playgrounds for City Schools" points out that the "creation of healthy social conditions will go a great way toward the elimination of crime." Riis's article is "very suggestive."

14   HENDERSON, C. R. "The New Books," Dial, 26 (16 June), 399.
      Reading Riis's Out of Mulberry Street, "One does not think of 'literature', but of life." These stories of "New York City life among the lowly" are written masterfully and with "mighty pathos." Riis and writers like

him are not to blame "If the public remains ignorant and apathetic in relation to the Unemployable."

1900 A BOOKS - NONE

1900 B SHORTER WRITINGS

1 ANON. "Among the New Books," Chicago Tribune (March). Scrpbk. pp. [173-75].
        A review of A Ten Years' War; Riis can see hope and encouragement for slum reform in spite of Tammany Hall's resistance. "Success and triumph have indeed begun to signalize this war" against the tenements. The book's style "reflects the character of its subject matter and is terse and forcible rather than graceful or elegant."

2 ANON. "Back to the Soil," Republican (12 December). Scrpbk. p. 175.
        "Making a Way Out of the Slums," Riis's article in the December Review of Reviews, is summarized.

3 ANON. "Battle of the Slums," Pittsburgh Commercial Gazette (16 February). Scrpbk. p. 161.
        Riis's talk, "The Battle of the slums," was delivered with "forcible language, interesting anecdotes and a series of graphic pictures." Introduced by Senator Arthur M. Kennedy, Riis spoke of the efforts to abolish the slums. That morning, at the Twentieth Century Club, he talked about "Tony's Hardships."

4 ANON. "Battle With the Slum," Rock Island Union (14 December). Scrpbk. pp. [175-77].
        In his speech, "The Battle With the Slum," Riis praised Roosevelt for his exertions in reform work when he was Police Commissioner. The lecture "did people good to hear it and to see with their own eyes what men of earnest purpose can accomplish for their fellow men."

5 ANON. "Battle With the Slums," Indianapolis Journal (18 February). Scrpbk. pp. [159-61].
        Speaking at Plymouth Church, Riis pointed out that "the solution of the tenement-house question is a matter on which the civil government of New York rests to-day, for municipal government is never either much worse or much better than its homes...."

1900

6   ANON.   "Battle With the Slums," Pittsburgh Dispatch
        (16 February). Scrpbk. p. 161.
            Riis spoke on "The Battle With the Slums" at the Carnegie
        Library Building. He argued that such a struggle was for
        "the American homes." He added, "As the home is, so is
        the citizenship." He related the work done by the Civic
        Club and other reform groups.

7   ANON.   "Battles with Slums," New York Times (10 March),
        p. 158.
            Examines Riis's arguments and lauds his book as "valu-
        able." Riis is credited with making New Yorkers aware of
        the conditions of poverty.

8   ANON.   "Chicago the Tramps' Paradise," Chicago Tribune
        (approx. November). Scrpbk. p. 92.
            Riis's view of tramps contrasted with that of Chicago's
        Mayor Harrison, who called himself "'a friend of the
        tramp.'" Riis seen as "a friend of the deserving poor,"
        Harrison as a friend of "the undeserving poor."

9   ANON.   "The Children of the Poor," Charities, 5
        (1 December), 20-21.
            Riis, at the annual meeting of the Children's Aid and
        Protective Society of the Oranges, argued that "he had
        found greater youthful depravity in some smaller places
        than in the slums of New York...." No children were bad
        by nature; "there was no such thing as total depravity."
        Riis pleaded for the construction of playgrounds "where
        the energy and spirit of these boys and girls may find
        vent in healthful exercise."

10 ANON.   "Children of the Slums," Indianapolis Journal
        (19 February). Scrpbk. pp. [159-61].
            Speaking again at Plymouth Church, this time about
        "Tony's Hardships," Riis painted the "little incidents of
        child life, showing how they were cared for and how,
        through wicked surroundings, evil associates and neglect
        by Christians in better circumstances, they grew up in
        evil ways."

11 ANON.   "Chronicle and Comment," Bookman, 11 (April), 103-4.
            Riis, according to this critic, is no ordinary police
        reporter. He is a student of life rather, who will not
        let injustice stand. He has accomplished much in the way
        of tenement house reform, yet remains humble and behind
        the scenes. A Ten Years' War, because of the optimistic
        spirit behind it, can be called "cheerful slumming."

12   ANON.   "Decoration for Jacob A. Riis," Brooklyn Eagle
         (1 October). Scrpbk. p. 178.
            Riis, "the well known writer on social questions," has
         been granted the decoration of the "Order of Dannebrog,
         the royal order of the Danish flag." It was presented to
         Riis by the Danish vice-consul at Riis's Richmond Hill
         home.

13   ANON.   "Decoration for Jacob A. Riis," New York Evening Sun
         (1 October). Scrpbk. p. 178.
            In a short paragraph, Riis is mentioned as having re-
         ceived the "gold cross of the order of Dannebrog," an
         award conferred by King Christian IX of Denmark.

14   ANON.   "Dedication of Alta House," Cleveland Plain Dealer
         (21 February). Scrpbk. pp. [154-59].
            Speaking at the dedication of Alta House, a social
         settlement project, Riis claimed that "the idea that
         heredity makes criminals is nonsense. It is environ-
         ment...that decides whether a child shall be a good man
         or not."

15   ANON.   Editorial, Churchman (3 March). Scrpbk. pp. [161-71].
            A puff for Riis's story about a visit to Ribe, the
         brief paragraph states that he "has held the attention"
         he won in How the Other Half Lives "by studies and stories
         that have blended the genius of the humorist with that of
         the artist, and suffused both with the glow of his enthu-
         siasm for social reform."

16   ANON.   Editorial, Hartford Courant (24 January).
         Scrpbk. pp. [154-59].
            Riis's address to the Civic Club is termed "in all
         respects choice." Riis is called "peculiarly magnetic
         and inspiring, and is an artist as well as a
         philanthropist."

17   ANON.   "Entertainments," no journal given (no date given).
         Scrpbk. p. 161.
            At the Cronkhite opera house in Little Falls, New York,
         Riis, on February 22, spoke about "Tony's Hardships."
         The lecture was termed "able" and "intensely interesting."

18   ANON.   "Evils of Tenements," New York Daily News
         (25 February). Scrpbk. p. 161.
            Under the auspices of the Tenement House Committee,
         Riis spoke about "what had been done in the past in the
         fight against tenement evils and of the way out of the
         difficulty."

1900

19   ANON.   "The Governor Goes Home," New York <u>Sun</u> (23 June).
          Scrpbk. p. 90.
             Governor Roosevelt, on June 22, visited Riis, who was
          recovering from an attack of angina pectoris, at his
          Richmond Hill home. The two men discussed Roosevelt's
          vice-presidential nomination.

20   ANON.   "Hear Riis Talk of Slums," <u>Chicago Tribune</u>
          (25 March). Scrpbk. p. 172.
             Addressing the housing conference at the Art Institute,
          Riis pointed out "how New York had gone wrong, and how
          it had been straightened out again." Riis argued "how
          Chicago should not go and how it should not build...."

21   ANON.   "Honored by the King of His Fatherland," <u>Richmond
          Hill Record</u> (6 October). Scrpbk. p. 178.
             An informal biography of Riis, occasioned by his being
          given the gold cross of the Order of Dannebrog. Riis's
          parlous New York days, his early jobs in America, and
          his success as a reporter and writer are described.

22   ANON.   Illegible title, illegible source (15 March).
          Scrpbk. p. 171.
             <u>A Ten Years' War</u> is "one of the most epoch-marking
          books that have appeared in many years." Riis's strug-
          gles against the evils bred by tenements are summarized.
          "One looks to see great results" from the book.

23   ANON.   "In Darkest Chicago," New York <u>Sun</u> (29 March).
          Scrpbk. p. 172.
             Riis's trip through "some of the worst districts on the
          West Side" is described. Riis "was reluctant to indulge
          in radical criticism of Chicago's city officials" but he
          did claim that those entrusted "with the enforcement of
          the city's sanitary regulations were grossly negligent."

24   ANON.   "In Slums of a Great City," <u>Omaha Bee</u> (7 December).
          Scrpbk. p. 90.
             Omaha people crowded Boyd's theater "to the limits of
          its capacity" in order to hear Riis talk about the slums
          and tenements of New York.

25   ANON.   "Jacob A. Riis," Chicago [illegible] (15 March).
          Scrpbk. p. 171.
             A tribute to Riis in which he is praised for his reform
          work and desire--in spite of his fame--to be "a simple
          working man." The eulogy ends with the thesis that "this
          is one secret of his success--believing much, to him is
          much given."

26   ANON.   "Jacob A. Riis Speaks to Large Audience," <u>Hartford
        Times</u> (24 January). Scrpbk. pp. [154-59].
            A report of Riis's talk given to the Civic Club. Riis's
        topic was "Boy" and dealt with "Tony," a street gamin.
        Riis described "Tony's" wretched life and pleaded for the
        establishment of more schools "so no children will run
        the streets...." Riis pointed out that play is the
        child's safety-valve.

27   ANON.   "Jacob A. Riis Tells of the Slums," <u>Syracuse Post-
        Standard</u> (28 November). Scrpbk. pp. [175-77].
            Riis's lecture, "The Battle with the Slums," is summa-
        rized. Riis described the evils of the tenements, the
        vested interests in slums, and the obstacles placed in
        the path of reform. Riis argued that a "cooking school
        would do more to knock out the liquor traffic than any-
        thing else. When a man does not get what he wants to
        eat...he resorts to liquors...."

28   ANON.   "Jacob Riis and His Compatriots," <u>Rockford Morning
        Star</u> (10 December). Scrpbk. p. 177.
            In an editorial, Riis is compared to Carl Schurz,
        Professor Goldwin Smith, and Mrs. Ballington Booth--
        reformers of foreign birth who made their home in America.

29   ANON.   "Jacob Riis' Epic of the Slums," <u>Chicago Times-Herald</u>
        (3 March). Scrpbk. p. 171.
            Sub-titled "Story of His Long Battle to Purify New York
        Plague Spots Now Put Between Covers," the review lauds
        Riis and <u>A Ten Years' War</u>. Riis is described as "an
        eminent authority on the conditions of life among the
        poor and criminal classes...." His style is described as
        "aphoristic and quotable and many of his incidents will
        bear repetition."

30   ANON.   "Jacob Riis on New York Slums," <u>Rockford Morning Star</u>
        (10 December). Scrpbk. p. 177.
            Called "one of the great men of the times," Riis spoke
        about "Tony's Hardships" in the Y.M.C.A. course at the
        opera house. Riis not only described Tony's life but also
        explained the changes reform had brought about in the last
        five years. He stressed the power of the environment in
        shaping the lives of slum dwellers.

31   ANON.   "Jacob Riis on the Tramp Nuisance," <u>Chicago Times-
        Herald</u> (approx. November). Scrpbk. p. 92.
            Riis's feelings about tramps are examined. Hoboes may
        get sympathy from Mayor Harrison, but Riis seems them as
        "irreclaimable blackguard[s] and lazy lout[s]."

1900

32   ANON.   "Jacob Riis's Lecture," <u>Hartford Courant</u>
     (24 January). Scrpbk. pp. [154-59].
        A summary of Riis's lecture, "Tony's Hardships," de-
     livered before the Civic Club. Riis stressed the need
     for "play" in the slums, since no "home and school priv-
     ileges" existed.

33   ANON.   "Jewish Success," <u>Outburst</u> (15 December).
     Scrpbk. p. 175.
        Riis's article describing the colony of resettled
     Russian-Jewish emigres in New Jersey ("Making A Way Out
     of the Slums") is summarized.

34   ANON.   "Letter," <u>Charities</u>, 4 (12 May), 14.
        Riis's remarks and investigation in Chicago are "bearing
     fruit" for many tenements are being condemned by the Board
     of Health.

35   ANON.   "Mr. Riis Lectures at Harvard on New York Slums," no
     journal given (21 January). Scrpbk. pp. [154-59].
        Riis's lecture, "The Battle with the Slums," is sum-
     marized. Riis contended that "as long as the slum remained,
     the safety of the home was endangered."

36   ANON.   "New Playgrounds for Cleveland," <u>Cleveland Plain
     Dealer</u> (18 February). Scrpbk. p. 159.
        Riis will speak at Association Hall. His struggle to
     eradicate New York's slums and his efforts to establish
     small parks and playgrounds are described. Riis "thinks
     that with the improvement of environment will come a bet-
     ter formation, which will dispense with the need of so
     much effort for reformation." Riis's ideas have importance
     for Cleveland.

37   ANON.   "New York Slums," <u>Indianapolis Journal</u> (18 February).
     Scrpbk. pp. [159-61].
        Speaking at Plymouth Church "before an audience of liter-
     ary club members," Riis dealt with "The Battle of the
     Slums." He contended "that man is his brother's keeper
     and bound up in his brother's concerns." He pointed out
     that the "battle of the slums is fought for decent living
     for the workers--not for the tramps and the shiftless...."

38   ANON.   "New York Slums Improved," <u>Cleveland Plain Dealer</u>
     (20 February). Scrpbk. pp. [154-59].
        Speaking about "The Battle With the Slums" at Associa-
     tion Hall, Riis related how the slums--thanks to the work
     started by Theodore Roosevelt and Col. George Waring--were
     "fast becoming decent places to live in...."

39   ANON.   No heading found, <u>Churchman</u> (approx. March).
          Scrpbk. pp. [173-75].
          <u>A Ten Years' War</u> is summarized. The description of the
      war against the slums is "an inspiration to read" for
      there have been "some notable victories for the cause of
      righteousness."

40   ANON.   No heading found, <u>Detroit Free Press</u> (no date given).
          Scrpbk. pp. [173-75].
          <u>A Ten Years' War</u> is a record of progress, for Riis has
      "lifted the veil that concealed the hideousness of the
      great city's under world." Riis is lauded as "the fore-
      most exponent of philanthropic endeavor in the submerged
      districts."

41   ANON.   No heading found, New York <u>Evening Sun</u> (10 March).
          Scrpbk. p. 161.
          <u>A Ten Years' War</u> is termed "interesting" and "instruc-
      tive." The book's contents are summarized.

42   ANON.   No heading found, <u>People's Monthly</u> (no date given).
          Scrpbk. pp. [173-75].
          <u>A Ten Years' War</u> "records so much good accomplished" but
      the "glimpse into the blackness beyond" fills the mind
      "with wonder and dread at the conduct of the majority of
      dwellers in the world of day."

43   ANON.   No heading found, <u>Richmond Hill Record</u> (29 December).
          Scrpbk. p. 151.
          In an article that deals with notable figures of Rich-
      mond Hill, Riis is described as a friend of Governor
      Roosevelt. The article points out that "The men are not
      unlike in a good many ways...." The piece ends with a
      wish that the country had more Roosevelts and "our town
      more Riises."

44   ANON.   No heading found, <u>St. Louis Globe-Democrat</u> (no date
          given). Scrpbk. p. 173.
          <u>A Ten Years' War</u> is of "high sociological value" and
      more interesting than <u>How the Other Half Lives</u>. The re-
      viewer adds that "Mr. Riis has been at the head and front
      of the crusade for municipal cleanliness and the trans-
      forming of the slum beast into a human creature."

45   ANON.   "The Overcrowded Poor," no journal given (24 November).
          Scrpbk. p. 195.
          Riis's testimony, at a public hearing concerning "The
      General Evils of the Tenement House Construction" is

summarized. At this hearing of the Tenement House Commission, Riis spoke about the conditions and uses of air-
shafts, and pointed out that fire escapes on the outside
of buildings were better than those in air-shafts. He
contended that prostitution in the tenements could be
checked if the landlord was held accountable for the number of people who slept in his building.

46   ANON.   "Playgrounds As a Cure for City Crime," Brooklyn
      Times (27 April). Scrpbk. p. 151.
        Speaking to the Brooklyn Society for Parks and Play-
      grounds for Children, Riis contended that the "'right of
      boys to play ball is as important to society as is the
      right of the citizen to the writ of habeas corpus.'" He
      claimed that "there was no such thing as a depraved child,
      and he characterized the theory that there were depraved
      children as rank nonsense."

47   ANON.   "Reform of New York's Morals," Brooklyn Eagle
      (23 April). Scrpbk. pp. [177-78].
        Referring to Riis's speech, delivered in Chicago, of the
      struggles and history of New York reform, the editorial
      mentions several major victories: the Lexow investigation,
      the anti-Tweed campaign, the movement against "dark and
      rear tenements." Riis "insists that there is increasing
      evidence that the public conscience has now become almost
      continually awake" and this produces "permanent" results.
      Riis contended New York had advanced far beyond Chicago;
      the Chicago of today reminded him of the New York of
      twenty-five years ago.

48   ANON.   "Reporter in Slums," Davenport Republican (13 December).
      Scrpbk. p. 177.
        Riis's lecture, "The Battle With the Slums," is called
      "entertaining" and "broad in scope, treating in a prac-
      tical way, of the features of tenement house life...."
      Riis explained model tenements, the problems facing slum
      children, and the effects of reform.

49   ANON.   "Riis Comes Tonight," Joliet Republican (4 December).
      Scrpbk. pp. [175-77].
        Riis, who would lecture that evening in a Y.M.C.A. course,
      "did not mince words in telling Mayor Harrison Saturday,
      where the fault lay with his administration in allowing
      Chicago to be infested with thieves and all sorts of
      thugs." Riis claimed that nightly holdups were the result
      of the attitudes held about the tramp; the professional
      tramp should be put in jail.

50   ANON.   "Riis on Slums," Des Moines State Register
         (9 December). Scrpbk. pp. [173-75].
         Riis, speaking at Drake University, is described as
         doing "more than any other man in New York to clean out
         the slums." Probably speaking about "The Battle with the
         Slums," Riis related the story of his newspaper career and
         his efforts to reform the tenements.

51   ANON.   "Riis on the Tenement Problem," Chicago Times-Herald
         (20 March). Scrpbk. pp. 172-73.
         This editorial disputes Riis's claim that the "suburbs
         offer the natural escape for the poor laborers of the
         congested districts." Laborers do not have the money to
         purchase lots, and do not have the time to journey into
         the city. It does agree with Riis that there is a need
         for small parks, and experiments with model tenements as
         part of the solution to the problem of the slums.

52   ANON.   "Riis on Tramp Problem," Chicago Times-Herald
         (4 December). Scrpbk. pp. [175-77].
         Riis, a "sociologist," believes that once the tramp
         problem is settled in Chicago, crime will be reduced. He
         pointed out the success of New York's municipal lodging
         houses.

53   ANON.   "Riis; One of 'Other Half,'" Chicago Tribune
         (22 April). Scrpbk. pp. [177-78].
         This short biographical sketch traces "what bearing his
         [Riis's] own life and experiences" have had upon his writ-
         ings. Riis's "hard knocks" as a young man, and immigrant,
         are recounted. Riis is quoted on the difficulty he had in
         finding a publisher for How the Other Half Lives.

54   ANON.   "Riis Visits the Slums," Chicago Tribune (28 March),
         p. 172.
         After traveling through some of the worst areas on the
         West Side, Riis claimed that conditions were worse than in
         New York. Accompanied by Gertrude Howe, a Hull House offi-
         cial, Riis wandered through such streets as Halsted, Polk,
         Ewing, and Clinton. Riis pointed out that Chicago needed
         an aroused "organized, active, powerful, public sentiment,"
         in addition to small parks, clean streets, and enforcement
         of sanitary regulations in order to remedy such horrible
         conditions.

55   ANON.   "Saviors of Society," Seattle Post-Intelligencer
         (16 December). Scrpbk. p. 175.

1900

In an editorial analyzing the impact of "intelligent
self-interest" upon economic laws and society, Riis's
"Making A Way Out of the Slums" is summarized.

56   ANON.   "Slumming with Mr. Riis," Berkshire Eagle
     (26 January). Scrpbk. pp. [154-59].
     At the First Congregational Church, Riis lectured on
     "The Battle with the Slums." Of him, the article states
     that "No one man has done more to bring about a reform in
     the slums of New York...." Riis spoke about the "relations
     of the home to the state," and "wanted to stamp out one of
     his greatest enemies--heredity, (which is nothing more or
     less than pure pessimism."

57   ANON.   "Sociological Work," Cleveland Leader (20 February).
     Scrpbk. pp. [154-59].
     An account of Riis's lecture at Association Hall. The
     talk was "illustrated with stereopticon views of New York
     slums, and also modern flat houses that have been erected
     to take their place...."

58   ANON.   "Some Tenement Problems," Chicago Times-Herald
     (25 March). Scrpbk. p. 172.
     Speaking at Fullerton Hall, in which the tenement-house
     conference was held, Riis devoted himself to "The Tenement
     Problem and the Way Out." He suggested that Chicago's
     solution to the problems of the slums should be different
     from New York's; the latter adopted certain measures be-
     cause it had to. Chicago's geography is different; it
     can expand. It is, Riis pointed out, "free, and its resi-
     dents can go into the suburbs."

59   ANON.   "The Struggle With the Tenement," Brooklyn Eagle
     (approx. March). Scrpbk. pp. [173-75].
     Riis's accomplishments are sketched. "Mr. Riis believes,
     with other workers in this wide field, that the children
     offer the only field that is capable of improvement. The
     parents are too deeply fixed by habit and association in
     old ways."

60   ANON.   "Talks of the Tenement House," Chicago Record
     (25 March). Scrpbk. p. 172.
     In this account of Riis's lecture at the Art Institute,
     Riis noted that Chicago was "fifty years behind New York
     on the tenement-house problem." He warned that Chicago
     could not allow such conditions to prevail longer.

61   ANON.   "Ten Years' War," Boston Daily Advertiser
        (23 February). Scrpbk. p. 173.
        In this review of A Ten Years' War, Riis is called "an
        unfailing source of reliable suggestions" about the prob-
        lems of the slums. Citing the chapter headings, the re-
        viewer lauds Riis's wit and optimism. "If ever there was
        a cheerful volume, this is the book. It is as full of
        life as a glorious June day...."

62   ANON.   "A Ten Years' War," Charities, 4 (26 May), 11-12.
        Riis is praised as a "reformer without the vice of re-
        form." A Ten Years' War strikingly illustrates the effec-
        tiveness of reform work which recognizes "the fact that
        human nature is everywhere the same...." The book should
        be "carefully studied" by those who are working for
        reform.

63   ANON.   "A Ten Years' War," Holyoke Transcript (no date given).
        Scrpbk. pp. [173-75].
        The optimist will be pleased with A Ten Years' War, for
        its "tone is most charming, showing as it does the wonders
        that have been accomplished in the New York slums...."
        Riis's commendations of Waring and Roosevelt are cited,
        and the reviewer contends that not even Tammany Hall can
        restore the old order after such progress.

64   ANON.   "A Ten Years' War," Literary Digest (14 April).
        Scrpbk. pp. [177-78].
        A Ten Years' War is seen against the background of a
        "long cherished project" of Riis's having come to fruition:
        the Tenement-House Exhibition, on Fifth Avenue, "designed
        to furnish an object-lesson to 'the First Half' of how
        'the Other Half' lives." The article quotes the major
        theses of Riis's book, and mentions the hopeful signs of
        present reform: cleaner streets, the destruction of un-
        sanitary tenements, public parks, recreation piers,
        playgrounds.

65   ANON.   "Tenement House Boy," Boston Herald (18 April).
        Scrpbk. p. 90.
        The Merchants' Club invited Riis to speak at their last
        meeting of the season. Riis spoke of the New York slum
        and of juvenile crime and reform. Boys should have schools
        with playgrounds, vacation schools, cooking schools, a
        place to play ball, and boys' clubs, he suggested.

66   ANON.   "Tenement House Reform in New York, 1834-1900," Annals
        of the American Academy of Political and Social Science,
        16 (July), 164-65.

A synopsis of the report Lawrence Vieller, Secretary of the Tenement House Commission, submitted to the Commission on May 8, 1900. It recounts the legislative history of tenement house reform in New York City, beginning with the Board of Health inspector's report in 1834 and ending with a compliment paid to the new Tenement House Commission of 1900. In between these dates it relates projects and incidents such as the "Workmen's Home Association" and the 1863 "draft riots" which shaped legislative attitudes toward tenement house reform. Riis is placed in a social and historical context.

67 ANON. "Tour of the Sweatshops," New York Sun (1 June). Scrpbk. p. 90.
    Report on Gov. Roosevelt's unexpected tour of the East Side sweatshops. James B. Reynolds and Riis accompanied Roosevelt.

68 ANON. "Training of the Youth," Indianapolis News (19 February). Scrpbk. pp. [159-161].
    In a summary of Riis's speech about "Tony's Hardships," emphasis is placed upon the evils of tenement houses and on the fight against "bad school houses." Riis stressed the need for "play" facilities in the slums.

69 ANON. "An Unpleasant Discovery," Chicago Tribune (29 March). Scrpbk. p. 173.
    Commenting upon Riis's description of Chicago's tenements, the article states that his criticism of the filthy conditions of the slum districts apply in varying degrees to the streets in all parts of the city.

70 ANON. "What to Do With the Slums," Syracuse Post-Standard (22 February). Scrpbk. p. 161.
    Speaking before the University Club, Riis described "the lives of the slums of New York and the factors which make up their character." He emphasized the need for educational reforms in the public schools.

71 AYRES, PHILLIP W. "The Summer School in Philanthropic Work," Annals of the American Academy of Political and Social Science, 15 (March), 297-300.
    Announces summer school project sponsored by the Charity Organization Society in New York City to be held from June 18 to July 28, 1900. Riis is listed "among those who have taken part in the work of the school in previous years, and who are expected this year."

72   McNUTT, GEORGE. "Riis's Fight on Slums," <u>Indianapolis News</u>
      (19 February). Scrpbk. pp. [159-61]
        After summarizing Riis's speech at Plymouth Church, Riis
      is called "a second Froebel" and characterized as having
      "a nose for news...a heart for humanity...."

73   MARSHALL, DEXTER. "Our New York Letter," <u>Port Jervis Evening
      Gazette</u> (23 January). Scrpbk. pp. [154-59].
        The letter opens with the controversy over Riis's efforts
      to get Hannigan, a policeman who shot a boy, out of prison.
      It quickly becomes a defense of Riis who is praised for his
      ideals and his refusal--in the face of fame--to give up his
      "chosen calling" of police reporting. Marshall states that
      "at present he is the real brains of the movement for puri-
      fying the morals of the east side."

74   STODDARD, RICHARD HENRY. "Literature," <u>Mail and Express</u>
      (22 March). Scrpbk. p. 173.
        Praising Riis for his efforts to clean up the slums,
      Stoddard warns the reader not to be complacent about pres-
      ent conditions; the fight has not been won yet. Explaining
      <u>A Ten Years' War</u>'s appeal, Stoddard says that Riis's bat-
      tles are "well told" and "popular in style." He concludes
      by pointing out how great a figure Riis is for the "moral
      and physical health of the community."

1901 A BOOKS - NONE

1901 B SHORTER WRITINGS

1   ANON. "Bishop Dedicates New Settlement," New York Herald
      (6 March). Scrpbk. pp. [189-91].
        Bishop Potter's speech, dedicating the Jacob A. Riis
      House, is summarized. Potter had described Riis as a man
      who "has got mother heart as well as father heart...."
      Moved by this tribute, Riis recounted the episodes of his
      boyhood "when he came here as a friendless stranger."

2   ANON. "Books Received from February 1, 1901 to April 1, 1901,"
      <u>Annals of the American Academy of Political and Social
      Science</u>, 17 (May), 525-27.
        Riis's <u>A Ten Years' War</u>, published by Houghton, Mifflin
      & Co., is listed as a new title.

3   ANON. "Children and Crime," <u>Chicago Record</u> (8 February).
      Scrpbk. p. 92.
        Before the Union League club, Riis not only criticized
      the people of Chicago for the conditions inside their

1901

police stations, but also pleaded for the poor children of Chicago's streets.

4   ANON.   "Home Named for Mr. Riis," New York World
        (6 March). Scrpbk. p. 191.
            In this account of the dedication of Jacob A. Riis House,
        Riis is quoted as saying that he received the "greatest
        encouragement" from his journalism career to engage in his
        philanthropic work. Bishop Potter had noted earlier that
        "To think of a modern reporter as a philanthropist rather
        taxes the imagination."

5   ANON.   "Honoring Jacob A. Riis," New York Tribune
        (6 March). Scrpbk. pp. [189-91].
            In this description of the dedication of the Jacob A.
        Riis House, it is pointed out that the ceremony occurred
        on Riis's twenty-fifth wedding anniversary. In a speech,
        Riis said that it "was his mother and his wife...who had
        been at the root of all the work that he had accomplished."
        A motion was made to have Mrs. Riis made honorary chairman
        of the House Committee.

6   ANON.   "Jacob A. Riis Honored," New York Times (6 March),
        p. 8.
            Calls Riis a "writer on sociological topics" and men-
        tions that his silver anniversary is being commemorated by
        the dedication of the Jacob A. Riis House.

7   ANON.   "The Jacob A. Riis House," Churchman (16 March).
        Scrpbk. pp. [191-93].
            The article--a brief description of the dedication of
        Riis House--states that Riis, in his address, spoke of the
        dignity "that might surround the journalist's profession,
        for which he had come to have a genuine reverence."

8   ANON.   "Jacob A. Riis in Detroit Last Week," Cleveland Jewish
        American (8 February). Scrpbk. p. 181.
            As a guest of the Fellowship Club, Riis, in Detroit,
        toured various reform institutions, such as a settlement
        and a mission.

9   ANON.   "Jacob A. Riis Speaks to Schoolboys," Brooklyn Standard-
        Union (23 March). Scrpbk. p. 189.
            Riis, addressing pupils at the Polytechnic Institute,
        spoke about "three men who occupy conspicuous places in
        history." Riis exhorted the students to "make an honor-
        able name" and cited as examples Patrick Mullen (an Astoria
        gunsmith), George E. Waring, and Theodore Roosevelt. His

speech was punctuated by cheers, and he told the audience
to follow Roosevelt's motto "Better be faithful than
famous."

10   ANON.   "Jacob A. Riis Was Anxious to See the Fire,"
      Cincinnati Tribune (28 January). Scrpbk. p. 91.
           The same night Riis spoke at Music Hall in Cincinnati to
      a crowd of 3,000 people, the Grand Opera House nearby
      caught fire. Riis talked afterwards to reporters about
      the Brooklyn theater fire, the worst fire he had ever
      witnessed.

11   ANON.   "Jacob Riis' Silver Wedding in His Little White House,"
      Brooklyn Eagle (2 March). Scrpbk. p. 189.
           In sketchy fashion, the article describes Riis's life in
      Denmark, his newspaper days, and friendship with Roosevelt.
      Of Mrs. Riis, it says that she is "musical" and at a re-
      cent "Danish afternoon," of the Twentieth Century Club,
      she "entertained the guests with some excellent Danish
      music." Riis's house is described, notice being taken of
      a replica of Thorwaldsen's Christ, a framed passport issued
      to Riis by "his friend, the Governor," and a framed letter
      with an offer of $1.00 "for his 'Other Half' people."

12   ANON.   "The King's Daughters' Settlement," Evangelist
      (14 March). Scrpbk. pp. [195-97].
           This description of the opening of the Jacob A. Riis
      House summarizes the tributes to Riis. He is called "the
      one from whom we have drawn our best inspiration in times
      of discouragement." A brief history of the settlement, and
      pictures of the Riis House are included.

13   ANON.   "Making a Way Out of the Slum," Jewish Chronicle
      (England) (11 January). Scrpbk. pp. [193-95].
           Above the heading, Riis had penned "The most influential
      Jewish paper in Europe." The article is a series of Riis's
      observations, taken from the American Review of Reviews,
      about the Woodbine colony: an experiment in resettling
      Russian-Jewish emigres in farming and manufacturing
      communities.

14   ANON.   "The Making of an American," Outlook, 69 (14 December),
      993.
           The "keynote" of Riis's autobiography "is that of hope-
      fulness and helpfulness."

15   ANON.   "Memorial of a Reporter's Service," New York Evening
      Post (4 March). Scrpbk. pp. [191-93].

1901

Invitations to the formal opening of the Jacob A. Riis
House have been sent out. Riis's career is briefly
sketched, and Roosevelt's tribute to Riis, in McClure's,
is quoted.

16   ANON.   "Mr. Jacob A. Riis," Jewish American (8 February).
Scrpbk. p. 181.
     Based on a day-long meeting with Riis, the editorial
calls him a "whole-souled man, all heart and good will
toward his fellow beings" and observes that "his simple
courtesy and kindly manner marks the true gentleman."
His zeal is mentioned in eradicating the slums.   In a
typographical error that Riis underlined and in the margin
penned three exclamation points the essay states that "Vice-
president Rosenfeld says that Jacob A. Riis had done more
for New York city than any man in America...."

17   ANON.   "Mr. Riis's Autobiography," New York Times
(7 December), p. 912.
     The Making of an American "is not so much a contribution
to literature as it is the outpouring of a man with whom
words have always been subordinated to fact."   Faults Riis
for revealing personal matters that should be kept private.
Noteworthy is a point critic and Riis hold in common:
that the emigrant should have first acquired "a realiza-
tion of his responsibilities as a citizen, before according him the privileges of a voter."

18   ANON.   "Named 'Jacob A. Riis House,'" New York Sun (6 March).
Scrpbk. pp. [189-91].
     In a short description of the dedication ceremonies,
Riis's early involvement with the King's Daughters is
related.

19   ANON.   "Naming a New Settlement House," New York Evening
Post (5 March).   Scrpbk. pp. [189-91].   In an account of
the dedication of the Jacob A. Riis House, Riis is described as "a New York reporter who has done much for
social improvement of the East Side, and he was the first
to suggest establishing the flower mission, from which
grew the settlement."   A description of the functions and
furnishings of the settlement is given.

20   ANON.   "The National Conference at Washington," Annals of the
American Academy of Political and Social Science, 18
(September), 373-74.
     On May 9-15, 1901, the National Conference of Charities
and Correction met in Washington, D.C.   "At the opening

session the principle addresses were delivered by
S. G. Smith of St. Paul, and Mr. Jacob A. Riis, of New
York."

21 ANON. No heading found, Charities, 7 (26 October), 344.
Brief entry: Riis's articles, "The Battle with the
Slums (Churchman, October 12, 19), are written "with his
characteristic vigor and optimism."

22 ANON. No heading found, Churchman (16 March).
Scrpbk. p. 195.
Riis's tribute to Dr. Rainsford, the rector of St.
George's, is quoted. Riis's remarks, "Religion by Human
Touch," were published in "The World's Work."

23 ANON. No heading found, Harper's Weekly (11 March).
Scrpbk. p. 193.
Everyone who reads newspapers knows something about Riis.
His activities as a reporter are described, and, it is
argued, that if he lives long enough, and has "the right
sort" of municipal government to aid him, "he will be a
notable power in the accomplishment of things more wonder-
ful still."

24 ANON. No heading found, New York Evening Post (11 March).
Scrpbk. p. 193.
In a brief editorial, Riis's work and struggles are
praised. "Journalism is under a debt to Mr. Riis for
showing how valuable to a community a reporter may become
who uses his eyes and exercises his thinking powers while
in the discharge of his duties as a newsgatherer."

25 ANON. No heading found, New York World (approx. 18 March).
Scrpbk. p. 195.
Speaking at Carnegie Hall, Riis compared efforts to
drive out vice to St. Patrick's expelling the snakes from
Ireland. He related stories of the "horrors surrounding
the children" in the tenements, and said that the meeting
"was really called by the children of the east side."

26 ANON. "A Notable Silver Wedding," Richmond Hill Record
(9 March). Scrpbk. p. 191.
In this substantial account of Riis's silver wedding,
mention is made of the festivities, presents, and guests.
In the margin, Riis corrected the errors. Prof. Finley,
Riis pens, does not occupy the chair of literature, but
"politics" at Princeton. He presented Riis with a copy
of Hamlet, "with his dedication," Riis notes.

1901

27   ANON.   "Notes," <u>Nation</u>, 73 (12 December), 454-55.
        Riis's autobiography is "the artless picture of a strong
        and generous nature bringing forth fruit after its kind."

28   ANON.   "The Rights of Children," <u>Charities</u>, 7 (13 July),
        47-49.
        Speaking at the library of the Charity Organization
        Society, Riis argues that "not all the science in the
        world...could take the place in dealing with the problems
        of charity, of the feeling that prompts a man to pick up a
        baby and fondle...it at sight...." Riis contended that
        the home was the instrument which would best regenerate
        the family.

29   ANON.   "Riis' Conquest of the Slums," <u>Detroit Journal</u>
        (25 January). Scrpbk. p. 91.
        Riis, in his Y.M.C.A. Star Course lecture at the Light
        Guard Armory, spoke about the slum and its inhabitants.
        The telltale sign that "the slum has come into your city,"
        he said, is the rise in juvenile crime.

*30   ANON.   "Riis, Jacob August," in <u>Who's Who in America; A Bio-</u>
        <u>graphical Dictionary of Notable Living Men and Women of</u>
        <u>the United States, 1900-1902</u>, edited by John Leonard.
        Chicago: A. N. Marquis & Company.

31   ANON.   "The Riis Silver Wedding," <u>Brooklyn Eagle</u> (6 March).
        Scrpbk. p. 191.
        The article, a brief description of Riis's celebration
        of his twenty-fifth wedding anniversary, describes the
        Riis home which displayed Danish and American flags. A
        guest list is included.

32   ANON.   "Short Interviews," <u>Port Huron Times</u> (25 January).
        Scrpbk. p. 91.
        Rev. John Munday, after hearing Riis speak in Buffalo,
        urged "everyone who is at all interested in sociology" to
        "make a point of attending his lecture."

33   ANON.   "Slum Battle," <u>Cincinnati Enquirer</u> (23 January).
        Scrpbk. p. 91.
        Riis spoke in Music Hall at the request of the Cincin-
        nati Y.M.C.A. He "earnestly advised all those interested
        in sociological and charitable schemes...to carefully
        distinguish between giving and aiding, since one makes
        citizens and the other makes weak, helpless paupers."

34   ANON.   "Slums of New York," <u>Muskegon Morning News</u>
        (27 January). Scrpbk. p. 91.
            In this lecture given at the city opera house, Riis
        talked of tenement reform measures, fresh air funds,
        Gov. Roosevelt's replacement of police lodging stations
        with municipal lodging houses, and the power of public
        opinion to curb greed.

35   ANON.   "Smashing the Frying-Pan and 'Ice-Water Coolers,'"
        <u>New York Evening Journal</u> (27 February). Scrpbk. p. 179.
            Riis "says of the excitable Mrs. Nation that if she
        would use her hatchet smashing the frying-pans of Kansas
        she would do more good than in demolishing much saloon
        glassware." Riis's point is well made, for poor cooking,
        concoctions soaked in grease, "washed down by horrible
        ice-water" cannot but help drive a man to drink. The
        piece concludes by suggesting that "When we learn how to
        cook; when the frying-pan and the ice-water tankard become
        obsolete, the drink question will have been largely
        solved."

36   ANON.   "Sociologist at a Dance," <u>Chicago Tribune</u> (8 February).
        Scrpbk. p. 92.
            After Riis spoke before the Union League, a reporter of
        the <u>Tribune</u> took him to the Hinky Dink Ball, which the
        First Ward Democrats held that evening. The reporter
        wrote this account of the ball and attributed it to Riis.

37   ANON.   "Stories of Slum Life," <u>Detroit Free Press</u>
        (25 January). Scrpbk. p. 91.
            Riis told listeners gathered at the Light Guard Armory
        that the battle against the slum should be fought with
        "sunshine and education."

38   ANON.   "Tammany versus Decency," <u>Outlook</u>, 69 (26 October), 482.
            Reference to Riis's article "Tammany the People's Enemy":
        "Mr. Jacob A. Riis points out...that the present government
        [of New York] as now conducted by Tammany, is an enemy of
        common decency and the aider and abettor of vice and crime."

39   ANON.   "Women Denounce Vice," <u>New York Tribune</u> (18 March).
        Scrpbk. p. 195.
            In Carnegie Hall, at a mass meeting called by women to
        protest the existence of "protected vice," Riis said that
        New York, because of its tenements, had been called the
        "homeless city." He "attacked the 'official discretion'
        clauses in the tenement house" and said that he believed
        police corruption was found "among the higher officials...."

1901

40 ANON. "World Is Good, Not Bad' Says Jacob A. Riis," <u>New York Journal</u> (6 March). Scrpbk. p. 191.
A short paragraph, the piece quotes Riis pointing out that it is not difficult for a reporter to be good.

41 ELSING, WILLIAM T. "The Autobiography of New York's Most Useful Citizen," <u>Book Buyer</u>, 23 (November), 272-75.
Riis romanticized. Finds in him more charm and in his life more adventure than in truth there was. Sees "flashes of genius" in Riis. Presents Elizabeth in the image of a dime novel heroine. Says the story of Riis's "adventures, struggles, sufferings, courage, hope, triumph, and love, will stir the hearts and ennoble the lives of all."

42 ROOSEVELT, THEODORE. "Reform through Social Work. Some Forces that Tell for Decency in New York City," <u>McClure's</u>, 16 (March), 448-54.
Roosevelt writes about New York philanthropists he admires. Of Riis he says, "the countless evils which lurk in the dark corners of our civic institutions, which stalk abroad in the slums, and have their permanent abode in the crowded tenement houses, have met in Mr. Riis the most formidable opponent ever encountered by them in New York City." Riis has the four qualities which distinguish the best reformers: courage, "disinterested desire to do good," intelligence, and "a sound sense of humor."

43 SILL, HENRY A. "A Ten Years' War," <u>St. Andrew's Cross</u> (January), 87, 88. Scrpbk. pp. [181]-187-[189].
In this, one of the longest reviews of <u>A Ten Years' War</u>, photographs are given of Riis, a model tenement, pushcarts on Hester Street, and an air-shaft. Sill argues that the problems of New York City are found in every large city; the "vote of Mulberry Bend might have decided a Presidential election." Riis's career is traced, emphasis being placed upon his crusade against the Bend. Sill describes other victories "more glorious than Manila or Santiago," such as school reform, and the building of model tenements. He argues that the "community is responsible for the evils due to the conditions it tolerates" and scores landlords, builders, and religious societies for having vested interests in the slums.

1902 A BOOKS - NONE

1902 B SHORTER WRITINGS

1 ANON. "Autobiography of an Immigrant," Current Literature,
       32 (January), 71-73.
           Praises Riis's book because it highlights "the struggles
       and discouragements which beset the average immigrant."

2 ANON. "Riis, Jacob August," in Harper's Encyclopaedia of
       United States History from 458 A.D. to 1902, edited by
       B. J. Lossing. New York: Harper & Brothers. 10 vols.
       Vol. 7, p. 439.
           Biographical sketch of Riis.

3 DEVINE, EDWARD T. "The Making of an American," Charities, 8
       (1 February), 124-25.
           The Making of an American is the "best" book that Riis
       "has written since his first." Riis's autobiography is
       as "vivid" and "intense" as How the Other Half Lives.

4 DUTTON, EDITH KELLOG. "The Making of an American," Dial, 32
       (1 January), 8-10.
           Good, short sketch of Riis's life to 1902. Feels Riis's
       philosophy--"to see each little day as an important item
       in a big account"--is valuable because of its practical
       nature. Says The Making of an American "freights no isms
       or ologies."

5 GILDER, JOSEPH B. "The Making of Jacob A. Riis," Critic, 40
       (January), 63-64.
           Review of The Making of an American. Finds Riis's
       egotism too pronounced and his phraseology clumsy, yet
       contends that "the personality of Mr. Riis is an excep-
       tionally interesting and attractive one, and the frankness
       of his self-revelation is the chief merit of his book."

6 HAPGOOD, HUTCHINS. "Jacob A. Riis's 'The Making of an Amer-
       ican,'" Bookman, 14 (January), 497-98.
           "Mr. Riis writes an absorbing autobiography, in which he
       shows concretely how one man has become an American citi-
       zen, and a good citizen." Hapgood calls Riis "a real
       power behind the machinery of reform."

7 LEE, JOSEPH. Constructive and Preventive Philanthropy.
       New York: Macmillan Company, pp. 56, 58, 62, 127, 141,
       165, 228.
           Riis is quoted about intemperance, and the lack of
       water in tenement houses. His interpretation of the
       character of anti-Roosevelt forces is mentioned.

1902

        With the publication of <u>How the Other Half Lives</u>, Riis "created an epoch in the history of the tenement-house...." Riis's efforts in destroying Mulberry Bend are mentioned.

<u>1903 A BOOKS - NONE</u>

<u>1903 B SHORTER WRITINGS</u>

1   ALLEN, WILLIAM H. "The Battle with the Slum," <u>Annals of the American Academy of Political and Social Science</u>, 21, 302.
        Review of Riis's seventh book: "the story of the battle for decent homes and clean atmosphere and free play can never be told too often by one with such broad human sympathy and wide experience as Jacob Riis."

2   ANON. "The Battle with the Slum," <u>Nation</u>, 76 (23 April), 338-39.
        Review of <u>The Battle with the Slum</u>. Finds Riis's enthusiasm and belief that "the slum is the measure of civilization" notable.

3   ANON. "Battle with the Slum (The)," <u>Outlook</u>, 73 (3 January), 89-90.
        In this new book Riis has "vitalized sociology." His is not "the optimism that produces smug complacency, but that which produces exalted endeavor."

4   ANON. "Book Department," <u>Annals of the American Academy of Political and Social Science</u>, 22 (July), 217-42.
        Footnote on page 222 reads: "'Constructive and Preventive Philanthropy' By Joseph Lee, with an Introduction by Jacob A. Riis. Pp x, 242. Price $1.00. New York: Macmillan Co., 1902."

5   ANON. "Books of the Week," <u>Outlook</u>, 73 (3 January), 89-90.
        A review of <u>The Battle with the Slum</u>; Riis "vitalizes every subject that he touches" and his optimism is not an ameliorative one. It argues that "all is going well if we struggle."

6   ANON. "Books of the Week," <u>Outlook</u>, 74 (27 June), 526.
        Calls <u>The Peril and the Preservation of the Home</u> the "quintessence of Mr. Riis's experience in tenement-house reform work...." The lectures are full of inspiration and information, rare qualities "in sociological lectures on any subject."

7   ANON.   "Contemporary Celebrities," Current Literature, 35
         (October), 410-13.
             A few paragraphs are devoted to Riis who in 1903 was
         still working for the New York Sun. Credits Riis for
         bringing "a veritable renaissance" to the East Side.

8   ANON.   "The Education of Mr. Riis' Burglar," Charities, 2
         (29 August), 178-79.
             A reader of Charities charges that the letter which Riis
         published in the July 25 issue and attributed to a boy
         imprisoned for burglary could not have been written--
         because of language and style--by an uneducated criminal.

9   ANON.   "From Oyster Bay to Hoboken," Syracuse Evening Herald
         (approx. 7 September). Scrpbk. pp. [197-end].
             At the top of this entry, Riis had written "The Presi-
         dent's train was 3/4 hour ahead of time." The article
         describes how Riis, after being summoned by message, had
         to sprint to the train station in order not to delay the
         President's train.

10   ANON.   "How Jacob A. Riis Became Roosevelt's Ideal American,"
         New York World (13 September), p. 3. Scrpbk. pp. [197-end].
             Called a "fighter, a hard worker," Riis's battles against
         the slum, and his friendship with Roosevelt are described.
         Article contains a biography of him, and pictures of his
         family and home.

11   ANON.   "Jacob A. Riis," Outlook, 75 (5 September), 16-17.
             Preface to Riis's editorial "Has Reform Made Good."
         Calls "Has Reform Made Good" a "companion picture to
         Mr. Riis's 'What Has Tammany Done for the People.'" Taken
         together the two articles state Riis's case against
         Tammany Hall.

12   ANON.   "Jacob Riis His Text," New York Times (11 July), p. 5.
             Rev. Charles T. Wheeler based his sermon at the South-
         west Tabernacle upon The Making of an American, saying
         that Riis's life "illustrates the keeping, purifying,
         stimulating power of love."

13   ANON.   No heading found, no journal given (no date given).
         Scrpbk. p. 193.
             An exchange of two letters, one by Mr. A. Lucas, Secre-
         tary of the Union of Orthodox Jewish Congregations of the
         United States and Canada, and Jacob Riis, over which Riis
         wrote "The 'creed' of the Jacob A. Riis Neighborhood Set-
         tlement." Lucas wrote to Riis, saying that unsubstantiated

1903

evidence indicated that the Riis Neighborhood House had
"been conducted in a spirit not commendable to our people,"
and that Riis had claimed that "the influence of the Home
is intended to be purely Christian," while, in fact, "the
great majority of the beneficiaries of the institution
are Jews." Riis replied that "the Gospel of Love" will be
"preached in that spot, at least as long as we live."
Moreover, Riis retorted, the great majority of beneficiaries were not Jews. He emphasized, "Jews or Christians,
however, they are all welcome."

14 ANON.   "President at Richmond Hill," Brooklyn Eagle
     (September). Scrpbk. pp. [197-end].
        This editorial is a description of the Riis-Roosevelt
     friendship, "a revelation of character on both sides."
     Riis and Roosevelt "are splendid citizens, with a consti-
     tutional habit of believing all over what they believe at
     all."

15 ANON.   "President at Riis's Home," New York Evening Post
     (8 September). Scrpbk. pp. [197-end].
        An account of Roosevelt's speech at Richmond Hill.
     Roosevelt is reported saying that "when I preach about
     decent citizenship, I can turn to him [Riis], and think
     he has practised just what I have been preaching." He
     added that Riis "would never have been of any use in the
     Police Department if he had always carried on a rosewater
     revolution."

16 ANON.   "President Roosevelt Stops at Richmond Hill," Richmond
     Hill Record (approx. 8 September). Scrpbk. pp. [197-end].
        Addressing 2,000 people at Richmond Hill, Roosevelt
     lauded Riis as a "decent citizen, because he practises what
     I have been preaching all along." Roosevelt termed Riis
     a man who "can practically apply the spirit of decency
     without mournfulness, a man without false pretenses."

17 ANON.   "President Roosevelt's Ideal Citizen Described by the
     Citizen Himself in His Remarkable Book 'The Making of an
     American,'" New York World (20 September).
     Scrpbk. pp. [197-end].
        The review is a series of excerpts from Riis's auto-
     biography. The book will allow others to assess "the sort
     of man President Roosevelt considers an ideal American."

18 ANON.   "Riis Is Called 'My Ideal Man' by Roosevelt," New York
     News (8 September). Scrpbk. pp. [197-end].

In this description of Roosevelt's speech at Richmond
Hill, Roosevelt is quoted as saying, "Now, friends, do you
know why I am fond of Mr. Riis? It is because when I
preach on decent citizenship I turn to him, your fellow
townsman, and say: 'Here is my ideal.' When you preach
decency, apply it to practise."

19 ANON. "Riis, Jacob August," in Who's Who in America; A Biographical Dictionary of Notable Living Men and Women of
the United States, 1903-1905, edited by John W. Leonard.
Chicago: A. N. Marquis & Company, p. 1246.
Biographical sketch of Riis.

20 ANON. "Roosevelt Back," New York Evening Sun (8 September).
Scrpbk. pp. [197-end].
An account of Roosevelt's speech at Richmond Hill, in
which Riis was called "an example of a decent citizen,
because he practises what I have been preaching all
along...."

21 ANON. "Roosevelt Likes Fighting Men," New York Evening World
(September). Scrpbk. pp. [197-end].
The article describes Roosevelt's appearance, movement,
and speech at Richmond Hill. Roosevelt, praising the
"fighting qualities" of good men, said, "I am very fond of
Mr. Riis. When I preach of good citizenship I can point
to Mr. Riis and say there is an example of what I preach.'
At the top of the page, Riis wrote: "On Sept. 7, 1903, I
went to Syracuse with the President as his guest. He
picked me up at Richmond Hill, and on the return, Tuesday
morning, Sept. 8, stopped at Richmond Hill and spoke to
my neighbors. Hence all this spread!"

22 ANON. "Sketches by Riis," New York Times (12 December),
p. 949.
Children of the Tenements is essentially a collection of
"newspaper 'stories'" showing Riis's "sympathy" for those
who live on the East Side. "As literature, pure and
simple,...the stories are not in any degree remarkable."

23 COCKERELL, T. D. A. "Battle with the Slums," Dial, 34
(16 February), 119-20.
Three "living realities" of the book are: that residents of the slums do not have a fair chance, that given
better conditions they improve themselves, and that justice cannot wait on philanthropy. Referring to the masses
of workers from overseas who are crowded into the slums,
Cockerell sees in the future a possible welding of this

"miscellaneous and at first sight unpromising material into the structure of a great nation."

24 DeFOREST, ROBERT W. and VIELLER, LAWRENCE, eds. The Tenement
    House Problem. 2 vols. New York: Macmillan Company.
    Vol. 1, pp. 105, 110. Vol. 2, p. 4.
        In a section entitled "The Work of Jacob A. Riis," Riis
    is credited with doing more to educate the general public
    about tenement-house reform than any other individual. He
    was instrumental in tearing down Mulberry Bend, and de-
    stroying numbers of unsanitary rear tenements. Riis's
    membership in the Tenement House Committee of the Charity
    Organization Society and the Small Parks Committee is
    cited.

25 HODGES, LEIGH MITCHELL. "The Optimist: A Little Look at the
    Brighter, Better Side," Philadelphia North American
    (22 January). Loose leaf, Box 7, Riis MSS, L.C.
        Short article, but full of praise. "Riis climbed a
    'depraved' stairway from poverty that most good persons
    would hesitate to go up."

26 STEFFENS, LINCOLN. "Jacob A. Riis: Reporter, Reformer,
    American Citizen," McClure's, 21 (August), 419-25.
        A kind, objective appraisal of Riis written by a friend
    and fellow reporter. Riis more than deserved the three
    titles "reporter, reformer, American citizen." Nobody
    devoted himself so completely to the welfare of New York
    City as did Riis. He was "poor in pocket" but "rich in
    sentiment, and strength, and courage."

1904 A BOOKS - NONE

1904 B SHORTER WRITINGS

1   ANON. "Archbishop Goes Slumming," New York Sun
    (30 September). Scrpbk. pp. [197-end].
        Riis is mentioned as conducting the Archbishop of
    Canterbury on a tour of the East Side. The journalist-
    reformer explained "all the changes that had been made in
    the district."

2   ANON. "The Housing Problem Facing Congress," Charities, 12
    (February), 161-66.
        Included in this article are "extracts from an address
    made by Jacob A. Riis at the annual meeting of the Asso-
    ciated Charities of Washington D.C., December 15, 1903."
    A day later Riis addressed Congress on problems facing
    American cities.

3   ANON.   "Is There a Santa Claus?," Independent, 57
            (15 December), 121.
            Is There a Santa Claus, written in Riis's "usual
         artistic style," has certainly "the merit of being timely."
         For Riis "Santa Claus is by no means altogether a myth";
         his story shows why.

4   ANON.   Jacob A. Riis; A Sketch of His Life and Work.   New
            York: Macmillan Company.
            In a pamphlet of 17 pages, Riis's career and adventures
         are briefly recounted. This publication may have been a
         "puff" for Riis's Macmillan publications. Riis is called
         a "lusty Danish emigrant, with a vigorous body, an undis-
         ciplined mind that grasps facts as he himself sees them,
         an imagination to reconstruct, emotion to suffer, and a
         kind, fighting spirit...."

5   ANON.   "Lights and Shadows of Slum Life in New York,"
            Spectator, 92 (24 June), 984-85.
            Discusses in detail Riis's stories "Midwinter in New
         York" and "Making a Way Out of the Slum." Of the latter,
         says it "effectually contradicts any suspicion of laissez-
         faire intention" on the part of Riis.

6   ANON.   "The Lounger," Critic, 44 (January), 10, 12-15.
            A look at Riis, fifty-four years old, after his retire-
         ment from newspaper work. Riis is described as a man who
         "shuns publicity and has never been wont to talk about
         himself." Since Riis recently completed a book on
         Roosevelt, much of the article is dedicated to the Riis-
         Roosevelt friendship.

7   ANON.   "Modern American Idealists," Chautauquan, 38 (January),
            477.
            Short article and photograph in honor of Riis. "Journal-
         ist, author, lecturer, social reformer and public-spirited
         citizen generally, Mr. Riis is a fine example of 'Modern
         American Idealists.'" Summary of Riis's accomplishments
         included.

8   ANON.   No heading found, New York Sun (no date given).
            Scrpbk. pp. [197-end].
            In a brief article, Riis's letter--sent to the editor
         of a Danish paper in Council Bluffs--is quoted. The public
         library board in that town had refused to put Riis's life
         of Roosevelt in the library, for fear it would help
         Roosevelt get elected. Riis quipped, "No help is needed
         to do that, but if any were, they have given him, and in-
         cidentally my book, an able lift all through the East."

1904

9   ANON.   No heading found, no journal given (27 October).
         Scrpbk. pp. [197-end].
           Riis, speaking about "The Battle with the Slums" to Yale
         students, was described as a "speaker whose English is per-
         haps the most simple and forcible of any man now appearing
         before the American public." Riis related the horrors of
         the slums, and "scored Tammany again and again." He also
         praised Roosevelt and Waring.

10   ANON.   "President Roosevelt," Bookman, 26 (June), 100-101.
           "Mr. Jacob A. Riis is a whole-hearted hero worshipper,
         and in 'Theodore Roosevelt: the Man and the Citizen,' he
         gives us a frankly enthusiastic appreciation of the god of
         his idolatry."

11   ANON.   Picture entitled "President Roosevelt at Chautauqua,"
         Christian Advocate (24 August). Scrpbk. pp. [197-end].
           Underneath a photograph of Roosevelt, Bishop John Heyl
         Vincent, and Riis, taken on August 11, Riis wrote, "Thus
         I came back to the place that saw me [illegible word]
         through the rain in 1871 [illegible word] a poor, dis-
         couraged boy. And, God help us, I am poorer now than ever,
         for she is dead, who was [illegible word], despite all dis-
         couragement, my hope and the bright light of my life."

12   ANON.   "Riis, Jacob August," in The Twentieth Century Bio-
         graphical Dictionary of Notable Americans, edited by
         Rossiter Johnson. Boston: The Biographical Society.
         Vol. 1, no page numbers given.
         Biographical sketch.

13   ANON.   "Riis Praises the President," Cleveland Leader
         (11 October). Scrpbk. pp. [197-end].
           Speaking about "Roosevelt the Man" at Oberlin, Riis in
         "one sense of the word" opened the Republican campaign.
         Riis described Roosevelt's life "from the beginning of his
         work in the slums of New York City up to his election to
         the Presidency...."

14   ANON.   "Roosevelt the Man--Roosevelt the Citizen," Critic,
         44 (May), 459-62.
           A review of Francis E. Leupp's The Man Roosevelt: A
         Portrait Sketch and Riis's Theodore Roosevelt the Citizen.
         Defends Riis's enthusiasm for Roosevelt. Describes Riis
         as a man who "has ideals that he believes in." Concludes
         that to a man of Riis's romantic temperament "devotion to
         President Roosevelt is very easy to understand."

15   ANON.   "Theodore Roosevelt the Citizen," Nation, 79
      (8 September), 204-5.
        Theodore Roosevelt the Citizen "may mark the beginning
of a new politico-literary era." The book "is strenuous,
it is loud, it is fervid, it is unmeasured, it is not
logical."

16   ANON.   "Theodore Roosevelt: the Man and the Citizen,"
      Atheneum (30 April), 554-55.
        Little reviewing done here. Reviewer is interested in
Roosevelt's reputation in England and on the Continent.
Comments on Roosevelt's "exasperatingly 'copybook' character." Of Riis's book says its "general effect is vivid
and even brilliant."

17   GLADDEN, GEORGE. "Theodore Roosevelt. Two New Books,"
      Current Literature, 36 (April), 390-97.
        Two books are reviewed in this article, Francis E.
Leupp's The Man Roosevelt and Riis's Theodore Roosevelt
the Citizen. Riis's treatment of Teddy Roosevelt as a
boy, a student, a legislator, a Civil Service Commissioner,
a soldier, and a family man is touched upon, as are Riis's
stated impressions of Roosevelt's personality. Gladden
labels Theodore Roosevelt the Citizen "eulogistic," yet
sees merit in Riis's partiality toward Roosevelt. "Cold
criticism has never been a characteristic of the best
biographies of living men," he asserts.

18   HUNTER, ROBERT. Poverty. New York: Macmillan Company,
      pp. 16, 22, 73, 74, 186, 194, 208, 271, 278.
        How the Other Half Lives is credited with placing "the
figures of distress" before the reader. Riis's proposals,
based on his knowledge of tenement-house life, have received "too little consideration" from municipal govern-
ments and teachers themselves. Riis's observations on
Italians are quoted, and Hunter argues that industry has
failed to absorb "some few at least of the new comers."

19   PECK, HARRY THURSTON. "Two Books about President Roosevelt,"
      Bookman, 19 (April), 181-82.
        Attacks Riis for his "Teddyism." "Mr. Riis's subject
is surely not the President of the United States. It is
just Teddy, tout court." Theodore Roosevelt the Citizen
"would have been sure of a warmer welcome had it appeared
about a year and a half ago when strenuous Teddyism was
for the moment popular."

1904

20   RICE, WALLACE. "President Roosevelt as a Hero," Dial, 36
     (16 March), 190-92.
          A review of two books: Theodore Roosevelt the Citizen
     by Riis and The Man Roosevelt by Francis E. Leupp. Takes
     Riis to task for his unqualified devotion to Roosevelt:
     "For all Mr. Riis's Americanism--and in other respects it
     is hardly to be called in question--this adopted citizen
     seems to have ingrained in his character a feudal devotion
     to princes." Challenges a number of Riis's statements
     concerning Roosevelt and the Spanish-American War, and
     Roosevelt and Civil Service.

21   TRENOR, J. D. "Proposals Affecting Immigration," Annals of
     the American Academy of Political and Social Science, 24
     (July), 221-36.
          Trenor, Chairman of the Committee on Immigration, de-
     fends liberal immigration policies. Of the immigrant in
     the slums he says, "it is the tenement, not the tenant,
     that makes the slum." To support this point he quotes
     Riis on the successful transformation of the Mulberry
     Bend district from "pigsty" to "park."

1905 A BOOKS - NONE

1905 B SHORTER WRITINGS

1   ANON. "Jacob A. Riis for Mayor?," New York Times (1 August),
     p. 12.
          Alderman Meyers suggests Riis is the ideal candidate to
     run for mayor on an anti-Tammany ticket. Calls "the Riis
     boom the real Simon-Pure article in non-partisanship."

2   ANON. "Mr. Riis as an Advance Agent of the Portland Con-
     ference," Charities, 13 (14 January), 373-74.
          Riis, on a lecture tour of the Pacific Coast, was com-
     missioned by the National Conference of Charities and
     Correction to announce its coming convention which was to
     be held in Portland.

3   ANON. No heading found, New York Sun (9 September).
     Scrpbk. pp. [197-end].
          Riis put an end to rumors suggesting that he would be a
     possible fusion candidate for Mayor. He pointed out that
     "I have no desire to be set up as a man of straw and
     knocked down to help make an election day." Above this,
     Riis penned "In the fall of 1905 repeatedly the suggestion
     was discussed in the newspaper to run me for Mayor on the
     anti-Tammany ticket. I killed it by coming out for

McClellan, the Tammany Mayor, who had made a very good
Mayor."

4   FIELD, CLARA. "Correspondence," Outlook, 80 (8 July), 645.
         An appeal for $1,500 from Clara Field, treasurer of the
    Jacob A. Riis House, to help pay for "work in the homes
    [Riis House and the Henry St. Home], the care of the sick,
    the distribution of flowers, [and] the arrangement of day
    excursions." Mentions Riis's "overwhelming sorrow"
    [caused by his first wife's death].

5   HUNTINGTON, J. O. S. "In Memoriam, Mrs. Jacob A. Riis,"
    Craftsman (July), p. 520.
         The staff of the Craftsman published this article to-.
    gether with "In the Valley of the Shadow," a poem, "as a
    brief expression of...sympathy" for Riis upon the death
    of Elizabeth.

1906 A BOOKS - NONE

1906 B SHORTER WRITINGS

1   ANON. "Jacob A. Riis Dissents," New York Times (22 September),
    p. 1.
         Spelling reform a bone of contention between Riis and
    Roosevelt. Riis disapproved of action taken by the Sim-
    plified Spelling Board to simplify the spelling of 300
    words, though President Roosevelt had approved of the
    Board's action. Said Riis: "While I have every respect
    for the President and his judgment in all matters, yet in
    spelling reform I must disagree with him."

2   ANON. "Jacob A. Riis Is Ill," New York Times (7 February),
    p. 9.
         Riis suffered an attack of angina pectoris upon his
    return from a visit to the White House. He was confined
    to bed in his Richmond Hill home.

3   ANON. "Jacob Riis Tells of His Early Trials," New York Times
    (29 October), p. 7.
         Interesting account of Riis's address to the West Side
    Y.M.C.A. on October 27, 1906, in which he talks of his
    life. At one point in his life Riis considered suicide--
    this before he began his work as a reporter. As usual he
    lauds Roosevelt.

1906

4   ANON.   "Riis Gymnasium Opens on Roosevelt Birthday," New
         York Times (28 October), p. 13.
            An account of the dedication ceremony of Roosevelt Gym-
         nasium, the newest addition to the Jacob Riis Settlement
         House.

5   ANON.   "Riis, Jacob August," in The National Cyclopaedia of
         American Biography. Vol. 13. New York: James T. White
         & Company, pp. 114-15.
            Riis's life and work sketched. Riis "plunged into every-
         thing for the benefit of mankind that came his way...."
         His life contains "the greatest moral lesson of recent
         years...."

6   ANON.   "Riis, Jacob August," in Who's Who in America; A Bio-
         graphical Dictionary of Notable Living Men and Women of
         the United States, 1906-1907, edited by John W. Leonard.
         Vol. 4. London: Kegan Paul, Trench, Trubner & Company,
         p. 1498.
            Brief sketch of Riis's life.

7   ANON.   "Roosevelt for Mayor," New York Times (1 February),
         p. 9.
            Riis's enthusiasm for Roosevelt at high pitch in 1906.
         On a return trip from a visit to the White House, Riis
         suggests that Roosevelt at the end of his term as Presi-
         dent in 1909 run for the office of Mayor of New York City,
         calling the idea "a splendid illustration of our
         democracy."

8   CUTTING, R. FULTON.   "President's Report," Sixty-Third Annual
         Report of the New York Association for Improving the Con-
         dition of the Poor, for the Fiscal Year Ending September 30,
         1906. New York, pp. 9-21.
            An A.I.C.P. advertisement, "Death by Milk or Earthquake,"
         quotes Riis: "You can kill a man with a tenement as well
         as with an axe." Riis is praised for helping build Sea
         Breeze Hospital. The children of the United States are
         "indebted for his eloquent...advocacy of their cause."

9   Editors of Outlook.   "Preface to "A Gift of Health," Outlook,
         83 (21 July), 654.
            Editors of the Outlook, in prefatory remarks to Riis's
         article, "A Gift of Health," congratulate the reformer on
         his successful campaign to raise money for the building of
         Sea Breeze Hospital.

10 HUEBNER, GROVER D. "The Americanization of the Immigrant," in
    Annals of the American Academy of Political and Social
    Science, 27 (May), 653-75.
        Discussion of factors influencing the Americanization of
    the immigrant: public school, trade unions, church, poli-
    tics, employment. In treatment of effects of public and
    other schools on immigrant children, Riis is quoted from
    his The Children of the Poor: "The industrial school
    plants itself squarely between the tenement and the public
    school."

11 STOY, ELINOR H. "Child-Labor," Arena, 36 (December), 584-91.
        Riis mentioned with other famous reformers at work to
    solve the child-labor problem: "Jacob Riis, Josephine
    Lowell, Jane Addams and others whose names you know. A
    mere handful it is true, where so many are needed to help
    do what they can to better the conditions of these infant
    toilers."

1907 A BOOKS - NONE

1907 B SHORTER WRITINGS

1 ANON. "The Greed of the Landlord," Charities and the Commons,
    19 (21 December), 1283-84.
        References in this article to correspondence between
    "the Harlem Property Owners' Association and Jacob A. Riis."

2 ANON. "Twenty-five Years and After," Charities and the Com-
    mons, 19 (4 December), 1136-37.
        Report on the anniversary conference of the Charity
    Organization Society. Points out where Riis and the COS
    were in agreement. Includes a story of how Riis's fellow
    reporters at the Mulberry Street headquarters were taken
    for money by a pauper.

3 ANON. "Two National Boys' Club Organizations," Charities and
    the Commons, 17 (March), 1109.
        Mentions that "Jacob Riis is president of the Federated
    Boys' Clubs."

4 KELLOGG, PAUL U. "What Jacob Riis and a Thousand Boys Are Up
    To: The Opening of the Roosevelt Gymnasium on Henry Street
    This Week," Charities and the Commons, 17 (no date given),
    167-70.
        Account of the history and activities of the Jacob Riis
    Neighborhood Settlement House on Henry Street. Tells how

1907

Riis's spirit inspires house and workers: "In truth it is
that spirit of the north country--mystic but strongly
human, which pervades this Henry Street settlement...."
Announces dedication of new Roosevelt Gymnasium.

5   WATERMAN, MRS. JOHN BARNETT. "The Poor White Boy of the South:
     The Mobile Boys' Club," Charities and the Commons, 18
     (7 September), 650-52.
       Argues that boys' clubs could help to develop "great
     leaders in Southern upbuilding." Mrs. Waterman quotes
     from a letter Riis sent her: "You can do nothing better
     for your city than have a boys' club sensibly run."

1908 A BOOKS - NONE

1908 B SHORTER WRITINGS

1   ANON.   "The Cost of a Lecture Trip," Charities and the Commons,
     19 (15 February), 1589.
       A criticism of Riis's lecture fees: "A lecture by Jacob
     Riis will soon have to be reckoned a direct element in the
     budget of a town where he speaks, and city councils will
     be figuring whether they can afford him. Viewing him only
     as a promoter of big enterprises and measuring results in
     the dollars and cents of public and private money expended,
     he ranks with many a captain of industry."

2   ANON.   "Mrs. Humphrey Ward on Play," Charities and the Com-
     mons, 20 (11 April), 79-81.
       Riis's conception of play as "a safety valve for riotous
     boyhood" is cited.

3   ANON.   "Riis, Jacob August," The New Encyclopedia of Social
     Reform, edited by William Dwight Porter Bliss and Rudolph M.
     Binder. New York: Funk & Wagnalls Company. Reprint.
     Arno Press, 1970, p. 1068.
       Brief description of Riis's work.

4   ANON.   "Riis, Jacob August," in Who's Who in America; A Bio-
     graphical Dictionary of Notable Living Men and Women of
     the United States, 1908-1909, edited by Albert N. Marquis.
     Vol. 5. Chicago: A. N. Marquis & Company, p. 1588.
       Biographical sketch of Riis.

5   ANON.   "Riis on Play and Playgrounds," Journal of Education,
     68 (3 December), 591-92.

In his lecture presented to the Playground Conference of the Massachusetts Civic League, Riis encouraged the people of Massachusetts to continue their efforts in playground development, arguing that playgrounds eliminate juvenile delinquency. Riis mentioned his disgust for child labor.

6   LEONARD, PRISCILLA. "The Christmas Stamp in America," Outlook, 90 (3 October), 265-68.
Describing the stamp's American history, Riis's efforts are summarized. He "had been struck by the possibilities of the government stamp in Denmark, put on sale each year in the holidays, to aid the anti-tuberculosis fight.... He desired to transplant it to America, and had suggested that the National Anti-Tuberculosis Society should take it up with the Government." Leonard describes how Riis achieved his goal by publicizing his efforts in the Outlook.

1909 A BOOKS - NONE

1   ANON. "Literary Notes," Independent, 67 (2 December), 1267.
A review of The Old Town. The book, dealing with the place of his birth and his childhood, is an "unaffected book of memories." Ribe of Riis's recollections no longer exists, for "in Europe, as well as here, modern civilization, with its rush and pressure, has killed it."

2   ANON. "The New Book," Outlook, 93 (6 November), 559.
Review of The Old Town: "There are a freshness and sincerity about all that Mr. Riis writes that invariably win a quick response from his readers."

3   ANON. "New Site for the House of Refuge," Charities and the Commons, 21 (9 January), 644-45.
Riis credited for bringing to light--six years before-- the obsolete condition of the New York House of Refuge which would not foster "a high grade of reformatory work."

4   GLADDEN, WASHINGTON. Recollections. Boston: Houghton Mifflin Company, Riverside Press, p. 1.
Gladden claims that his autobiography "follows no such romantic paths as those in which Jacob Riis has led us."

1910 A BOOKS - NONE

1910

<u>1910 B SHORTER WRITINGS</u>

1   ANON. "In Memory of Mr. Gilder," <u>Outlook</u>, 94 (5 March), 516.
      Riis, before an audience gathered in memory of Richard
      Watson Gilder, spoke of "the human fellowship side of
      Mr. Gilder's career," and of "his deep sympathy with the
      people in the tenement-houses."

2   ANON. "The New Books," <u>Outlook</u>, 96 (15 October), 372.
      Review of <u>Hero Tales of the Far North</u>. Says Riis writes
      about Americans of "great deeds and patriotic ideals" in a
      style full of "animation and zest."

3   ANON. "The Question of Ready-Made Farms," <u>Craftsman</u>, 18
      (June), 401.
      Riis is mentioned as a supporter of a plan "to have an
      incorporated association, with plenty of capital at its
      command, [to] locate well-stocked model farms in various
      States and allot them to promising applicants."

4   ANON. "Riis, Jacob August," in <u>Who's Who in America; A Bio-</u>
      <u>graphical Dictionary of Notable Living Men and Women of</u>
      <u>the United States, 1910-1911</u>, edited by Albert N. Marquis.
      Vol. 6. Chicago: A. N. Marquis & Company, p. 1610.
      Biographical sketch.

5   HUNTINGTON, J. O. S. "Jacob Riis Revivalist," <u>Survey</u>, 24
      (7 May), 200-202.
      Describes successful lecture tour Riis made through
      Indiana. He spoke in South Bend, Terre Haute, Evansville,
      and Indianapolis. Riis's speeches for the cause of housing
      reform filled listeners with "the new zeal and fervor of
      a real awakening."

<u>1911 A BOOKS - NONE</u>

<u>1911 B SHORTER WRITINGS</u>

1   ANON. "The A.I.C.P. in Three Campaigns," <u>68th Annual Report</u>
      <u>of the New York Association for Improving the Condition</u>
      <u>of the Poor</u>, September 30, 1911. New York: no publisher
      given, pp. 95-105.
      Riis is called "indefatigable" for his "tireless energy"
      in the campaign to establish "Seaside Park" and a hospital.

2   ANON. "Offers Brighton for Park," <u>New York Times</u>
      (1 September), p. 4.

Reports a lively exchange between Riis and Mayor Gaynor arose over "the proposed acquisition by New York City of the Dreamland or the Rockaway Park beach fronts for a seaside park." Riis felt that $2,250,000 was a fair price for the land. The Mayor accused Riis of seeing only the humanitarian side of the matter.

3   PERRY, ARTHUR. "Wider Use of the School Plant," Craftsman, 20 (September), 634.
     Perry argues for a broadening of the role of the public school. He quotes Riis, who saw as the ultimate goal of settlement work the development of the public school.

1912 A BOOKS - NONE

1912 B SHORTER WRITINGS

1   ANON. "Blackwell's Island for Playground," Survey, 28 (18 May), 300.
     Speaking at the National Arts Club in New York, Riis urged that Blackwell's Island be made a public playground. Riis had also proposed this "nearly a generation ago" when he was a member of the Small Parks Commission.

2   ANON. "The Press in Social Work," 69th Annual Report of the New York Association for Improving the Condition of the Poor, September 30, 1912. New York: no publisher given, pp. 109-14.
     Riis's praise of the A.I.C.P. is quoted.

3   ANON. "Riis, Jacob August," in Who's Who in America; A Biographical Dictionary of Notable Living Men and Women of the United States, 1912-1913, edited by Albert Nelson Marquis. Vol. 7. Chicago: A. N. Marquis & Company, p. 1761.
     Biographical sketch of Riis.

1913 A BOOKS - NONE

1913 B SHORTER WRITINGS

1   ANON. "Tammany Versus the People," Outlook, 105 (4 October), 253-54.
     Argues "If organizations were judged by their deeds, as individual men are, and according to moral standards by which individual men are measured, Tammany Hall would not have had its history of power." Cites Riis as one who has spoken the truth about Tammany Hall.

1913

2   ROOSEVELT, THEODORE. An Autobiography. New York:
        Macmillan Company, pp. 48, 70, 185 seq., 211, 213, 218-19.
        Terms How the Other Half Lives an "enlightenment and
        an inspiration." Riis is called "the best American I
        ever knew."

3   ROOSEVELT, THEODORE. "The New York Police," Outlook, 104
        (26 July), 660-81.
        Roosevelt describes his activities as President of the
        Police Commission of New York, an office he held for two
        years beginning in 1895. A few paragraphs are devoted to
        Riis and to Riis's How the Other Half Lives. Roosevelt
        writes, "The man who was closest to me throughout my two
        years in the Police Department was Jacob Riis.... 'How
        the Other Half Lives' had been to me both an enlightenment
        and an inspiration."

4   WINSHIP, A. E. "Roxy and Timon of Hester St.," Journal of
        Education, 77 (12 June), 652-54.
        The stories of two children, Roxy and Timon, who bene-
        fited from Riis's reform work in the Hester Street district
        of New York. In the opening paragraph Winship credits Riis
        with having made "the beginning of the greatest movement
        for the betterment of children America has ever known,"
        and goes on to say that "behind all the later movements in
        which Jane Addams, William R. George, Judge Lindsey, and
        John E. Gunckel have won international renown, stands
        Jacob Riis in his first attack on vicious child conditions
        in the Hester St. district."

1914 A BOOKS - NONE

1914 B SHORTER WRITINGS

1   ANON. "Boys Honor Jacob Riis," New York Times (25 June),
        p. 20.
        Report on the gathering of 400 boys of the Jacob A. Riis
        Neighborhood Settlement who met "to pay tribute to the
        dead philanthropist." Charities Commissioner Kingsbury
        told the crown how Riis influenced his life and led him
        into social welfare work.

2   ANON. "Casual Comment," Dial, 56 (16 June), 487-88.
        A review of The Making of an American. Riis's autobiog-
        raphy is "one of the great and lasting books of its kind."
        Riis's life is the story of "hard won," "highly honorable
        success" by an immigrant with almost all the odds against
        him.

90

1914

3   ANON.   "Current Events Pictorially Treated," <u>Outlook</u>, 107 (13 June), 345.
      A picture of Riis with the caption "Jacob A. Riis." This portrait is the first in a series depicting important men and events in the news.

4   ANON.   Editorial, <u>Survey</u>, 32 (4 July), 379.
      Requests Riis's letters for a book in his memory being compiled by Mrs. Riis. Riis is described as having been a prodigious letter writer. An anecdote about a correspondence between Riis and a young stranded immigrant who requests money of Riis is related.

5   ANON.   "A Great Hearted American," <u>Outlook</u>, 107 (6 June), 267.
      Warm praise for Riis after his death: contains a brief historical sketch of Riis's life; talks of Riis's efforts to provide parks and playgrounds for the people of New York City; compares his <u>The Making of an American</u> to Lincoln's <u>Speeches</u>, Emerson's <u>Essays</u>, Mary Antin's <u>The Promised Land</u>; and claims "It is safe to say that no man has ever more vitally and faithfully expressed and interpreted the American Spirit than Jacob Riis."

6   ANON.   "Jacob A. Riis," <u>Literary Digest</u>, 48 (6 June), 1372, 1374, 1375.
      An article in honor of Riis at the time of his death. Includes a biography of Riis, a word on his relationship with Teddy Roosevelt, and a summary of his accomplishments.

7   ANON.   "Jacob A. Riis Buried," <u>New York Times</u> (29 May), p. 11.
      Notice of Riis's burial in Barre, Massachusetts: "Simple funeral services for Jacob A. Riis were held in the farm house on Hubbardston Road where the author and social worker breathed his last.... Only members of the family and intimate personal friends attended the services."

8   ANON.   "Jacob A. Riis Collapses," <u>New York Times</u> (11 May), p. 1.
      On his way from the sanitarium in Battle Creek, Michigan to his summer home in Barre, Massachusetts, on May 10, Riis collapsed.

9   ANON.   "Jacob A. Riis Dying," <u>New York Times</u> (21 May), p. 1.
      According to this article, Dr. Bates, Riis's physician, regards Riis's condition as critical; says Riis has been failing for several days and has, at the most, another month to live.

1914

10 ANON. "Jacob A. Riis Dying," New York Times (26 May), p. 1.
Further report on Riis's health: "A marked turn for the
worse was reported in the condition of Jacob A. Riis....
Mr. Riis was much weaker, partook of little nourishment,
and was in a semi-conscious condition most of the day."

11 ANON. "Jacob A. Riis Improves," New York Times (12 May),
p. 1.
Report on Riis's condition. The day after his collapse
in Coldbrook, Massachusetts, Riis showed a marked improvement in health and was able to complete his trip to Barre,
Massachusetts. His wife said the journey from Michigan
had strained his already weakened heart.

12 ANON. "Jacob A. Riis Park," New York Times (28 May), p. 19.
Reports that the proposal, initiated by Commissioner of
Charities John A. Kingsbury, to change the name of
Telawanna Park to Jacob A. Riis Park, in memory of the
"writer and worker among the poor, has been adopted by the
Board of Managers of the New York Association for Improving
the Condition of the Poor." Article, in addition, gives
arrangements for Riis's burial.

13 ANON. "Jacob A. Riis, Reformer, Dead," New York Times
(27 May), p. 11.
This article, which announces Riis's death, gives details of his last days, an account of his "lifelong battle for others," a short biography, and a description of
his heart disease.

14 ANON. "Jacob A. Riis, Roosevelt's Ideal Citizen," American
Review of Reviews, 50 (July), 97-98.
Written not long after Riis's death, this article pays
homage to the reformer. In one and a half pages it reviews
Riis's life and presents the impressions he left on three
of his esteemed friends: Theodore Roosevelt, who called
him "the ideal citizen"; Jane E. Robbins, "headworker of
the Jacob A. Riis Neighborhood House," who said he was
"the finest immigrant that we have ever known"; and
James Russell Lowell, who after reading How the Other Half
Lives, told Riis, "I felt as Dante must have when he
looked over the edge of the abyss."

15 ANON. "Jacob A. Riis Weaker," New York Times (22 May), p. 13.
Riis reported weaker; W. S. Bates, his doctor, abandons
hope for his recovery. Mrs. Riis received--among hundreds
of inquiries--a telegram from Col. Roosevelt.

16 ANON. "Jacob A. Riis Weaker," New York Times (23 May), p. 11.
      Riis, seriously ill, had a very bad night May 22.

17 ANON. "Jacob Riis and His Work," New York Times (28 May),
      p. 12.
        Article suggests Riis's "service to the public did not
      so much lie in what he personally and directly did in the
      way of reforming social conditions as in calling the atten-
      tion of many with more power than himself to 'the other
      half' and the way it lived." Also suggests similarities
      between Riis's use of the English language and Joseph
      Conrad's use of it.

18 ANON. "Jacob Riis: Friend of the American People,"
      Craftsman, 26 (July), 459-61.
        In an eloquent eulogy, Riis is described as "a man whom
      America could ill have spared in the story of her spiritual
      progress. Although a foreigner...coming here very poor,
      very lonely, very young, yet we shall always think of him
      as a friend of America and especially a friend of the young
      American." Riis had turned down a cabinet position because
      he "felt himself drawn so closely to the work of helping
      the New York boys at that time."

19 ANON. "The Jacob Riis Park," Outlook, 107 (13 June), 329-30.
        Outlook urges New York City to accept Theodore Roosevelt's
      suggestion that Sea Breeze--a seaside park for the poor and
      crippled, rendered possible by Riis--have its name changed
      to Jacob Riis Park.

20 ANON. "Jacob Riis Seriously Ill," New York Times (19 April),
      p. 1.
        Reports condition of Riis on Saturday, April 18, 1914, as
      he lay near death in a sanitarium in Battle Creek, Michigan.
      Riis had suffered two heart failures during recent lecture
      tours. Physicians in Battle Creek held out "little hope
      for his ultimate recovery." Riis, breathing with difficulty,
      was quoted as saying, "Now that I have to fight for almost
      every breath of air, I am more thankful than ever that I
      have been instrumental in helping the children of the tene-
      ments to obtain fresh air."

21 ANON. "Jacob Riis Still Improves," New York Times (13 May),
      p. 11.
        Continued improvement reported in the condition of Riis.

1914

22   ANON.   "Jacob Riis's Books," Survey, 33 (26 December), 345.
           The Russell Sage Foundation has received about 200
        volumes from Riis's collection. Many of the works have
        Riis's autograph or "inscriptions to him from the
        authors...." Other volumes have Riis's annotations.

23   ANON.   "Jacob Riis's Health Improving," New York Times
        (9 May), p. 11.
           Progress report on Riis's health: "Jacob Riis, who for
        several weeks has been ill at a local health resort, has
        so far improved that an effort will be made to move him to
        his summer home near Springfield, Mass."

24   ANON.   "Jacob Riis's Will Gives All to Widow," New York Times
        (21 June), p. 15.
           Reports Edward Riis made public his father's will: Riis
        "left the bulk of his estate" to Mary Riis, and left noth-
        ing to the children of his first wife "since they had
        already been provided for by a deed of trust." Article
        includes text of the will that refers to the Jacob A. Riis
        Settlement.

25   ANON.   "Literary Necrology," Bookman, 39 (July), 491, 493.
           Announces recent deaths of "several conspicuous men of
        letters" among whom Riis is mentioned. Riis, "probably
        more than any other man, was responsible for reclaiming
        New York City from the contamination of the slums."

26   ANON.   "Lose Hope for Jacob Riis," New York Times (25 May),
        p. 5.
           "'Slowly sinking' was the report...regarding the condi-
        tion of Jacob A. Riis, who is ill of heart trouble."

27   ANON.   "Memorial Service for Riis," New York Times (13 June),
        p. 5.
           Report of the memorial service held for Riis in Plymouth
        Church, Brooklyn. One of many speakers, Ernest K. Coulter,
        founder of the Big Brothers Society, recalled times with
        Riis "when both were engaged in newspaper work."

28   ANON.   "Memorial Service to Jacob A. Riis," New York Times
        (11 June), p. 11.
           Announces "a memorial service to Jacob A. Riis, writer,
        social worker, and head of the Henry Street Settlement,

will take place tomorrow evening in Plymouth Church,
Brooklyn.... All of those who will take part were friends
of Mr. Riis."

29 ANON. "A Monument to Jacob A. Riis," Outlook, 108
        (11 November), 570-71.
        Argues Riis's "untimely death was in no small part
        caused by the self-sacrificing expenditure of his time,
        strength and money for the benefit of his fellow-citizens
        of all conditions of life." Includes a plea, in the name
        of Riis, for contributions to the Jacob A. Riis Neighbor-
        hood Settlement.

30 ANON. "Riis, Jacob August," in Who's Who in America; A Bio-
        graphical Dictionary of Notable Living Men and Women of
        the United States, 1914-1915, edited by Albert Nelson
        Marquis. Chicago: A. N. Marquis & Company, p. 1973.
        Brief biographical sketch of Riis's life.

31 ANON. "Riis's Condition Grave," New York Times (23 April),
        p. 10.
        Claims Riis, suffering from "organic heart trouble,"
        has lost ground in his fight against death. Riis's son
        arrived in Michigan from Barre, Massachusetts, to be with
        his father.

32 ANON. "Riis's Condition Unchanged," New York Times (24 May),
        p. 9.
        Report on Riis's health. Riis's condition remains
        serious; restless and delirious at night, he sleeps some
        in the morning.

33 ANON. "Roosevelt in 1916," New York Times (14 January), p. 2.
        Report on Riis's announcement that Theodore Roosevelt
        will run for the presidency in 1916 provided the people
        want him. Riis is fully quoted. He comments on the pos-
        sibility of Roosevelt accepting the Republican nomination,
        and expresses amazement at "'the force of character dis-
        played by President Wilson.'"

34 ANON. "Roosevelt Mourns for Riis," New York Times (27 May),
        p. 11.
        Roosevelt, "shocked" when he learned of Riis's death,
        telegraphed his condolences to Mrs. Riis.

1914

35 ANON. "A Seer," Survey, 33 (12 December), 299-300.
Eulogy. Sums up Riis's accomplishments. Says Riis
brought to philanthropy "the Scandinavian genius for the
moving drama of life," and that his gift was not one of
philosophy but "of tongue, and eye, and heart."

36 ANON. "Thanks from Riis Family," New York Times (2 June),
p. 11.
Edward V. Riis expresses his "deep thanks and that of
all the [Riis] family for the many touching and beautiful
tributes" to his father.

37 ANON. "To Name a Park for Jacob Riis," Survey, 32 (6 June),
249.
Announces that John A. Kingsbury, Commissioner of the
New York City Department of Public Charities, initiated a
drive "to change the name of Telawana Park at Rockaway
Beach to Jacob A. Riis Park."

38 ANON. "Tributes to Riis by Social Workers," New York Times
(1 June), p. 20.
At the Intercity Settlement Workers' Conference, tribute
was paid to the memory of Riis. Lillian D. Wald read a
"resolution of respect and sympathy." Dr. Jane Robbins
commented on Riis's passion for facts and his disappoint-
ment that little was being done to eliminate the misery
in the tenements.

39 ANON. "Want Riis Honored," New York Times (7 June), p. 1.
Reports that residents of Rockaway Park favor changing
the name of Telawana Park to Jacob A. Riis Park.

40 ANON. "Widow Seeks Riis Will," New York Times (7 June),
p. 4.
Mary Riis was granted permission "to open a safe deposit
box in the Colonial Branch of the Equitable Safe Deposit
Company in Manhattan to prosecute a search now being bade
to find her husband's will." Article reveals that Riis,
after moving to New England, "retained a voting residence
in Richmond Hill, Queens Borough."

41 ROBBINS, JANE E. "A Maker of Americans," Survey, 32 (6 June),
285-86.
An article in the Survey honoring Riis after his death:
"To most of us Jacob Riis was the finest immigrant that we

have ever known. To all of us, from editor to office boy,
he was a friend." There is a large photograph of Riis on
the cover of this issue.

42 ROGERS. "A 'Jacob A. Riis Park,'" New York Times (25 May),
p. 10.
Since Riis will not live much longer, this admirer of
Riis, in a letter to the editor, suggests that the name
of Mulberry Bend Park be changed to Jacob A. Riis Park
"at the earliest possible moment."

43 ROOSEVELT, THEODORE. "Jacob Riis," Outlook, 107 (6 June), 284.
Roosevelt commemorates Riis: "Jacob Riis was one of
those men who by his writings contributed most to raising
the standard of unselfishness, of disinterestedness, of
sane and kindly good citizenship, in this country."

44 WINSHIP, A. E. "Jacob Riis," Journal of Education, 79
(4 June), 631.
A tribute by the editor to Riis one month after Riis's
death. Winship recalls times when Riis expressed his
devotion to Teddy Roosevelt.

1915 A BOOKS - NONE

1915 B SHORTER WRITINGS

1 ANON. "Memorial Service for Riis," New York Times (1 January),
p. 10.
"Five hundred members of singing societies and others"
attended a service New Year's Eve dedicated to Riis's
memory. The service was held in Madison Square. Exercises
began at 11:00; two minutes before midnight taps were
played.

2 ANON. "A Memorial to Jacob Riis," Outlook, 111 (22 December),
926, 929.
Riis initiated in 1913 a public New Year's celebration
of his own held in Madison Square. He believed an organized
songfest could replace the riotous celebrations New York
had come to know. This article is a plea for support of
the gathering in 1915.

3 ANON. "Songs to Keep Jacob Riis' Memory Green," Survey, 35
(25 December), 339.
Announcement of plans for songfest in memory of Riis to
be held on New Year's Eve 1915. Theodore Roosevelt heads

1915

the committee directing the affair. Among the participants
will be boys from the Jacob A. Riis Settlement.

4   BAY, J. CHRISTIAN, ed. Denmark in English and American Literature: A Bibliography Edited for the Danish American Association. Introduction by C. H. W. Hasselriis. Chicago:
The Danish American Association, pp. 60-61.
A listing of Riis's writings about Denmark.

5   BURTON, MARGARET E. "A Servant of the City," Comrades in
Service. New York: Missionary Education Movement of the
United States and Canada, pp. 1-23.
Short, simple biography of Riis, with photograph;
stresses Riis's consecration of his pen to reform in·the
ultimate service of God.

6   WALD, LILLIAN D. The House on Henry Street. New York: Henry
Holt and Company, p. 67.
Quotes Riis's belief that "As a nation we must rise or
fall as we serve or fail these future citizens [children
surrounded by dirt, ignorance, crime, and anarchy]."

1916 A BOOKS - NONE

1916 B SHORTER WRITINGS

1   GILDER, ROSAMOND, ed. Letters of Richard Watson Gilder.
Boston: Houghton Mifflin Company, pp. 274, 275, 380, 400.
Letters to and about Riis. Topics include Riis's proposal for a Bureau of Municipal Statistics, the naming of
a park in what was Mulberry Bend, a projected article for
the Century, and Riis's mention of Gilder's service to the
inhabitants of tenement districts.

2   WADE, MARY. "Jacob Riis," Pilgrims of To-Day. Boston:
Little, Brown and Company, pp. 54-111.
A retelling of Riis's career.

1917 A BOOKS - NONE

1917 B SHORTER WRITINGS

1   CARY, H. M. "A Modern Book of Acts II. A Knight in the Slums--
Jacob August Riis," Homiletic Review, 41 (January), 14-20.
An account of Riis's life; emphasis is placed upon
Christian virtues and dedication to the social problems of

the day. Riis not only demonstrated that the "Christian profession" is "attainable and practicable," but also "translated Christian idealism into terms of action adjusted to an environment" that is part of "the world we know."

2   PARKMAN, MARY R. "A Modern Viking: Jacob Riis," St. Nicholas, 44 (January), 208-13.
     A biography of Riis written for adolescents. It is a condensed version of Riis's autobiography The Making of An American. Riis is compared to the Northmen of old: "The dauntless Northmen, who pushed across the seas and discovered America, could not have thrilled more at the sight of their Vinland than did this Dane of our own day when he saw the sky-line of the great city." Stresses throughout Riis's "boundless enthusiasm and tireless industry," also the "many honors" that were his. Two pictures are included: one of Riis and one of the Jacob A. Riis Settlement.

1918 A BOOKS - NONE

1918 B SHORTER WRITINGS

1   ANON. "League to Promote American Ideals," New York Times (6 November), p. 6.
     Max Henius named his organization to promote the "Americanization" of immigrants after Riis, calling it "The Jacob A. Riis League for Patriotic Service." Article relates Henius's ideas for teaching the spiritual meaning of America to recent immigrants.

2   O'BRIEN, FRANK M. The Story of the Sun; New York, 1833-1918. New York: George H. Doran Company, p. 398.
     Mentions Riis's joining the Evening Sun, and Roosevelt's interest in Riis's writing.

1919 A BOOKS - NONE

1919 B SHORTER WRITINGS

1   CALKINS, RAYMOND. Substitutes for the Saloon. Boston: Houghton Mifflin, Riverside Press, pp. 267, 278.
     Quotes Riis's A Ten Years' War on the problems of social environment and on the attraction of the saloon in the slums.

1919

2   ROOSEVELT, THEODORE. "Introduction," in The Making of an
        American, by Jacob A. Riis. New York: Macmillan Company,
        p. xi.
            An excerpt from the Outlook of June 6, 1914; Roosevelt
        praised Riis's achievements in "raising the standard of
        unselfishness, of disinterestedness, of sane and kindly
        good citizenship, in this country."

3   THAYER, WILLIAM ROSCOE. Theodore Roosevelt; An Intimate
        Biography. Boston: Houghton Mifflin Company, pp. 35, 70,
        103-4, 137, 138, 139, 266.
            Describes Riis's tours of the city by night with Roose-
        velt, and quotes Riis on Roosevelt's governorship. Riis's
        campaign biography of Roosevelt is cited.

1920 A BOOKS - NONE

1920 B SHORTER WRITINGS

1   BISHOP, JOSEPH BUCKLIN. Theodore Roosevelt and His Time.
        2 vols. New York: Charles Scribner's Sons. Vol. 1,
        pp. 67, 118; Vol. 2, p. 19.
            Riis-Roosevelt friendship is cited, as well as Riis's
        efforts to get Roosevelt, then governor of New York, to
        pardon a woman convicted of murder; Riis's plea for com-
        mutation of the death sentence was ineffective. Roosevelt's
        letter (June 26, 1906) to Riis, containing advice about
        answering criticism directed at Roosevelt, is quoted.

2   HUSBAND, JOSEPH. "Jacob A. Riis," in Americans by Adoption;
        Brief Biographies of Great Citizens Born in Foreign Lands.
        Boston: Atlantic Monthly Press, pp. 140-53.
            Riis's life in Denmark and America, his reform efforts,
        and work as a police reporter are recounted.

1921 A BOOKS - NONE

1921 B SHORTER WRITINGS

1   GILLIN, JOHN LEWIS. Poverty and Dependency; Their Relief and
        Prevention. New York: The Century Company, p. 593.
            Retells Riis's anecdote about the little girl from the
        tenements who was sent by a "fresh-air charity" to the
        country. She wrote to her mother that the farmer did not
        get his milk out of a can but "pulled it out of a cow."

2   GILMAN, BRADLEY. <u>Roosevelt, the Happy Warrior</u>. Boston:
      Little, Brown, and Company, pp. 6, 77, 121-23, 126, 132,
      165, 169, 176.
         Describes the history of the Riis-Roosevelt friendship.
      Roosevelt's Tenement House Commission Bill was first sug-
      gested by Riis. Riis's "struggle for the redemption of
      the city was not occasional. It was continuous." When
      Roosevelt aided Riis, they formed "one of the noblest,
      purest coalitions in all history."

3   RAINWATER, CLARENCE E. <u>The Play Movement in the United States;</u>
      <u>A Study of Community Recreation</u>. Chicago: The University
      of Chicago Press, p. 61.
         The story of children injured while playing in the open
      space of what was formerly Mulberry Bend gave Riis an
      opportunity to protest the lot's condition. The authori-
      ties were compelled to act. Mulberry Bend Park was then
      finished...."

<u>1922 A BOOKS - NONE</u>

<u>1922 B SHORTER WRITINGS</u>

1   DEVINE, EDWARD T. <u>Social Work</u>. New York: Macmillan Company,
      p. 28.
         "Striking experiments may become contagious." Riis's
      efforts, like those of Fry and Addams, "may give direction
      to innumerable individual impulses."

2   FARIS, JOHN T. "From Carpenter's Apprentice to Philanthropist,"
      in <u>Men Who Conquered</u>. New York: Fleming H. Revell Com-
      pany, pp. 21-33.
         Riis's life in Ribe, and struggles in America are
      sketched.

3   HOLDEN, ARTHUR C. <u>The Settlement Idea; A Vision of Social</u>
      <u>Justice</u>. New York: Macmillan Company, pp. 19-20, 77, 78.
         Riis will "not be remembered primarily as a settlement
      worker...." However, no history of the movement is com-
      plete without mention of his name. Riis was "notably the
      educator of the early reform movement in New York...."
      His influence was far reaching; contemporary slums are not
      those "which disgraced our civilization in the closing
      quarter of the last century."

4   RAINSFORD, W. S. <u>The Story of a Varied Life; An Autobiography</u>.
      Garden City, New York: Doubleday, Page & Co., pp. 236,
      255, 369.

1922

> Riis was a "lover of, a believer in the East Side
> boy...." Riis and Father McGlynn "knew the poor of New
> York, and were loved by them more than any other men in my
> time." Rainsford recalls St. George's on the East Side
> where he first met the street urchin Riis immortalized as
> "Tony."

5   WATSON, FRANK DEKKER. <u>The Charity Organization Movement in</u>
     <u>the United States; A Study in American Philanthropy</u>. New
     York: Macmillan Company, p. 305.
          Mentions that Riis, with Jane Addams and Joseph Lee, was
     on the publication committee of the New York Charity Organ-
     ization Society. This committee's aim was to "give national
     breadth and effect" to <u>Charities</u>.

1923 A BOOKS - NONE

1923 B SHORTER WRITINGS

1   ANON. "Why Their Names Are in the Town Hall," New York <u>Town</u>
     <u>Hall Bulletin</u>, 2 (1 December), 13.
          Tells why Riis's name is honored at City Hall. The last
     decades of the nineteenth century "saw a new conception of
     man's obligation to his fellows, a new social conscience;
     and the man who was as responsible for this advance as any
     was Jacob A. Riis...."

2   CHARNWOOD, LORD. <u>Theodore Roosevelt</u>. Boston: The Atlantic
     Monthly Press, pp. 45-46.
          <u>How the Other Half Lives</u> turned Roosevelt's attention to
     "things dreadfully wrong in poor city homes, which good
     police and sanitation could...help."

3   HAGEDORN, HERMANN, ed. <u>The Americanism of Theodore Roosevelt;</u>
     <u>Selections from His Writings and Speeches</u>. Boston:
     Houghton Mifflin Company, p. 201.
          Cites Roosevelt's praise that there "was never a better
     American than Jacob Riis, who was born in Denmark and whom
     I always thought about the best American I ever knew."

4   JOHNSON, ROBERT UNDERWOOD. <u>Remembered Yesterdays</u>. Boston:
     Little, Brown and Company, p. 112.
          The <u>Century</u> was a "fellowship of goodlie men" and Riis
     was "a rare spirit."

1924 A BOOKS - NONE

1924 B SHORTER WRITINGS

1 JENSEN, OSKAR. <u>Dansk-Amerikaneren Jacob A. Riis</u>. København:
   Johs, G. Gielsen & Company.
     A Danish pamphlet about Riis. Written by a priest, the
   story of Riis's life was used as a lecture to raise money
   for a church at Husum.

2 ROOSEVELT, THEODORE. <u>Letters from Theodore Roosevelt to Anna
   Roosevelt Cowles, 1870-1918</u>. Compiled by Anna Roosevelt
   Cowles. New York: Charles Scribner's Sons, pp. 187, 188,
   203.
     Riis is "a dear who has helped me much in my police
   work..." (July 19, 1896). In a letter dated July 26, 1896,
   Roosevelt mentions that Professor Smith, Jacob Riis, and
   Stephen Crane "turned up, and dined with me." In a letter
   of January 31, 1897, Roosevelt mentions Riis's presence at
   Clarendon Hall.

1925 A BOOKS - NONE

1925 B SHORTER WRITINGS

1 ANON. "$231,698.81 for the Neediest," <u>New York Times</u>
   (4 January), p. 6.
     Riis's work mentioned in relation to "The Hundred Need-
   iest Cases," a relief campaign run by the <u>Times</u>. <u>How the
   Other Half Lives</u>, says writer, "had a wide appeal and a
   wholesome influence in helping the people in this city to
   a consciousness of the misery surrounding them and stirring
   them to an effort to make things better."

2 GOMPERS, SAMUEL. <u>Seventy Years of Life and Labor</u>. 2 vols.
   New York: E. P. Dutton Company. Vol. 1, pp. 434, 436.
     Riis was active in the Social Reform Club "composed of
   trade unionists and others interested in the improvement
   of the conditions of wage-earners...." Riis was also a
   member of the Advisory Council of the People's Institute.

3 LODGE, HENRY CABOT, ed. <u>Selections from the Correspondence of
   Theodore Roosevelt and Henry Cabot Lodge, 1884-1912</u>.
   2 vols. New York: Charles Scribner's Sons. Vol. 1,
   p. 165.
     In a letter of August 22, 1895, Roosevelt recalls that
   last Sunday he and Riis drove and walked for nine hours
   "to see for ourselves exactly how the Excise Law was
   enforced."

1926

1926 A BOOKS - NONE

1926 B SHORTER WRITINGS

    1   SULLIVAN, MARK. Our Times; The Turn of the Century. 6 vols.
        New York: Charles Scribner's Sons. Vol. 1, p. 288.
          Riis recounted the story of a Harvard instructor ques-
        tioning a graduate about his future work. "'Oh,' said
        the latter, with a little yawn, 'really, do you know,
        Professor, it does not seem to me that there is anything
        that is much worth while.'" Roosevelt, when hearing this
        story, regarded the graduate's remark with scorn.

1927 A BOOKS - NONE

1927 B SHORTER WRITINGS

    1   RIIS, ROGER WILLIAM. "Worms for Bait," Survey Graphic, 58
        (1 August), 447.
          Riis's son recalls a fishing trip he took with his father
        when he was a boy. Riis tells of the same trip in The
        Making of an American. Article includes a picture of Riis
        in a dress suit and derby.

1928 A BOOKS - NONE

1928 B SHORTER WRITINGS

    1   WEINSTEIN, GREGORY. Reminiscences of an Interesting Decade;
        The Ardent Eighties. New York: International Press,
        pp. 111, 114.
          Riis was a member of the Social Reform Club, formed "for
        the interchange of views between employers and representa-
        tive labor leaders." When Roosevelt, then Police Commis-
        sioner of New York, had his methods and policies "scathingly
        attacked" by the Club, he wrote Riis "requesting him to
        resign...."

1930 A BOOKS - NONE

1930 B SHORTER WRITINGS

    1   ANON. "One Minute Biographies. Who: Jacob A. Riis."
        Christian Science Monitor (21 June), 19.

Argues Riis "succeeded in rousing the public conscience" because "he was a born fighter and the battles which he fought were always for others."

2   EINSTEIN, LEWIS. Roosevelt, His Mind in Action. Boston: Houghton Mifflin, p. 24.
     Cites Roosevelt's remark that he was tempted to call Riis the "best American I ever knew."

1931 A BOOKS - NONE

1931 B SHORTER WRITINGS

1   FAULKNER, HAROLD UNDERWOOD. The Quest for Social Justice, 1898-1914. New York: Macmillan Company, pp. 23, 240.
     Riis's descriptions of the poor "equalled, if they did not surpass, the statistics collected by Booth and Rowntree for London." Riis is credited with helping fight the war against tuberculosis by promoting the sale of Christmas seals.

2   HARRISON, SHELBY M. The Social Survey; The Idea Defined and Its Development Traced. New York: Russell Sage Foundation, p. 12.
     Riis's books "pictured out of firsthand experience un-healthful, insanitary, and oppressive surroundings" that menaced the slum dwellers.

3   STEFFENS, LINCOLN. The Autobiography of Lincoln Steffens. New York: Harcourt, Brace and Company, pp. 203 seq.; 218, 223, 290.
     Steffens describes Riis's activities while covering police headquarters, and during the crusades against vice. Riis "passionately hated all tyrannies, abuses, miseries, and he fought them. He was a 'terror' to the officials and landlords responsible, as he saw it, for the desperate condition of the tenements where the poor lived." Steffens points out that Riis "was interested not at all in vice and crime, only in the stories of people and the condi-tions in which they lived." Riis's incredulity at the existence of homosexuals is recounted.

1932 A BOOKS - NONE

1932

1   Editors of <u>Fortune</u>. <u>Housing America</u>. New York: Harcourt,
     Brace & Company, p. 21.
          Riis, as journalist and reporter, "dramatized the slum."
     He was instrumental in destroying the police lodging room
     and transforming "The Bend."

2   ROGERS, JAMES EDWARD. <u>The Child and Play</u>. New York: The
     Century Company, p. 147.
          During Riis's struggle for small parks in New York City,
     he termed the existing city parks as "breathing spaces,
     where one can do little else."

1933 A BOOKS - NONE

1933 B SHORTER WRITINGS

1   ANON.   "Completed Jacob Riis Park, Seaside Resort Within City,
     to Reopen to Public Sunday," <u>New York Herald Tribune</u>
     (7 May), p. 5.
          An informative article which gives a short history and
     detailed description of Riis Park, a biographical sketch
     of Riis, and a few comments on the Jacob A. Riis Settlement
     House. Riis Park had an uncertain history from the time
     Riis was first "impressed by the possibilities of Rockaway
     Peninsula," through the city's purchase of the 262 acres,
     to completion of the park in 1933. A description of the
     park--"in atmosphere it is not unlike the English seaside
     resorts"--its environs, and its possible future improve-
     ments is given. The article claims that, contrary to
     fact, Riis was a "well-educated man in his own language,"
     and that <u>How the Other Half Lives</u> had wide public appeal
     because it "was so convincing, so simple and realistic."

2   LONGWORTH, ALICE ROOSEVELT. <u>Crowded Hours</u>. New York:
     Charles Scribner's Sons, p. 15.
          Longworth does not recollect whether, as a child, she
     was told much about Roosevelt's "nocturnal expeditions"
     with Riis.

3   SCHLESINGER, ARTHUR M. <u>The Rise of the City, 1878-1898</u>.
     New York: The Macmillan Company, pp. 110, 194.
          Riis aided philanthropic citizens and organizations that
     both "insistently agitated for stricter housing laws" and
     built decent lodgings. Riis's newspaper work was an
     "important training school" for authorship.

1934 A BOOKS - NONE

1934 B SHORTER WRITINGS

1   LENS, SIDNEY. Poverty; America's Enduring Paradox. New York:
      Thomas Y. Crowell Company, pp. 199, 214.
        How the Other Half Lives is a "masterly reportage" of
      the hardships of slum life, "drawn from direct observation
      without interpretive embellishments." Riis's works "opened
      many a complacent eye...." Riis founded Neighborhood House
      in New York in 1888, a year before Hull House was
      established.

2   NEVINS, ALLAN. Abram S. Hewitt: with Some Account of Peter
      Cooper. New York: Harper & Brothers, pp. 504-5, 537.
        Describes Riis's efforts to have small parks built, and
      his efforts in transforming Mulberry Bend. Hewitt insisted
      Riis be appointed secretary of the Small Parks Committee.

3   WALD, LILLIAN D. Windows on Henry Street. Boston: Little,
      Brown, and Company, p. 11.
        Quotes Riis's anecdote about his trouble in drawing up a
      "suitable statement" to present before a "learned group."
      Riis said, "I find I don't know how to get statistics. I
      am like the man in a Western village who, when asked by a
      research student from the East, 'What is the death rate
      here'? replied, 'I guess it's about one death for every
      person.'"

1935 A BOOKS - NONE

1935 B SHORTER WRITINGS

1   HOLMES, JOHN HAYES. "Riis, Jacob August," in Dictionary of
      American Biography, edited by Dumas Malone. Vol. 15.
      New York: Charles Scribner's Son's, pp. 606-8.
        Description of Riis's life and work. Riis's "exuberance"
      was sometimes "mistaken for roughness or crudity, but at
      heart was a tenderness as of a woman, and a sensitiveness
      as of a child."

2   JOSEPH, SAMUEL. History of the Baron De Hirsch Fund; The
      Americanization of the Jewish Immigrant. No place of pub-
      lication given: Jewish Publication Society, pp. 27, 44,
      68.
        Riis described the Baron De Hirsch Fund census, and re-
      ported that "the cause of progress along the safe line is

1935

holding its own." Riis's "Making a Way Out of the Slums" described the orderly conditions of Woodbine in contrast to the slums of the East Side.

1937 A BOOKS - NONE

1937 B SHORTER WRITINGS

1 ANON. "The Christmas Seals," New York Times (3 December), p. 22.
     Credits Riis for an article he wrote in his day that "led to the first experiment in the use of Christmas seals in the United States."

2 DORF, A. T. "Danish Americans," in Our Racial and National Minorities, edited by Francis J. Brown and Joseph Slabey Roucek. New York: Prentice-Hall, pp. 124-36.
     Riis's The Making of an American showed the process of Americanization to be "an easy and pleasant one." Riis's career is briefly summarized.

3 FLYNN, CLARENCE. "Jacob A. Riis," American Scandinavian Review, 25 (June), 134.
     A fourteen line poem in honor of Riis: "He went into the dismal wilderness of human squalor / where hearts cringe and bleed / and raised a voice to herald their distress...."

4 MORRIS, RICHARD B. "The Metropolis of the State," in History of the State of New York in Ten Volumes, edited by Alexander C. Flick. Vol. 10. New York: Columbia University Press, pp. 173-214.
     Riis was one of the "closest students of tenement conditions in New York" and discovered the tenements "concealed gambling dens, policy shops, joss houses, 'greengoods bedrooms' and worse."

1938 A BOOKS

1 WARE, LOUISE. Jacob A. Riis; Police Reporter, Reformer, Useful Citizen. Introduction by Allan Nevins. Foreword by Roger William Riis. New York: D. Appleton-Century Company.
     First full-length biography of Riis. Complete coverage of reformer from his boyhood days in Ribe, Denmark to his last years at Pine Brook Farm in Barre, Massachusetts.

Ware sees Riis as "a plain man" who cared little for out-
ward form, whose message was one of Christian sociology,
and whose books combined human interest with telling statistics about the slum. She believes that the power of
Riis's dramatic appeal was more important than his ideas
and accomplishments. The "cheerful fighting spirit of
Jacob Riis" is needed in contemporary social work.

1938 B SHORTER WRITINGS

1 DUFFUS, R. L. Lillian Wald, Neighbor and Crusader. New York:
    Macmillan Company, pp. 5, 33, 61, 71, 87.
       Riis is described as "fiery" and "impulsive." Roosevelt
    visited the Henry Street Settlement "under escort of his
    admiring friend, Jacob Riis...." Mentions Riis's praise
    of a speech Wald made, and Riis's meeting Minnie Wald.

2 MOTT, FRANK LUTHER. A History of American Magazines, 5 vols.
    Cambridge, Mass.: Harvard University Press.
    Vol. 2, p. 512; vol. 3, pp. 430, 486.
       Walter Hines Page had Riis write about his social work
    for the Atlantic. Mentions that Riis contributed to the
    Delineator, and that The Making of an American was pub-
    lished serially in the Outlook.

3 NEVINS, ALLAN. "Introduction," in Jacob A. Riis; Police
    Reporter, Reformer, Useful Citizen, by Louise Ware. New
    York: D. Appleton-Century Company, pp. v-viii.
       Riis, "an unsurpassed publicist," believed that the slum
    was not the "sole root of social evil," for no less impor-
    tant were liquor and unrestricted immigration. Riis "took
    the slum as the principal gauge of our urban civilization."

4 OAKLEY, AMY. Scandinavia Beckons. New York: D. Appleton-
    Century Company, p. 340.
       The commemorative tablet on Riis's house in Ribe is
    described.

5 RIIS, ROGER WILLIAM. "Foreword," in Jacob A. Riis; Police
    Reporter, Reformer, Useful Citizen, by Louise Ware. New
    York: D. Appleton-Century Company, pp. ix-xv.
       Reminiscences of Riis's son. Roger Riis first explains
    the "remote resentment" he felt at the world's interest in
    his father; next he compliments Louise Ware on the thor-
    oughness of her study; and then he discusses his father.
    His father's anger over the tenements grew, he says, out
    of a knowledge of two worlds: the world of Denmark's
    North Sea Coast and the world of New York City's slums.

He further remembers his father as being quick-tempered,
a great story teller, a long letter writer, and a "swift"
disciplinarian when necessary. He says, in conclusion,
his father was a friend.

6   _____. "My Father," Survey Graphic, 27 (March), 182-83.
        Reminiscences of Riis's son that also appear in the
    "Foreword" to Jacob A. Riis by Louise Ware. Roger W. Riis
    had been asked to write this recollection twelve years be-
    fore by Paul Kellogg, editor of the Survey Graphic.

7   SIMKHOVITCH, MARY KINGSBURY. Neighborhood; My Story of Green-
        wich House. New York: W. W. Norton & Company, pp. 88-89.
        Riis was one of the incorporators of the Cooperative
    Social Settlement Society; the CSSS developed a variety
    of approaches to social problems; Riis's "was for slum
    clearance."

8   Workers of the Federal Writers' Union Project, Works Progress
        Administration in the City of New York. The Italians of
        New York; A Survey. New York: Random House, pp. 14-15,
        19.
        Cites Riis's observations of the padrone who often
    fleeced the Italian immigrant, and quotes Riis on the
    poverty and misery in which many of the Italian immigrants
    lived.

1939 A BOOKS - NONE

1939 B SHORTER WRITINGS

1   DAVID, HENRY. "Notices and Reviews of Books," New York History,
        20 (July), 351-53.
        Review of Jacob A. Riis; Police Reporter, Reformer, Use-
    ful Citizen, by Louise Ware. David says Ware's book is
    "worthwhile" but too "sympathetic." He argues that Riis's
    "reform philosophy was frequently narrow and short-sighted"
    and "always colored by a romantic sentimentality." He
    also faults Riis for being opposed to the organized labor
    movement and "to all radical solutions of social problems."

2   DEVINE, EDWARD T. When Social Work Was Young. New York:
        Macmillan Company, pp. 69, 73, 96, 110.
        Riis "had told 'how the other half lives' in words of
    blistering indignation." Mentions that Riis was a member
    of the Tenement House Committee of the Charity Organization
    Society, that he spoke at the Sixth International Congress

on Tuberculosis meeting in Washington in 1908, and that
he was on the National Publication Committee of the C.O.S.

3   FILLER, LOUIS. <u>Crusaders for American Liberalism; The Story
     of the Muckrakers</u>. New York: Harcourt, Brace & Co.,
     pp. 45-48, 50, 54, 92, 269.
        Analyzes the Riis-Roosevelt friendship. Riis "was the
     typical successful reformer of that time, thoroughly of
     New York...." Riis had no understanding of national
     policy. When the muck-raking era began, Riis's "work was
     done." Of his friendship with Roosevelt, Filler argues
     Riis hated politics. Roosevelt "spoke vigorous words and
     got things done."

4   OWRE, J. RIIS. "Genealogy of the Riis Family," L.C., Riis
     MSS, box 6.
        The family tree. Includes Riis's ancestors, relations,
     and descendants, also the Gortz family. The male line of
     Riis has died out in both America and Denmark.

5   SMITH, WILLIAM CARLSON. <u>Americans in the Making; The Natural
     History of the Assimilation of Immigrants</u>. New York:
     D. Appleton-Century Company, pp. 41, 44, 49, 123, 144,
     392, 436.
        Riis's efforts "aroused" New York to clear the slums,
     establish parks, and enact better housing laws.

1940 A BOOKS - NONE

1940 B SHORTER WRITINGS

1   GABRIEL, RALPH. <u>The Course of American Democratic Thought;
     An Intellectual History Since 1815</u>. New York: The
     Ronald Press Company, p. 332.
        Progressivism transcended the "humanitarianism" of
     reformers such as Riis and Jane Addams.

2   JOSEPHSON, MATTHEW. <u>The President Makers; The Culture of
     Politics and Leadership in an Age of Enlightenment, 1896-
     1916</u>. New York: Harcourt, Brace and Company, p. 54.
        Mentions Roosevelt's friendship with Riis and Lincoln
     Steffens. Roosevelt attributed his belated awareness of
     the contrast between wealth and poverty to the influence
     of "tender-hearted" Riis.

3   LOTZ, CHARLES J. "Jacob Riis--Journalist." In <u>Creative Per-
     sonalities; Vocations and Professions</u>, edited by Philip
     Henry Lotz. New York: Association Press, pp. 33-41.

1940

An interpretive biography of Riis that emphasizes his
industry and compassion. Riis was not only a journalist
but also one "who cared about the events he chronicled."
A short bibliography of works by and about Riis is
appended.

4   POOLE, ERNEST. The Bridge; My Own Story. New York:
     Macmillan Company, p. 66.
        Poole "hungrily" read How the Other Half Lives; tenement
     life appealed to him "as a tremendous new field, scarcely
     touched by American writers...."

1942 A BOOKS - NONE

1942 B SHORTER WRITINGS

1   Blue Network Co. "The Making of an American." Script of a
     radio play produced by the Little Blue Playhouse, Radio
     City, New York, N. Y., 5 September 1942. L.C., Riis
     MSS, box 7.
        Biographical skit.

2   RIIS, ROGER WILLIAM. "The Most Unforgettable Character I've
     Met," Reader's Digest, 41 (December), 48-52.
        Roger William Riis sketches his father's personality
     by relating the lessons he learned from him and recalling
     the incidents between them that shaped the son's admiration
     for the father. Riis was a sincere man with a "passion
     for workmanship," who had special affection for men having
     "no conception of defeat." Riis's "zest for living sprang
     from his unorthodox feeling about God." Many of the inti-
     macies exchanged between father and son, their outings in
     the Catskills, their travels, the passwords kept between
     them, and their "rough passages" which drew them closer
     together are recalled.

1943 A BOOKS - NONE

1943 B SHORTER WRITINGS

1   ABELL, AARON IGNATIUS. The Urban Impact on American Protes-
     tantism, 1865-1900. Cambridge, Mass.: Harvard University
     Press, pp. 220-21.
        Riis credited with helping organize the King's Daughters'
     Settlement at 48 Henry Street.

2   ANON. "Riis, Jacob August," in Who Was Who in America, 1897-
        1942. Chicago: A. N. Marquis Company, p. 1035.
        Dates of Riis's life and works.

3   CURTI, MERLE. The Growth of American Thought. New York:
        Harper & Row, p. 589.
        Riis was among the "able champions" of social justice.

4   HURWITZ, HOWARD LAWRENCE. Theodore Roosevelt and Labor in
        New York State, 1880-1900. New York: Columbia University
        Press, pp. 172, 198, 204, 206, 231, 291.
        Studies influence of Riis upon Roosevelt; Riis's
        services--taking Roosevelt on a tour of sweatshops,
        accompanying him to Clarendon Hall, investigating the
        O'Leary affair, and securing "reliable data as to the true
        feelings of the drug clerks"--are detailed.

1946 A BOOKS - NONE

1946 B SHORTER WRITINGS

1   ROOSEVELT, THEODORE. Letters to Kermit from Theodore Roosevelt,
        1902-1908. Edited with Introduction and Prefaces by Will
        Irwin. Biographical Index by Nora E. Cordingley. New
        York: Charles Scribner's Sons, pp. 100, 200.
        In a letter dated May 7, 1905, Roosevelt wrote that "I
        quite sympathize with your feeling about your not going in
        to hear dear Jacob Riis because you knew he would be say-
        ing complimentary but embarrassing things about me." The
        collection has a short biography of Riis by Nora Cordingley.

2   WITTKE, CARL. We Who Built America; The Saga of the Immigrant.
        New York: Prentice-Hall, Inc., p. 296.
        Riis is cited as an example of Danish-American sentiment
        favoring "progressive movements."

1947 A BOOKS - NONE

1947 B SHORTER WRITINGS

1   ALLAND, ALEXANDER, et al. "'The Battle with the Slum' 1887-
        1897," in U.S. Camera 1948, edited by Tom Maloney. New
        York: U.S. Camera Publishers, pp. 11-18, 345, 346.
        A representation of text, captions, and many of Riis's
        photographs that were displayed, in special exhibition,
        at the Museum of the City of New York. This essay was one

of the first to explore Riis's success as a pioneering
photojournalist.

2   ANON.   "The Battle with the Slum," Hobbies, 52 (September), 21.
         A review of the exhibition--held at the Museum of the
     City of New York--of Alexander Alland's prints which were
     made from Riis's original negatives. Argues that Riis
     "found the lens, which could not lie or understate, a
     mightier weapon than the spoken word, a living proof to
     supplement the pen."

3   ANON.   "Riis Photos Show City's Old Slums," New York Times
         (21 May), p. 31.
         Fifty photographic prints Alexander Alland made from
     Riis's original glass negatives were shown in "the last
     exhibition of the season at the Museum of the City of
     New York." Riis is applauded in this review for his
     thirty-five year struggle "to abolish the most sordid
     aspects of slum life."

4   ATKINS, GORDON. "Health, Housing, and Poverty in New York
         City, 1865-1898." Ph.D. dissertation, Columbia University,
         1947, pp. 208-29.
         "Riis, Adler and Better Housing" studies Riis's activities
     against the background of the war for the eradication of the
     slum. How the Other Half Lives is compared to Dickens'
     portrayal of poverty. Both Riis and Dickens had "a keen
     insight into the problems of the people which had hitherto
     been neglected."

5   DUMOND, DWIGHT LOWELL. America in Our Time, 1896-1946.
         New York: Henry Holt and Company, pp. 21, 76.
         As an example of one whose life offered "no other value
     so incomparably rich as constructive service," Riis dedi-
     cated his years to aiding the children of the tenements.
     His efforts "resulted in a gradual shifting of emphasis"
     in the development of social service and public welfare.

1948 A BOOKS - NONE

1948 B SHORTER WRITINGS

1   ANON.   "Battle with the Slums," Survey Graphic, 37 (November),
         464-66.
         Alexander Alland's photographic prints, taken from the
     original negatives Riis made during his wanderings through
     New York's tenement districts, inspired this article which

claims little has been done in two generations to improve the lot of New York's slum dwellers: "The costumes are changed and the beards have been shaved. But quite as many people sleep in one room today as sixty years ago." Article includes five of Alland's prints.

2   BRUNO, FRANK. Trends in Social Work as Reflected in the Pro-
    ceedings of the National Conference of Social Work, 1874-
    1946. New York: Columbia University Press, pp. 72, 226,
    251.
        Riis is credited with inspiring the Christmas seal cam-
    paign. Bruno argues that "Harriet Fullmer, of the Visiting
    Nurses Association of Chicago, and Jacob Riis, of New York,
    in 1911 and 1919 argued that poor housing was expensive
    since it caused many of the ills with which the Conference
    [National Conference of Social Work] was dealing."

3   Community Service Society of New York. Frontiers in Human
    Welfare; The Story of a Hundred Years Service to the Com-
    munity of New York, 1848-1948. New York: Community Ser-
    vice Society of New York, p. 24.
        Riis "preached reform with all the vehemence of the muck-
    raking era...." The Tenement House Committee of the C.O.S.
    sent a papier-mache model of a tenement block to the
    Legislature; Riis commented upon the reproduction by
    noting that "Not to understand after one look at the
    poverty and disease maps that hung on the wall was to
    declare oneself a dullard."

4   HARTMANN, EDWARD GEORGE. The Movement to Americanize the
    Immigrant. New York: Columbia University Press, pp. 23,
    39.
        Riis, with other leaders of the settlement house move-
    ment, was "ever alert to the great assimilative role"
    which the institution played for the immigrant. Riis is
    mentioned as a member of the North American Civic League
    for Immigrants.

5   NEVINS, ALLAN. "Past, Present, and Future," in The Greater
    City New York, 1898-1914, edited by Allan Nevins and
    John A. Krout. New York: Columbia University Press,
    pp. 1-39.
        Riis had pointed out that approximately 10 percent of
    the city's inhabitants could not afford a "decent grave"
    and had to be buried in Potter's Field.

1949 A BOOKS - NONE

1949

1949 B SHORTER WRITINGS

1   ANON.   "In Memory of Jacob Riis," New York Times (3 May),
       p. 24.
       "We in the newspaper world take pride in the memory of
       Riis because he was a newspaperman," claims the editor of
       this centennial tribute to Riis. A "burning conscience
       and sympathy for those living in the squalor of the slums"
       drove Riis in his day to startle "a complacent New York
       into a sense of responsibility on slum conditions...."

2   ANON.   "In the Footsteps of Jacob Riis," Survey, 85 (June),
       329.
       A report on the gathering of 300 people at the Waldorf-.
       Astoria in New York on May 5, 1949, to celebrate the 100th
       anniversary of Riis's birth. Distinguished speakers were
       Mrs. Franklin Roosevelt, Henrick A. de Kauffmann,
       Mrs. Mary K. Simkhovitch, and Mrs. Riis. Harold S.
       Buttenheim, President of the Citizens Housing and Planning
       Council of New York, discussed the terrible tenement con-
       ditions still extant thirty-five years after Riis's death.
       It was agreed that improvement had not been "great enough
       nor fast enough," and "that war against the slums must
       still be waged."

3   ANON.   "Jacob A. Riis," Social Service Review, 23 (June), 231.
       Brief biographical sketch of Riis, celebrating the cen-
       tenary of his birth. Picture of Riis on the opposite page.

4   ANON.   "Mrs. Roosevelt Asks Tolerance of Views," New York
       Times (4 May), p. 36.
       States that thousands of Danes gathered at Riis's birth-
       place in Ribe to celebrate the centenary of Riis's birth,
       while in New York Mrs. Franklin D. Roosevelt said, at a
       dinner in Riis's honor, that if Riis were still alive he
       would speak up for the strength of democracy.

5   ANON.   "Riis Week Proclaimed," New York Times (26 April),
       p. 27.
       Reports Mayor O'Dwyer proclaimed May 1 to 8 "'Jacob A.
       Riis Week.'"

6   BUTTENHEIM, HAROLD S.   "Jacob Riis Valiant Foe of the Slum."
       Paper delivered at the Riis Centennial Dinner, 5 May 1949,
       New York, New York. L.C., Riis MSS, box 7.
       Riis's example will "always be a challenge and an inspi-
       ration to us to carry on."

Jacob Riis: A Reference Guide

7 Citizens' Housing and Planning Council of New York. "The
      Story of Jacob A. Riis: A Dramatic Narration for Radio."
      L.C., Riis MSS, box 6.
        Script prepared for a thirty minute radio broadcast.
      Four voices: narrator's, first man's, second man's, and a
      woman's. Close: "His success was great for what one man
      could accomplish alone but, yet, as we look about today,
      we still have with us the slums, the poverty and under-
      privileged children."

8 HODGES, LEIGH MITCHELL. "Story by Jacob Riis Recalled," New
      York Times (9 May), p. 24.
        Hodges criticizes the editor of the New York Times for
      forgetting to mention in the editorial tribute to Riis on
      the hundredth anniversary of his birth his promotion of
      the Christmas seal in this country.

9 MOSES, ROBERT. "The Living Heritage of Jacob Riis," New York
      Times Magazine, 98 (1 May), pp. 12, 13, 59, 60, 61.
        A centennial salute to Riis. Moses admires the manner
      in which Riis assimilated himself into American life: he
      did not come "to sit in the seat of the scornful--to harp
      on the old culture of Europe...or to preach disaffection
      and revolution"; rather, "His Americanism was deep and
      undiluted." Article includes a biography, a description
      of the streets and alleys Riis knew first-hand, such as
      Five Points, Mulberry Bend, and Bottle Alley, and a list
      of the reforms he brought about in his lifetime.

10 SIMKHOVITCH, MARY KINGSBURY. Here Is God's Plenty; Reflections
      on American Social Advance. New York: Harper & Brothers,
      p. 29.
        How the Other Half Lives added to the growth of the
      community's social conscience; it publicized the efforts
      of the tenement reform movement.

1950 A BOOKS - NONE

1950 B SHORTER WRITINGS

1 SCHLESINGER, ARTHUR M. The American as Reformer. Cambridge,
      Mass.: Harvard University Press, p. 51.
        How the Other Half Lives is a "conscience-stirring" work,
      along with Looking Backward, The Jungle, and The Grapes of
      Wrath. Authors enlisted in the cause of reform "often
      carry conviction where the professional agitator batters
      against stone walls."

1951

1951 A BOOKS - NONE

1951 B SHORTER WRITINGS

1   MORRIS, LLOYD. <u>Incredible New York; High Life and Low Life</u>
     <u>of the Last Hundred Years</u>. New York: Random House,
     p. 277.
         Riis, "a talented writer," had undergone most of the
     hardships that afflicted the foreign-born poor. His anger
     at the conditions of the tenement and its populace "boiled
     up" in <u>How the Other Half Lives</u>. Riis "became a powerful,
     insistent crusader for reform."

2   ROOSEVELT, THEODORE. <u>The Letters of Theodore Roosevelt; The</u>
     <u>Square Deal, 1901-1903</u>. Vol. 3. Selected and edited by
     Elting E. Morison; John M. Blum, Associate Editor;
     Hope M. Wigglesworth, Assistant Editor; Sylvia Rice, Copy
     Editor. Cambridge, Mass.: Harvard University Press,
     pp. 32, 55, 113, 186, 243-44, 376, 377, 410, 564, 575,
     646, 693.
         References; letters to and about Riis; topics include a
     coal strike settlement, a trip to Tuskegee, Riis's biog-
     raphy of Roosevelt, Riis's possible governorship of the
     Virgin Islands, and Schmittberger.

3   _____. <u>The Letters of Theodore Roosevelt; The Square Deal,</u>
     <u>1903-1905</u>, Vol 4. Selected and edited by Elting E.
     Morison; John M. Blum, Associate Editor; Hope M.
     Wigglesworth, Assistant Editor; Sylvia Rice, Copy Editor.
     Cambridge, Mass.: Harvard University Press, pp. 752, 794,
     977, 982, 1057, 1282.
         References; letters to and about Riis; topics include
     Roosevelt's campaign, a trip with Riis to visit poor
     children in Westchester, requested legislation about tene-
     ments, support for Wilcox, Riis's photographs of
     Roosevelt.

4   _____. <u>The Letters of Theodore Roosevelt; The Years of</u>
     <u>Preparation, 1898-1900</u>. Vol 2. Selected and edited by
     Elting E. Morison; John M. Blum, Associate Editor: John J.
     Buckley, Copy Editor. Cambridge, Mass.: Harvard Univer-
     sity Press, pp. 887, 921, 938, 960, 961, 965, 986, 994,
     1010, 1012, 1113, 1122, 1150, 1195, 1199, 1237, 1283-4,
     1292, 1294, 1312, 1376-77, 1396, 1448.
         References; letters to and about Riis; topics include
     appointment of factory inspectors, the bill about drug
     clerks, the O'Leary episode, sweatshops and tenements.

1952

5 _____. *The Letters of Theodore Roosevelt; The Years of Preparation, 1868-1898.* Vol. 1. Selected and edited by Elting E. Morison; John M. Blum, Associate Editor; John J. Buckley, Copy Editor. Cambridge, Mass.: Harvard University Press, pp. 278, 409, 410, 419, 472, 550, 573, 576-77, 596, 599, 612, 618, 635, 665, 698.
   References; letters to and about Riis; topics include Riis's influence, the Clarendon Hall incident, and meetings with labor leaders.

1952 A BOOKS - NONE

1952 B SHORTER WRITINGS

1   BROOKS, VAN WYCK. *The Confident Years: 1885-1915.* New York: E. P. Dutton, pp. 13-14, 120-22.
    Describes Riis's energy and passion for "making the crooked straight." Riis was one of the "imaginative minds" of the 1890's "obsessed" with the social problems the tenements represented and engendered. Roosevelt, "partly through the influence" of Riis, moved towards Progressivism.

2   BROWN, FRANCIS J. and JOSEPH S. ROUCEK, eds. *One America.* New York: Prentice-Hall, p. 83.
    A history of ethnic groups in the United States. Riis is an example of the Danish contribution to American life. He was "bent upon aiding the poor through better housing, better recreational facilities, opposition to child labor, and remedial and preventive legislation."

3   BUELL, GEORGE C. "A Man in Mulberry Street: Jacob A. Riis and the Awakening of Social Conscience in America (1870-1914)." Senior thesis, Princeton University.
    "Warm, friendly, and agressive," Riis's life pointed out that "the immigrant did have a place in American society."

4   HIGHAM, JOHN. "Origins of Immigration Restriction, 1882-1897: A Social Analysis," *Mississippi Valley Historical Review*, 39 (June), 77-88.
    The movement to restrict the flow of immigrants to the U.S., lasting from 1882 to 1897, had four roots: the reform movement, ethnic antipathy, anti-Catholicism, and economic fear. It stemmed from "a rising concern over urban problems and only indirectly from an objective change in urban conditions." Riis's *How the Other Half Lives* "first spread fully before the public" the evils of tenement life. Yet the conditions he described were not new;

twenty-five years before, the abject plight of the immigrant tenement dwellers "attracted little comment."

5 PHILLIPS, HARLAN B. "Walter Vrooman: Agitator for Parks and
Playgrounds," New York History, 33 (January), 25-39.
  Walter Vrooman, a reporter for the World, during the
1890s fought like Riis to establish parks and playgrounds
for the children of New York. Phillips argues that if
the slum children "found their most effective propagandist
in Jacob Riis," in Walter Vrooman they found "a willing
and spirited champion," who, unlike Riis, was not content
merely to point out "the human waste in children."
Vrooman stepped further than Riis. Riis protested against
the harshness of the tenements; Vrooman felt "the injustice
of slum life."

6 ROOSEVELT, THEODORE. The Letters of Theodore Roosevelt; The
Big Stick, 1905-1907. Vol. 5. Selected and edited by
Elting E. Morison; John M. Blum, Associate Editor;
Alfred D. Chandler, Jr., Assistant Editor; Sylvia Rice,
Copy Editor. Cambridge, Mass.: Harvard University Press,
pp. 212, 267, 317.
  References; letters to and about Riis. Topics include
Roosevelt's "sane and courageous radicalism," Riis as part
of an "incongruous lot" at the White House, Riis as a
"good public servant."

7 _____. The Letters of Theodore Roosevelt; The Big Stick,
1907-1909. Vol. 6. Selected and edited by Elting E.
Morison; John M. Blum, Associate Editor; Alfred D.
Chandler, Jr., Assistant Editor; Sylvia Rice, Copy Editor.
Cambridge, Mass.: Harvard University Press, pp. 1100,
1160-61, 1195, 1284.
  References to Riis. Items include Riis's "good advice"
when Roosevelt was Police Commissioner, Riis's support of
Hughes, Riis's report that there is political apathy in
the West among farmers, Riis's struggle against the
tenements.

1953 A BOOKS - NONE

1953 B SHORTER WRITINGS

1 KOUWENHOVEN, JOHN ATLEE. The Columbia Historical Portrait of
New York; An Essay in Graphic History in Honor of the Tri-
centennial of New York City and the Bicentennial of
Columbia University. Garden City, N.Y.: Doubleday &
Company, Inc., pp. 349, 381-86.

1954

"How the Other Half Lives" was a phrase that did not originate with Riis; it had been used as the subtitle of a series of articles, "Our Homeless Poor," in Frank Leslie's Illustrated Newspaper in 1872. Many of Riis's photographs are reproduced.

2 REZNECK, SAMUEL. "Unemployment, Unrest, and Relief in the United States during the Depression of 1893-97," Journal of Political Economy, 61 (August), 324-45.
   A discussion of social ills introduced to the United States by the depression which began on 'Industrial Black Friday,' May 5, 1893. About relief programs Rezneck says: "the novelty and variety of relief projects adopted particularly during 1893-94 were perhaps more remarkable than the actual amount of relief provided." Cites Josephine Shaw Lowell who saw the relief programs as morally damaging to recipients. Riis is numbered among those who favored sound relief programs.

1954 A BOOKS - NONE

1954 B SHORTER WRITINGS

1 EMERY, EDWIN and HENRY LADD SMITH. The Press and America. New York: Prentice-Hall, Inc., pp. 390, 450, 506-7.
   Riis was one of the great reporters of the Sun; he had been trained by Chester S. Lord and Selah M. Clarke. The dramatic impact of Riis's articles about the slums is mentioned.

2 MANN, ARTHUR. Yankee Reformers in the Urban Age. Cambridge, Mass.: Belknap Press, pp. 3, 172.
   Riis, with Jane Addams and Charles Booth, is credited with showing that "the slum was the microcosm of the evils which beset Western civilization." Mentions that Riis was invited to address the Twentieth Century Club.

3 ROOSEVELT, THEODORE. The Letters of Theodore Roosevelt; The Days of Armageddon, 1914-1919. Vol. 8. Selected and edited by Elting E. Morison; John M. Blum, Associate Editor; Alfred D. Chandler, Jr., Assistant Editor; Sylvia Rice, Copy Editor. Cambridge, Mass.: Harvard University Press, pp. 959, 1027, 1051.
   References to Riis and family. Roosevelt recalls that Riis was among the men who provided him with the most help; Riis's sons are examples of the problems of dual citizenship; Mrs. Riis was a member of the Women's Roosevelt League.

1954

4 _____. The Letters of Theodore Roosevelt; The Days of
Armageddon, 1909-1914. Vol. 7. Selected and edited by
Elting E. Morison; John M. Blum, Associate Editor;
Alfred D. Chandler, Jr., Assistant Editor; Sylvia Rice,
Copy Editor. Cambridge, Mass.: Harvard University
Press, pp. 242, 298, 672.
 References to Riis's interest in Roosevelt's "ticket,"
Riis's conversation with Roosevelt about Judge Lindsey,
and Riis's possible appearance as a character witness in
Roosevelt's libel suit against George A. Newett.

1955 A BOOKS - NONE

1955 B SHORTER WRITINGS

1 HIGHAM, JOHN Strangers in the Land; Patterns of American
Nativism, 1860-1925. New Brunswick, N. J.: Rutgers
University Press, pp. 40, 67.
 Explores the nature of Riis's Social Gospel: Riis
warned that only a "Christian sense of justice could stop
the dreadful wedge that greed was driving between the tenement dwellers and the upper classes. Since the slums and
the foreign quarters coincided, Riis treated them as syn-
onomous." Through his picture of slum life, he exposed
"the disorganization and squalor of their foreign residents." Even though Riis wrote about the immigrants with
warmth, and ascribed the evils of the slum to the larger
political environment, his book "aroused anti-foreign as
well as anti-tenement attitudes."

1956 A BOOKS - NONE

1956 B SHORTER WRITINGS

1 BREMNER, ROBERT H. From the Depths; The Discovery of Poverty
in the United States. New York: New York University
Press, pp. 4, 65, 68-69, 70, 82, 83, 84, 105, 116, 149,
154, 204, 205, 269.
 Studies Riis's activities against a solid, empirical
background of social reform and reformers. Riis's opinions
on the problems of tenements, poverty, and intemperance
are cited.

2 STILL, BAYRD. Mirror for Gotham; New York as Seen by Contem-
poraries from Dutch Days to the Present. Washington
Square, N.Y.: New York University Press, pp. 211, 215,
217, 245-47.

Riis presented "graphic evidence" of the miserable conditions in which "increasing thousands of New Yorkers
dwelt." Cites Riis's observations of the lower East Side
culled from How the Other Half Lives "published in 1888."

1957 A BOOKS - NONE

1957 B SHORTER WRITINGS

   1   BIGELOW, DONALD N. "Introduction," in How the Other Half
       Lives; Studies Among the Tenements of New York, by
       Jacob A. Riis. New York: Hill and Wang, pp. vii-xiv.
       Bigelow quickly explains the influence of the book.
      What is emphasized is Riis's understanding of the social
      scene he encountered. As Bigelow points out, "Although
      the book discusses what has been done and what could be
      done to cure some of the evils which are portrayed, most
      of its suggestions are technical and temporary. Riis's
      interest in the economic basis of the problem is slight."
      Bigelow emphasizes Riis's concern with the tenant's moral
      and physical reconstruction, and explores Riis's sense of
      practical action.

   2   BRUNO, FRANK J. and LOUIS TOWLEY. Trends in Social Work 1874-
       1956; A History Based on the Proceedings of the National
      Conference of Social Work. New York: Columbia University
      Press, pp. 72, 226, 251.
      Bruno's earlier work (see 1948.B2) brought up to date.

1958 A BOOKS - NONE

1958 B SHORTER WRITINGS

   1   ANDREWS, AVERY DELANO. "Theodore Roosevelt as Police Commis-
       sioner," New York Historical Society Quarterly, 42 (April),
      117-41.
      A history of Roosevelt's years as Police Commissioner
      of New York. Article is taken from General Andrews' unpub-
      lished memoirs. What emerged from the Roosevelt term in
      office, argues Andrews, was a police force with "Morale."
      Mentions of Riis and references to his book, Theodore
      Roosevelt The Citizen, run throughout the article.
      Andrews remembers Riis as "the widely beloved humanitarian
      and authority upon the life and the social problems of the
      East Side, and author of a book that became famous, How
      the Other Half Lives." He goes on to say that "Roosevelt

had great respect and admiration for Riis, as indeed did
all of us who had an opportunity to know his gentle yet
fearless nature."

2   BREMNER, ROBERT H. "The Big Flat: History of a New York
    Tenement House," American Historical Review, 64 (October),
    54-62.
       Bremner traces the history of "Big Flat," a New York
    tenement house constructed in 1855 by the New York Asso-
    ciation for the Improvement of the Condition of the Poor.
    Riis, who described Big Flat as "a regular hotbed of
    thieves and peace-breakers," was delighted to see it
    demolished and a carriage factory erected in its place.
    In his time, he came to believe that business "had done
    more than all other agencies together to wipe out the
    worst tenements." Bremner disagrees: "The onward march
    of industry and the 'beneficent spirit of business,'"
    which Riis and a host of reformers had lauded, occasionally
    destroyed bad tenements but rarely created good ones. "The
    overwhelming weight of evidence presented in tenement house
    inspections and investigations made in the 1890's leads to
    the conclusion that the dispossessed tenants of the Big
    Flat benefited little from its destruction." Article, in
    addition, furnishes concrete evidence of the prostitution,
    child mortality rates, overcrowding, stale beer saloons,
    opium traffic, and filth associated with the tenements of
    Riis's time and outlined in his How the Other Half Lives.

3   MEYER, GRACE M. Once Upon a City; New York from 1890-1910 as
    Photographed by Byron and Described by Grace M. Meyer.
    New York: Macmillan Company, pp. 128, 143.
       Riis's photographic concerns are studied; a "pictorial
    approach" gave impact to his stories. His use of flash
    powder is described. His efforts to rescue the boy from
    the gang through the Small Parks Committee are described.

4   POLLACK, PETER. The Picture History of Photography, from the
    Earliest Beginnings to the Present Day. New York:
    Harry N. Abrams, Inc., p. 298.
       Riis would not have considered "his pictures works of
    art; he would not have indulged in such discussions." His
    concern was to produce clear, detailed photographic evi-
    dence to illustrate his stories. Yet, Riis "left a mighty
    series of pictures motivated by the depth of his humani-
    tarian feelings." Several of Riis's photographs are
    reproduced.

1960

5   WAGENKNECHT, EDWARD. The Seven Worlds of Theodore Roosevelt.
         New York: Longmans, Green & Company, pp. 109, 117.
             Riis's years spent with Roosevelt were, so Riis observed,
         "the happiest he ever had." Riis's wearing a decoration at
         an event "where everybody else was plainly attired" is used
         to illustrate Roosevelt's consideration for others.

1959 A BOOKS - NONE

1959 B SHORTER WRITINGS

1   FAULKNER, HAROLD U. Politics, Reform, and Expansion, 1890-1900.
         New York: Harper, pp. 31-32.
             Riis, "more than any other individual," brought to the
         attention of Americans the plight of the slum dweller.
         "No amount of legislative investigations and reports"
         would have equalled the impact of Riis's "sustained rhet-
         oric." Riis's work "called attention to problems which
         technology then had to solve...."

2   GULLASON, THOMAS ARTHUR. "The Sources of Stephen Crane's
         Maggie," Philological Quarterly, 38 (October), 497-502.
             Material for Crane's Maggie came in part from the writer's
         association with Riis: "There is a strong possibility that
         Crane got some valuable details, not only from Riis's lec-
         ture and later conversations with him, but also from his
         clinical study of the New York slums, How the Other Half
         Lives." Themes common to both Riis's book and Crane's
         (conditions of the slums, slum youth, the sufferings of
         young working girls) are identified and compared.

3   LORANT, STEFAN. The Life and Times of Theodore Roosevelt.
         Garden City, N.Y.: Doubleday & Company, pp. 269, 277.
             Quotes Riis about his nocturnal inspections with
         Roosevelt; presents Nast's cartoon, "Roosevelt Upholds the
         Law," and quotes Roosevelt about a nine hour tour he and
         Riis took to see how the Excise Law was enforced.

1960 A BOOKS - NONE

1960 B SHORTER WRITINGS

1   SWETT, STEVEN C. "The Test of a Reformer: A Study of Seth
         Low, New York City's Mayor, 1902-1903," New York Histor-
         ical Society Quarterly, 44 (January), 4-41.

1960

> In 1894 Low declined membership in anti-Tweed "Second
> Committee of Seventy" which gave birth to the Citizens
> Union made up of Republicans hoping to reform municipal
> politics. "Among the Union's 165 founders were financier
> J. Pierpont Morgan, lawyer and later Secretary of State
> Elihu Root, and social worker and critic Jacob Riis."

1961 A BOOKS - NONE

1961 B SHORTER WRITINGS

1   CARTER, RICHARD. The Gentle Legions. New York: Doubleday &
     Company, p. 76.
         Riis's campaign to have the government sell a special
     Christmas stamp in order to gain revenue to combat tuber-
     culosis is cited. Riis's idea was derived from the Danish
     government's fight against the disease.

2   CREMIN, LAWRENCE A. The Transformation of the School; Pro-
     gressivism in American Education, 1876-1957. New York:
     Alfred A. Knopf, pp. 58, 86, 184.
         Riis, with humanitarians "of every stripe," believed
     that education was "at the heart" of social reform. Riis
     asked, "Do you see how the whole battle with the slum is
     fought out in and around the public school"? With the
     rise of "professionalism," fewer people like "Jane Addams,
     Jacob Riis, Theodore Roosevelt, and Walter Hines Page con-
     cerned themselves directly with educational reform...."

3   HARBAUGH, WILLIAM HENRY. Power and Responsibility; The Life
     and Times of Theodore Roosevelt. New York: Farrar,
     Straus and Cudahy, pp. 120, 225-26.
         Roosevelt's letter to Riis, explaining the decision to
     "veto a bill to reduce the long hours of drug clerks" is
     quoted. Roosevelt's explanation to Riis about a pension
     order for Civil War Veterans is cited.

4   LUBOVE, ROY. "Lawrence Veiller and the New York State Tene-
     ment House Commission," Mississippi Valley Historical
     Review, 47 (March), 659-77.
         Contrasts Veiller to Riis: unlike Riis, Veiller "con-
     ceived of a universe in which power regulated human affairs
     more decisively than did love or the milk of human kind-
     ness," and though he lacked "the bubbling optimism and
     winsome personal warmth" of Riis, "he was no less committed
     to better housing in the name of justice to the individual
     and the well-being of the community."

1962 A BOOKS - NONE

1962 B SHORTER WRITINGS

1   BURGESS, CHARLES O. "The Newspaper as Charity Worker: Poor
     Relief in New York City, 1893-1894," New York History,
     43 (July), 249-68.
         Riis, during the depression of 1893, was part and parcel
     of the battle which ensued when professional charity
     organizations criticized the newspapers for what they con-
     sidered indiscriminate relief. Burgess in this article
     examines the battle between newsmen and charity workers
     which ensued. "Jacob Riis," states Burgess, "rated dis-
     crimination as the mark of a business-like approach to
     reform and charity."

2   LUBOVE, ROY. The Progressives and the Slums; Tenement House
     Reform in New York City, 1890-1917. Pittsburgh: Univer-
     sity of Pittsburgh Press, pp. 49-80, 247-50.
         Riis was "squarely in the American entrepreneurial
     tradition." The virtues he extolled were based on an
     individualism tempered by "justice, moral responsibility
     and Christian love...." Riis's vision of the "real Amer-
     ica" resembled Ribe, the place of his birth. The rural
     virtues of hard work, the dignity of labor, reverence for
     the divine and nature, and a close family "insured the
     individual's proper moral respect."

3   RISCHIN, MOSES. The Promised City; New York's Jews, 1870-1914.
     Cambridge, Mass.: Harvard University Press, pp. 125, 144,
     196-97, 213, 214.
         Riis and Byron, utilizing the latest techniques in
     photography, brought "realistic portraits of the city's
     worst features to public attention." Riis's rebuttal
     against a "metaphysical crank" at the Labor Temple is
     mentioned as well as Riis's observations on the strongest
     virtue of the Jew, patriarchal family life.

4   WIEBE, ROBERT H. Businessmen and Reform; A Study of the Pro-
     gressive Movement. Cambridge, Mass.: Harvard University
     Press, p. 19.
         Riis, with a committee from the Cleveland Chamber of
     Commerce, developed a housing code which was brought before
     the state legislature.

1963 A BOOKS - NONE

1963

1963 B SHORTER WRITINGS

1 DESTLER, CHESTER McARTHUR. <u>Henry Demarest Lloyd and the</u>
  <u>Empire of Reform</u>. Philadelphia: University of Pennsylvania Press, p. 475.
     Riis supported Lloyd's call for emergency nationaliza-
  tion of "coal carriers and mines backed by martial law"
  if coal production was not resumed by September 1, 1902.

2 FILLER, LOUIS. "Riis, Jacob A.," in <u>A Dictionary of American</u>
  <u>Social Reform</u>. New York: Philosophical Library, p. 659.
     Biographical entry; Riis is credited with helping improve
  the slum conditions of his time. He was not a profound
  thinker, and was "naive" in his admiration of Roosevelt.
  He helped organize "moderate reform opinion."

3 GREEN, CONSTANCE McLAUGHLIN. <u>Washington; Capital City, 1879-</u>
  <u>1950</u>. 2 vols. Princeton, N. J.: Princeton University
  Press, Vol. I, pp. 152-53.
     Riis spoke before a joint session of the House and
  Senate. He pointed out that "Negro alley dwellers" in
  Washington, D.C., lived in worse conditions than in the
  "grimmest" tenements of New York. Moreover, "one-room
  families" were more numerous in the capital than in New
  York.

4 McKELVEY, BLAKE. <u>The Urbanization of America, 1860-1915</u>.
  New Brunswick, N. J.: Rutgers University Press, pp. 120,
  163.
     Riis's statistics on tenements are quoted. <u>How the Other</u>
  <u>Half Lives</u> provided data "for innumerable sermons" and
  sparked investigations in many towns. Riis's arguments
  for playgrounds, day nurseries, and fresh-air funds are
  cited.

*5 WISE, WILLIAM. <u>The Story of Mulberry Bend</u>. New York:
  E. P. Dutton.

1964 A BOOKS - NONE

1964 B SHORTER WRITINGS

1 KLEIN, WOODY. <u>Let in the Sun</u>. New York: Macmillan Company,
  pp. 64-65.
     Riis's newspaper career is briefly summarized. Riis
  probably had no peer in striving for tenement-house reform.

2   NEWHALL, BEAUMONT. The History of Photography, from 1839 to
      the Present Day. Rev. and enlarged edition. New York:
      The Museum of Modern Art, pp. 139-140.
         The difficulties of reproducing Riis's photographs for
      How the Other Half Lives are explained. When the book
      was published, seventeen illustrations were "halftones,
      but of poor quality...." Nineteen photographs "were shown
      in drawings made from them: some are signed 'Kenyon Cox,
      1889, after photograph.'" Alland's work in reproducing
      Riis's photographs is described. Riis chose "unerringly"
      the camera position that would best "tell the story."

3   SCHEINER, SETH M. "The New York City Negro and the Tenement,"
      New York History, 45 (October), 304-15.
         Argues that during the period 1880-1910 "difficulties
      that the New York City Negro faced in the area of housing--
      poor living conditions, high rents, segregation, and dis-
      crimination--were not only problems for the Negro, but for
      the entire housing situation in the city." Relates that
      Riis in 1890 wrote about the unbearable housing conditions
      and excessive rental charges Negroes faced in the city.

1965 A BOOKS - NONE

1965 B SHORTER WRITINGS

1   BELLAMY, DAVID G. "Riis, Jacob August (1849-1914)," in
      Encyclopedia of Social Work, edited by H. Lurie. New
      York: National Association of Social Workers, pp. 666-67.
         Biographical sketch. Riis inspired a generation of
      writers to describe the other half with "pitiless honesty
      rather than with amused or horrified condescension."

2   CHESSMAN, G. WALLACE. Governor Theodore Roosevelt; The Albany
      Apprenticeship, 1898-1900. Cambridge, Mass.: Harvard
      University Press, pp. 66, 201, 204, 205, 209, 211, 213,
      214.
         Riis's participation in Roosevelt's administration is
      sketched through such events as the O'Leary incident and
      the Kelley affair.

3   CHURCHILL, ALLEN. The Roosevelts; American Aristocrats.
      New York: Harper & Row, pp. 189-90.
         Recounts episode in which Riis and Steffens were rebuked
      after asking then Police Commissioner Roosevelt if he
      sought the Presidency.

1965

4   DANIELS, JONATHAN. <u>They Will Be Heard; America's Crusading
    Newspaper Editors</u>. New York: McGraw-Hill, p. 258.
        Riis's service to Police Commissioner Roosevelt is
    described. Riis had Roosevelt see the "alliance of graft,
    politics and crime."

5   FELT, JEREMY P. <u>Hostages of Fortune; Child Labor Reform in
    New York State</u>. Syracuse, N. Y.: Syracuse University
    Press, p. 97.
        Riis had urged the substitution of a birth certificate
    for a parental affadavit for establishing an individual's
    legal age for work. The Child Labor Committee realized
    this would not solve the problem of the law's evasion.
    Many immigrant children could not obtain the needed docu-
    ment from Central and Eastern Europe.

6   GERNSHEIM, HELMUT with ALISON GERNSHEIM. <u>A Concise History of
    Photography</u>. New York: Grosset & Dunlap, pp. 148, 190.
        Riis made a "poignant series" of photographs between
    1887 and 1892 of the poor. Riis, like Hine and others
    who "used the camera instinctively as an objective com-
    mentator on life," prepared the way for modern photography
    before World War I.

7   MARCUSE, MAXWELL F. <u>This Was New York!; A Nostalgic Picture
    of Gotham in the Gaslight Era</u>. New York: LIM Press,
    pp. 61, 75-76, 99.
        <u>How the Other Half Lives</u> "deeply influenced"
    Mrs. Simkhovitch. Riis was "<u>the</u> crime reporter of his
    time" and he believed that the neglect of law in the
    tenements was brought about by the greater neglect of law
    by the public and its official indifference regarding the
    plight of the slum dweller.

1966 A BOOKS - NONE

1966 B SHORTER WRITINGS

1   BANNISTER, ROBERT C. <u>Ray Stannard Baker; The Mind and Thought
    of a Progressive</u>. New Haven, Conn.: Yale University
    Press, p. 145.
        Quotes Baker's journal entry of August 31, 1912, in
    which he reflected that the Progressive's social justice
    group--of whom Riis, Pinchot, and Addams were part--"and
    I say it with no intent to disparage, feel more deeply
    than they think."

Jacob Riis: A Reference Guide

2   BLUMBERG, DOROTHY ROSE. Florence Kelley; The Making of a
       Social Pioneer. New York: Augustus M. Kelley Publishers,
       pp. 172-74.
         Riis tried to arrange a meeting between Roosevelt and
       Kelley in order to have her appointed Factory Inspector
       of New York State. The first meeting did not, as Riis
       hoped, take place. A second meeting ensued with Riis,
       Roosevelt, and Jane Addams; Kelley did not gain the post.

3   DORN, JACOB HENRY. Washington Gladden; Prophet of the Social
       Gospel. Columbus, Ohio: Ohio State University Press,
       pp. 86, 132, 276, 287.
         Gladden's awareness of slum conditions is, in part,
       traceable to Riis's books. Gladden's sermons were based
       on "realistic studies" such as How the Other Half Lives.
       Riis is mentioned as a member of the Commission on Labor
       established by the General Convention of the Protestant
       Episcopal Church in 1901.

4   ELLIS, EDWARD ROTH. The Epic of New York City. New York:
       Coward-McCann, Inc., pp. 435-37.
         Riis's association with Roosevelt when he was Police
       Commissioner is traced.

5   KEEFER, TRUMAN FREDERICK. Ernest Poole. New York: Twayne
       Publishers, Inc., p. 25.
         How the Other Half Lives, claimed Poole, changed the
       course of his life. His "latent sympathies" for the
       other half were "aroused" by Riis's book.

6   LUBOVE, ROY. "Introduction," in The Making of an American,
       by Jacob A. Riis, edited by Roy Lubove. New York:
       Harper & Row, pp. xi-xxvi.
         Riis's social program and his impact upon later urban
       planners are discussed. Riis's theory of "renewal" is
       superior to the present one "with its emphasis upon the
       revitalization of downtown." His approach suggests a
       "diffused renewal": improvements are made across the
       entire city.

7   ZIFF, LARZER. The American 1890s; Life and Times of a Lost
       Generation. New York: Viking Press, pp. 152, 153-155,
       161, 164.
         How the Other Half Lives is a "model work" of "human
       interest" and sociological reporting. Riis's work en-
       couraged that of Walter Wyckoff.

1967

1967 A BOOKS - NONE

1967 B SHORTER WRITINGS

1   DAVIS, ALLEN F. Spearheads for Reform; The Social Settlements
     and the Progressive Movement. New York: Oxford University
     Press, pp. 38, 62, 67, 172.
        How the Other Half Lives might have inspired college
     students, sending them from the campus to the slums. The
     book, a "plea for sympathy and a demand for justice," con-
     tained elements of "nostalgic agrarianism...." Riis, more
     than any other person, brought the conditions of poverty
     to the attention of Americans.

2   ELLIS, DAVID M.; FROST, JAMES A.; SYRETT, HAROLD C. and
     CARMEN, HENRY J. A History of New York State. Rev. ed.
     Ithaca, N. Y.: Cornell University Press, pp. 479-620.
        Americans depended upon Riis to analyze the significance
     and conditions of the city, immigrant neighborhoods, and
     poverty. The poor provided Riis with an invaluable source
     of material.

3   GLAAB, CHARLES N. and A. THEODORE BROWN. A History of Urban
     America. New York: Macmillan Company, pp. 94, 139, 216,
     217, 241, 244, 247, 248.
        Riis's use of the metaphor of a many-colored quilt to
     chart population patterns is cited, a technique used by
     his contemporaries, "particularly in commenting on New
     York." Riis's emphasis upon environmental causation is
     mentioned.

4   NEIDLE, CECYLE S. The New Americans. New York: Twayne
     Publishers, pp. 145-49.
        An essay on Riis is included in a chapter devoted to
     immigrants—successful in one way or another—who came to
     America between the years 1830 and 1880. The essay is
     divided into two parts: a biographical sketch in four
     paragraphs, and three pages of excerpts from The Making of
     an American.

5   MARTIN, JAY. Harvests of Change; American Literature, 1865-
     1914. Englewood Cliffs, N. J.: Prentice-Hall, p. 246.
        Riis's revelations about the East Side's population
     density, "'the most densely populated district in all the
     world, China not excluded,'" provided sensational contrasts,
     "characteristic of muckraking journalism...." The por-
     trayal of such urban conditions "always compelled and
     fascinated middle-class readers."

6   WIEBE, ROBERT H. The Search for Order, 1877-1920. New York:
        Hill & Wang, pp. 88-89.
        How the Other Half Lives, like other works of the time,
        intimated that barbarism would not completely die in the
        face of social reform.

1968 A BOOKS - NONE

1968 B SHORTER WRITINGS

1   CADY, JOSEPH LAWRENCE. "The Containment of Chaos; The Repre-
        sentation of Poverty in Fiction by Authors Associated with
        the Dominant Literary Culture in Late Nineteenth Century
        America." Ph.D. dissertation, University of California,
        Berkeley, 1968, pp. 131-132.
        Analyzes Riis's style and tone in How the Other Half
        Lives. The book, filled with "aggressive rhetoric" has a
        number of "simulated visits." Some of these convey the
        impression that Riis's audience "merely needs contact with
        poverty in order to understand how wretched it is."

2   CORDASCO, FRANCESCO, ed. Jacob Riis Revisited; Poverty and the
        Slum in Another Era. Introduction by Francesco Cordasco.
        Garden City, N. Y.: Doubleday and Company, Anchor Books,
        pp. xiii-xxi.
        Riis's career and program of reform are explored. Riis
        was a victim of the prejudices of his time. We can under-
        stand him neither if we focus solely on his crude carica-
        tures of the immigrant poor, nor on his concept of
        Americanization. With the reform age, he emphasized
        "commitment"; he attacked social evils with the epoch's
        "buoyant optimism which prophesied inevitable change...."

3   GARRATY, JOHN A. The New Commonwealth, 1877-1890. New York:
        Harper & Row, p. 205.
        Reformers, though sincere and dedicated, nevertheless
        often applied derogatory labels to national groups. In
        How the Other Half Lives, Riis "characterized the Irish
        as belligerent, the Italians as dirty, the Jews as grossly
        materialistic."

4   TRATTNER, WALTER I. Homer Folks; Pioneer in Social Welfare.
        New York: Columbia University Press, p. 75.
        Riis supported Folks's nomination for Commissioner of
        Charities under the Low administration.

JACOB RIIS: A REFERENCE GUIDE

1969

1969 A BOOKS - NONE

1969 B SHORTER WRITINGS

1   CERILLO, AUGUSTUS, JR. "Reform in New York City: A Study of
        Urban Progressivism." Ph.D. dissertation, Northwestern
        University, pp. 43, 53, 129.
           Riis's efforts to secure better housing, schools, and
        health facilities for slum neighborhoods are mentioned.
        Riis gave Roosevelt further insight into slum life.

2   CHESSMAN, G. WALLACE. Theodore Roosevelt and the Politics of
        Power. Boston: Little, Brown and Company, pp. 72-73.
           Riis's writings allowed Roosevelt to see what needed to
        be done "towards giving a better chance for respectability
        and usefulness to the people in the lower wards."

3   FINE, DAVID MARTIN. "The Immigrant Ghetto in Fiction, 1885-
        1917." Ph.D. dissertation, University of California at
        Los Angeles, pp. 23-25, 59-62, 127.
           Riis's importance lay in his crying out the need for
        tenement reform, thereby preparing the way for future
        legislation, "climaxed by the work of the Tenement House
        Commission of 1900."

*4   GERNSHEIM, HELMUT with ALISON GERNSHEIM. The History of
        Photography from the Camera Obscura to the Beginning of
        the Modern Era. New York: McGraw-Hill Book Company.
           Riis listed under the genre of Social Documentation; his
        intentions are compared to those of Thomas Annan who photo-
        graphed the Glasgow slums during the years 1867 to 1877.
        Riis called America's "first photo-reporter."

5   HOLL, JACK M. "The George Junior Republic and the Varieties
        of Progressive Reform," New York History, 50 (January),
        43-60.
           A study of the activities and underpinnings of the
        George Junior Republic boys' camp. Holl contends that
        "because it both reflected and blurred all shades of
        ideology and commitment, George Junior Republic produced
        its own microcosmic version of the stormy Progressive
        Era." Riis's influence and attitude toward George Junior
        Republic are discussed. Riis felt that boys' clubs and
        camps were the answer to vandalism, and that the milita-
        ristic organization of such clubs and camps was not dan-
        gerous. He said it was better for the boys to march with
        a "gun on the shoulder" than with "stripes on the back."

6   KOBRE, SIDNEY. Development of American Journalism. Dubuque,
    Iowa: William C. Brown Company, p. 369.
        Mentions that Dana secured Riis for the Evening Sun.
    Describes the numerous reforms Riis waged through the
    medium of journalism. Cites Riis's use of the camera and
    flashlight powder.

7   LANDESMAN, ALTER F. Brownsville; The Birth, Development and
    Passing of a Jewish Community in New York. New York:
    Bloch Publishing Company, pp. 51, 107.
        Riis called Brownsville a "nasty little slum." Riis,
    like John Swinton, Hutchins Hapgood, and Lillian Wald,
    postulated that Brownsville and the East Side were sui
    generis, and not representative of America. Such places
    were "what the stream of newcomers from the Old World had
    helped to make them."

8   THOMAS, LATELY. The Mayor Who Mastered New York; The Life &
    Opinions of William J. Gaynor. New York: William Morrow
    & Company, p. 292.
        Riis, in Denmark, sent a telegram to Gaynor, during the
    latter's struggle to recover from an assassination attempt
    in 1910.

1970 A BOOKS

1   LANE, JAMES B. "Bridge to the Other Half: The Life and Urban
    Reform Work of Jacob A. Riis." Ph.D. dissertation, Univer-
    sity of Maryland.
        A scholarly biography divided into twelve chapters which
    thoroughly cover Riis's life from childhood to his later
    years. Lane argues that Riis "bridged the gap between the
    two Americas that he confronted as an immigrant. He walked
    with the rich and powerful while retaining his bond with
    the slum resident." He isolates factors in Riis's Danish
    background that shaped his character, such as a love of
    nature, a belief in hard work, Danish nationalism, and an
    impulsive, adventurous spirit. Lane then explains how
    Riis affected and was affected by young, industrial America.
    This dissertation served as the basis of Lane's book Jacob
    A. Riis and the American City, 1974.

1970 B SHORTER WRITINGS

1   CARLSON, ROBERT A. "Americanization as an Early Twentieth-
    Century Adult Education Movement," History of Education
    Quarterly, 10 (Winter), 440-64.

1970

Carlson argues that the educational programs to Americanize the ethnic cultures of cities like New York in the
Progressive Era were started in an altruistic spirit, but
ended up as a means of forcing minorities to conform to
middle-class standards. He mentions Riis as one of the
muckraking journalists whose The Battle with the Slum
(1902) seriously disturbed middle-class complacency.

2   CORDASCO, FRANCESCO. "Introduction," in The Children of the
      Poor, by Jacob A. Riis. New York: Garrett Press, Inc.,
      pp. iii-xi.
        This is a reprint of Cordasco's "Introduction" to Jacob
      Riis Revisited: Poverty and the Slum in Another Era
      (New York: Doubleday, 1968), pp. xiii-xxii.

3   GARTNER, CAROL BLICKER. "A New Mirror for America: The Fic-
      tion of the Immigrant of the Ghetto, 1890-1930." Ph.D.
      dissertation, New York University, pp. 10, 20-21, 41, 81,
      175.
        Riis, in How the Other Half Lives, powerfully evokes the
      atmosphere and detail of the physical ghetto. When he
      wrote fiction, he "merely rearranged true stories...."
      Abraham Cahan was given a letter of introduction by
      Steffens to Riis. Riis taught Cahan the aspects of his
      job, and helped him meet reporters and public officials
      at police headquarters.

4   MEYER, ISIDORE S. "Book Reviews," American Jewish Historical
      Quarterly, 59 (June), 545-48.
        A review of The Spirit of the Ghetto, by Hutchins Hapgood.
      Hapgood's vision of the ghetto differed sharply from Riis's
      vision. Characteristic of Riis's descriptions of the
      ghetto is "the home-mission evangelistic imagery of the
      patronizing uncomprehending reformer." Hapgood, on the
      other hand, sensed "a spirit of seriousness, melancholy,"
      and "high idealism" in the ghetto. He judged Yiddish New
      York "sympathetically," recognizing "its inner ardor and
      idealism." He saw the East Side as "a source for reform
      in greater America."

5   NOBLE, DAVID W. The Progressive Mind, 1890-1917. Chicago:
      Rand McNally & Company, pp. 74, 162.
        Riis is an example of a popular middle-class hero as
      muckraker. Riis is quoted on Roosevelt's belief in the
      "gospel of the will."

6   OWRE, J. RIIS. "Preface" and "Epilogue," in The Making of an
      American. New York: Macmillan Company, pp. xi-xii,
      285-337, respectively.

In an essay motivated by abiding interest and deep
affection, Owre says that "it falls to me, grandson of
its [The Making of an American] author, to bring the story
to a close, to tell of the last years of his life." His
study, the closest we have to an "inside" portrait, deals
with Riis's lectures during, and after, 1902, the death
of Lammet, his remarriage, and his family.

7   SKOLNIK, RICHARD. "Civic Group Progressivism in New York City,"
    New York History, 51 (July), 410-39.
        The story of civic group progressivism in New York City.
    New York in the Progressive Era experienced a rush of
    civic group activity. Riis was always wary of group re-
    form, but at times acted as an agent for specific reform
    clubs. Though the civic groups of New York brought sig-
    nificant changes to the city, their elitism and casual
    attitudes in part confirmed Riis's skepticism.

8   STINSON, JOHN D. "The Papers of Jacob A. Riis and of the
    Jacob A. Riis Neighborhood Settlement in the New York
    Public Library," Social Service Review, 44 (June), 201-4.
        Announces that Riis's papers in the custody of the New
    York Public Library since 1936 have been officially donated
    to the library by his heirs, and that the library has also
    recently received as a gift "records of the Jacob A. Riis
    Neighborhood Settlement." Riis's papers (of which brief
    descriptions are given) consist of "seven manuscript boxes
    of letters, manuscripts of books, notes and drafts of lec-
    tures and speeches, pocket diaries, memorandum books, and
    miscellaneous papers for the period 1871-1916." The
    records of Jacob A. Riis Neighborhood Settlement or "Riis
    House" cover the period 1892-1962 and "provide an inter-
    esting account of settlement house work on Manhattan's
    Lower East Side and in the Bedford-Stuyvesant section of
    Brooklyn."

9   TRATTNER, WALTER I. Crusade for the Children; A History of the
    National Child Labor Committee and Child Labor Reform in
    America. Chicago: Quadrangle Books, p. 32.
        In The Children of the Poor, Riis brought to light the
    "gross evasion" of child labor laws in New York.

10 VECOLI, RUDOLPH. "Introduction," in The Children of the Poor,
    by Jacob A. Riis. New York: Johnson Reprint Corporation,
    pp. v-xiii.
        Riis's work as a reformer and his newspaper career are
    detailed. Riis was a "thoroughgoing environmentalist."
    Riis rejected hereditary influences; they were an obstacle

to reform. Riis believed that human nature was fundamen-
tally good. If a youth turned to crime, it was because
"evil influences" had shaped his character. The thesis
of <u>The Children of the Poor</u> is that the "total environment of slum youth worked for their <u>moral corruption</u>."

11   WARNER, SAM BASS, JR. "Editor's Introduction," in <u>How the</u>
      <u>Other Half Lives; Studies Among the Tenements of New York</u>,
      by Jacob Riis, edited by Sam Bass Warner, Jr. Cambridge,
      Mass.: Harvard University Press, Belknap Press, pp. vii-
      xix.
          Explores Riis's battle against the slum. No less impor-
      tantly, Riis's literary style and tactics are analyzed.
      The "mixture of crime and poverty" in <u>How the Other Half</u>
      <u>Lives</u> "joined literary tradition with special urban spacial
      patterns." As a police reporter, Riis made the "conven-
      tional links" among "slum, revolution, and criminality."

<u>1971 A BOOKS - NONE</u>

<u>1971 B SHORTER WRITINGS</u>

1   ASTOR, GERALD. <u>The New York Cops; An Informal History</u>. New
      York: Charles Scribner's Sons, pp. 18-19, 79, 82, 100,
      101.
          Cites Riis's observations on the wretched conditions of
      slum dwellers, and Riis's disgust at Inspector Williams'
      brutal treatment of suspected criminals. Riis "distinctly
      approved of club work on young toughs."

2   BRANDES, JOSEPH and MARTIN DOUGLAS. <u>Immigrants to Freedom;</u>
      <u>Jewish Communities in Rural New Jersey since 1882</u>.
      Philadelphia, Pa.: University of Pennsylvania Press,
      pp. 41, 175.
          In the <u>Review of Reviews</u>, Riis hailed experiments in
      South Jersey in which Jewish farming communities were
      established; Riis called for such colonies in the age of
      rapid urbanization. Points out that even though many
      Americans were not bigots, cliches and stereotypes could
      not be easily shaken. Riis, for example, claimed that
      money is the God of the Russian Jews.

3   HOLL, JACK M. <u>Juvenile Reform in the Progressive Era;</u>
      <u>William R. George and the Junior Republic Movement</u>.
      Ithaca, N. Y.: Cornell University Press, pp. 43, 60, 63,
      64, 66, 67, 91, 93, 103, 125, 155, 156, 185, 187, 225, 286,
      301.

1971

While having scattered references to Riis, this study
of George's life devotes attention to Riis's influence
upon, and friendship with, the founder of the Junior
Republic. It brings to our attention joint tours Riis
and George made to the "tenements and sweatshops of
'Jewtown.'"

4 LANE, JAMES B. "Unmasking Poverty: Jacob A. Riis and How the
   Other Half Lives," Maryland Historian, 2, 27-39.
      Lane contends Riis's "most impressive accomplishment as
   a crusader for social justice...was his ability to subject
   affluent Americans vicariously to the reality of poverty."
   Riis's background enabled him to do this; in Ribe Riis
   "learned to revere...family, church, community, and nation."
   His cultural heritage, therefore, was akin to that of the
   upper classes in America.

5 LEVINE, DANIEL. Jane Addams and the Liberal Tradition.
   Madison, Wis.: State Historical Society of Wisconsin,
   pp. 132-133.
      How the Other Half Lives signals a change in attitude
   toward poverty. While Riis condemned the shiftless and
   the tramps, his harrowing picture of slum life demonstrated
   that the slum inhabitants hated their abject quarters, and
   that not all of them were "idlers."

6 LEVINE, JERALD ELLIOT. "Police, Parties, and Polity: The
   Bureaucratization, Unionization and Professionalization
   of the New York City Police, 1870-1917." Ph.D. dissertation, University of Wisconsin, pp. 245, 247
      Mentions Riis's night tours with Roosevelt and the lat-
   ter's interest in Riis's judgment, which he could trust.
   Riis's drawing of the two "making the rounds" is included.

7 MADISON, CHARLES A. "Preface," in How the Other Half Lives;
   Studies Among the Tenements of New York, by Jacob A. Riis.
   New York: Dover, pp. v-viii.
      Riis's newspaper days are placed in the context of Amer-
   ican economic conditions. Riis's achievements in photography are also discussed. How the Other Half Lives
   revealed Riis to be "relatively unsophisticated and of
   limited political perspective...." Riis often overlooked
   the "healthier shoots" in the tenements and was not able
   to overcome his racial prejudices. Nonetheless, Riis is
   not to be faulted for being a product of his times, and
   Madison explores the book's impact and theme.

1971

8   NOVOTNY, ANN. Strangers at the Door; Ellis Island, Castle
     Garden, and the Great Migration to America. Riverside,
     Conn.: Chatham Press, pp. 81, 101-2.
        Contains brief biography of Riis and photographs.

1972 A BOOKS - NONE

1972 B SHORTER WRITINGS

1   CORDASCO, FRANCESCO and SALVATORE LaGUMINA. Italians in the
     United States; A Bibliography of Reports, Texts, Critical
     Studies and Related Material. New York: Oriole Editions,
     pp. 49, 53.
        Riis's discussions plus photographs of Italian-American
     life, in How the Other Half Lives, are cited, as well as
     his Century article of August, 1899 ("Feast-days in Little
     Italy").

2   FURER, HOWARD B., ed. and comp. The Scandinavians in America
     986-1970; A Chronology and Fact Book. Dobbs Ferry, N. Y.:
     Oceana Publications, p. 61.
        The book is divided into four parts: "Chronology,"
     "Documents," "Bibliographical Aids," and "Index." Riis is
     listed under Chronology, April 1890. Riis is called the
     "most well-known Danish-American." How the Other Half
     Lives "succeeded in arousing the social conscience of New
     York City to improve life in the slums and among the poor."

3   WHISNANT, DAVID E. "Selling the Gospel News, or: The Strange
     Career of Jimmy Brown the Newsboy," Journal of Social
     History, 5 (Spring), 269-309.
        Myths, such as that of the American newsboy, "that have
     followed from the peculiarities of our national ideology"
     have blocked at times, Whisnant argues, the way to social
     reform. Riis, who separated fact from fancy in most of
     his reform work, encouraged in How the Other Half Lives
     the newsboy stereotype. "In view of the uncertainty of
     so perceptive a critic as Riis," he concludes, "one may
     well understand why it was to take the American public in
     general until the late 1930s to admit that the abuses [of
     the newsboy] existed and to agree at least to alleviate
     them."

1973 A BOOKS - NONE

1973 B SHORTER WRITINGS

1 DILLARD, IRVING. "Six Decades Later," in Muckraking; Past, Present, and Future, edited by John M. Harrison and Harvey H. Stein. University Park, Pa.: Pennsylvania State University Press, pp. 1-10.
     Riis's career and legacy are traced. Riis's war upon the slums, embracing a twenty-five year span, was directed against exploiting landlords and employers who were responsible for the wretched "physical, moral and spiritual" poverty of many of the city's inhabitants.

2 GARDENER, JOSEPH L. Theodore Roosevelt as ex-President. New York: Charles Scribner's Sons, pp. 4, 311.
     Riis's trips by train with Roosevelt are cited. When Roosevelt was told of Riis's death, he "took time"--while traveling to Washington--"to dictate a thoughtful statement to the press."

3 KINGSDALE, JON M. "The 'Poor Man's Club': Social Functions of the Urban Working-Class Saloon," American Quarterly, 25 (October), 472-89.
     Saloons in the period 1890-1920 helped shape the values and behavior of the urban working class. "Jacob Riis, in How the Other Half Lives, described the lowest of the low in a New York tenement slum...."

4 LANE, JAMES B. "Jacob A. Riis and Scientific Philanthropy During the Progressive Era," Social Service Review, 47 (March), 32-48.
     An analysis of the "paradoxical relationship" between Riis and the New York Charity Organization Society. Riis's attitude toward urban reform evolved in four stages in relation to the C.O.S., Lane argues. During the 1880s he became a convert to the philanthropic theories of Josephine Shaw Lowell and the charity organization movement. In the 1890s Riis was emphasizing "prevention rather than correction." At the end of the century he was again working with the C.O.S. "to institutionalize social control of the environment." In later life he rebelled against the "formalized methodology and bureaucratic structure of the COS."

5 TRIPP, WENDELL. "Recent Publications," New York History, 54 (January), 124.
     Dover Press in 1971 republished How the Other Half Lives. Tripp finds this new edition, with its preface by Charles A. Madison, its additional sixty photographs, and its over-all better design, an improvement on the original edition.

Jacob Riis: A Reference Guide

1974

1974 A BOOKS

1   ALLAND, ALEXANDER. <u>Jacob A. Riis; Photographer & Citizen</u>.
Millerton, N. Y.: Aperture. Preface by Ansel Adams.
Riis used the camera to record not to create, says
Alland. Riis's pictures were "sordid documents...that
led to many vital reforms." The first half of the book is
a biography of Riis; the second half is a collection of
Alland's excellent, detailed reproductions of photographs
taken by Riis. Without a look at this pictorial history
of Riis's studies of the poor, one does not have a true
appreciation of Riis's work.

2   LANE, JAMES B. <u>Jacob A. Riis and the American City</u>. Port
Washington, N. Y.: Kennikat Press.
A contemporary biography of Riis, based on Lane's doctoral dissertation. Riis "thought in terms of the person
rather than the mass" and Lane stresses Riis's optimism
and "humane touch." His examination of Riis's personal
life reveals the complexity and difficulties of the reformer who stressed the virtues of close family life and
patriarchal values.

3   MEYER, EDITH PATTERSON. <u>"Not Charity but Justice"; The Story</u>
<u>of Jacob A. Riis</u>. New York: Vanguard Press.
This biography is based upon much of Riis's own writings.
Riis's voice for social justice was not a solitary one,
but probably the "most powerful of the times...." It was
the right moment for an "able and concerned" reporter to
arouse the public to the plight of the slum-dwellers.

1974 B SHORTER WRITINGS

1   ADAMS, ANSEL. "Preface," in <u>Jacob A. Riis; Photographer &</u>
<u>Citizen</u>. Millerton, N. Y.: Aperture, pp. 6-7.
Riis's work is a <u>unit statement</u>. Riis's photographs
have an intense <u>living</u> quality.

2   CAINE, STANLEY P. "The Origins of Progressivism," in <u>The</u>
<u>Progressive Era</u>, edited by Lewis L. Gould. Syracuse,
N. Y.: Syracuse University Press, pp. 11-34.
<u>How the Other Half Lives</u> is a "stirring expose" of
tenement life. Riis's photographs of living areas could
only be made after the development of flash photography--
so dark were the dwellings of the poor.

3   HARAP, LOUIS. <u>The Image of the Jew in American Literature;</u>
<u>from Early Republic to Mass Immigration</u>. Philadelphia:
Jewish Publication Society of America, pp. 441-442, 564.

Riis echoed anti-Semitic notions, and his own attitude
towards Jews was "not free from conventionality."

4   KAPLAN, JUSTIN. Lincoln Steffens, A Biography. New York:
     Simon and Schuster, pp. 59, 61, 69, 70, 72, 73, 76, 78,
     84, 132, 305.
        Riis's influence upon and friendship with Steffens are
     traced. Riis showed Steffens that the journalist, "as
     man of good will, had a social obligation: to make things
     happen."

5   RAVITCH, DIANE. The Great School Wars: New York City, 1805-
     1973; A History of the Public Schools as Battlefield of
     Social Change. New York: Basic Books, pp. 122-123, 130.
        The Children of the Poor is discussed, and Riis's pro-
     posals for educational reform are traced. Riis's sympathy
     for the immigrant is explored.

6   SKARDAL, DOROTHY BURTON. The Divided Heart. Lincoln, Neb.:
     University of Nebraska Press, pp. 46, 115.
        Riis is grouped with other Scandinavian-American writers
     who felt at home with the American language. Skardal
     points out that in Enok Mortensen's novel, Thus I Became
     Homeless, about a fictitious immigrant named Niels Nord a
     reference is made to Riis: "'On reading Jacob Riis'
     autobiography, How I Became an American, Niels lost his
     doubt once more.'"

1975 A BOOKS - NONE

1975 B SHORTER WRITINGS

1   ANON. "Exhibition on the City's Not-So-Good Old Days," New
     York Times (8 March), pp. 27, 52.
        Riis's photographs exposing the underbelly of New York
     City in his age are centered on the exhibition walls of
     the Museum of the City of New York as part of a show
     entitled "How Grim Was My City," a portrait of New York.

2   DOCTOROW, E. L. Ragtime. New York: Random House, pp. 15-16.
        In this historical meditation, Riis appears as a "tire-
     less newspaper reporter and reformer." Doctorow constructs
     Riis's interview with Stanford White.

3   KAY, JANE HOLTZ. "Recording the Innocent," Christian Science
     Monitor (22 July), p. 24.

1975

Kay argues that "the dilemma of documentary photographs
[as evidenced in the reprints Alexander Alland made of
Riis's work] is this: given time, given talent, dirt may
become picturesque, 'ugliness' turn to 'beauty,' social
ills evolve into art." In Alland's collection "the squalor
seems somewhat sanitized; views are quaint, ragamuffins
and even ragged old men more engaging than wretched."

4   WEISS, MARGRET R. "The Formidable Frances B. Johnston,"
        Saturday Review (23 August), pp. 51-53.
        The story of Frances B. Johnston, "pioneer among photo-
     journalists" in the 1890s, who photographed "the daily
     life of Theodore Roosevelt's children for a Ladies' Home
     Journal feature by Jacob Riis."

Index

Note: References in the following index are to year of publication,
category, and item within a category. 1891.B2, for example,
represents item 2, Shorter Writings (B), 1891; 1974.A1 refers
to item 1, Books (A), 1974. Items with the same author and
title listing have been further alphabetized according to
source (e.g., Anon., "The Battle with the Slum," *Hobbies*,
1947.B2; Anon., "The Battle with the Slum," *Nation*, 1903.B2).

Abell, Aaron Ignatius, The Urban
Impact on American Protes-
tantism, 1865-1900, 1943.B1
Adams, Ansel, "Preface," in
Jacob A. Riis; Photographer &
Citizen, 1974.B1
Alland, Alexander, et al., "'The
Battle with the Slum' 1887-
1897," 1947.B1
Alland, Alexander, Jacob A. Riis;
Photographer & Citizen,
1974.A1
Allen, William H., "The Battle
with the Slum," 1903.B1
Andrews, Avery Delano, "Theodore
Roosevelt as Police Commis-
sioner," 1958.B1
Anon.:
"The A.I.C.P. in Three
Campaigns," 1911.B1
"Abandoned Farms," 1893.B1
"Abandoned Farms," 1893.B2
"Abandoned Farms," 1893.B3
"About the Slums," 1899.B1
"Aid to State Charities,"
1895.B1
"Ambitious King's Daughters,"
1890.B1
"Americanism in Municipal
Politics," 1895.B2
"Among the New Books,"
1900.B1

"Archbishop Goes Slumming,"
1904.B1
"Arraigned by a Universalist,"
1894.B1
"Autobiography of an
Immigrant," 1902.B1
"Back to the Soil," 1900.B2
"Battle of the Slums,"
1900.B3
"The Battle with the Slum,"
Hobbies, 1947.B2
"The Battle with the Slum,"
Nation, 1903.B2
"Battle with the Slum,"
Rock Island Union, 1900.B4
"Battle with the Slum (The),"
1903.B3
"Battle with the Slums,"
Indianapolis Journal,
1900.B5
"Battle with the Slums,"
Pittsburgh Dispatch,
1900.B6
"Battle with the Slums,"
Survey Graphic, 1948.B1
"Battle with Slums," 1900.B7
"Bishop Dedicates New Settle-
ment," 1901.B1
"Blackwell's Island for Play-
ground," 1912.B1
"Book Department," 1903.B4

"Book Notices," New York
  Evening Sun, 1893.B4
"Book Notices," *Silver Cross*
  (February), 1891.B2
"Book Notices," *Silver Cross*
  (January), 1891.B1
"Book of Today," 1893.B5
"Books about Four Great
  Cities," 1891.B3
"Books of the Week,"
  Outlook, 1903.B5
"Books of the Week,"
  Outlook, 1903.B6
"Books Received from August 1,
  1902 to December 1, 1902,"
  1903.B7
"Books Received from Febru-
  ary 1, 1901 to April 1,
  1901," 1901.B2
"Booth and Riis," 1890.B2
"Boys Honor Jacob Riis,"
  1914.B1
"Casual Comment," 1914.B2
"Charities," 1895.B2
"Charles Scribner's Son's
  New Books," 1891.B4
"The Chautauqua Press Club,"
  1891.B5
"Cheer of St. Nicholas,"
  1896.B1
"Chicago the Tramps'
  Paradise," 1900.B8
"Children and Crime,"
  1901.B3
"Children as Workers,"
  1895.B3
"Children of the Poor,"
  Boston Transcript, 1894.B2
"The Children of the Poor,"
  *Buffalo Christian Advo-
  cate*, 1892.B1
"The Children of the Poor,"
  Charities, 1900.B9
"The Children of the Poor,"
  Christian Register,
  1892.B2
"The Children of the Poor,"
  Christian Union, 1892.B3
"'The Children of the Poor,'"
  Critic, 1892.B4

"'The Children of the Poor,'"
  *Five Points House of
  Industry Report*, 1893.B6
"'The Children of the Poor,'"
  Humanity and Health,
  1893.B7
"Children of the Poor,"
  London *Public Opinion*,
  1893.B8
"The Children of the Poor,"
  *Monthly Bulletin of St.
  John's Guild*, 1892.B5
"'Children of the Poor,'"
  New Bedford *Evening
  Standard*, 1893.B9
"Children of the Poor,"
  New York *Evening Sun*,
  1892.B6
"The Children of the Poor,"
  New York *Evening World*,
  1893.B10
"The Children of the Poor,"
  New York Tribune, 1900.B9
"Children of the Poor,"
  Providence Journal, 1898.B1
"Children of the Poor," *San
  Francisco Chronicle*,
  1892.B7
"'The Children of the Poor,'"
  Zion's Herald, 1892.B8
"Children of the Slums,"
  1900.B10
"Children of the Tenements,"
  1895.B4
"Christian at Work," 1891.B6
"The Christmas Seals,"
  1937.B1
"Chronicle and Comment,"
  1900.B11
"The Church Club of New York,"
  1897.B1
"Citizens Dine Roosevelt,"
  1899.B2
"Citizenship in the Tenements,"
  1897.B2
"The City Child's Case,"
  1898.B2
"Completed Jacob Riis Park,
  Seaside Resort Within City,
  to Reopen to Public Sunday,"
  1933.B1

INDEX

"Congregational Association,"
1895.B5

"Conlin Disobedient,"
1897.B3

"Contemporary Celebrities,"
1903.B7

"Corruption Not the
Trouble," 1896.B2

"The Cost of a Lecture Trip,"
1908.B1

"Current Events Pictorially
Treated," 1914.B3

"Darkest New York," 1890.B3

"The Day of Little Things,"
1896.B3

"Decoration for Jacob A.
Riis," *Brooklyn Eagle*,
1900.B12

"Decoration for Jacob A.
Riis," New York *Evening
Sun*, 1900.B13

"Dedication of Alta House,"
1900.B14

"Discussing Some Social
Problems," 1891.B7

"Discussion before the
Nineteenth Century Club,"
1894.B3

"Dr. Adler on Poverty,"
1890.B4

Editorial, *Churchman*,
1900.B15

Editorial, *Hartford Courant*,
1900.B16

"Editorial Notes," 1891.B8

Editorial, *Survey*, 1914.B4

"The Education of Mr. Riis'
Burglar," 1903.B8

"Edward Atkinson's Figures,"
1896.B4

"An English Journal on 'How
the Other Half Lives,'"
1891.B9

"Entertainments," 1900.B17

"Evils of Tenements,"
1900.B18

"Evils of the Tenements,"
1897.B4

"Exhibition on the City's
Not-So-Good Old Days,"
1975.B1

"The Factor of Character,"
1893.B11

"Facts about the Poor,"
1893.B12

"The Federation of Churches
and Christian Workers in
New York City," 1898.B3

"Feeding Her Audience,"
1891.B9

"Filled with Misery,"
1891.B10

"Flowers for Poor Children,"
1889.B1

"For Little Orphans,"
1897.B5

"A Free Employment Bureau,"
1894.B4

"Fresh-Air Charity," 1897.B6

"The Fresh-Air Fund," 1897.B7

"The Fresh Air Work," 1893.B13

"From Oyster Bay to Hoboken,"
1903.B10

"Fruit of the Slums," 1891.B11

"The Genesis of the Gang,"
1897.B8

"A Golden Opportunity,"
1895.B6

"Good Government Club Plans,"
1896.B5

"Good Side of the Slums,"
1898.B4

"Good Work," 1898.B5

"Good Work for Charity,"
1894.B5

"The Governor Goes Home,"
1900.B19

"Graveyard; Playground,"
1897.B9

"A Great Hearted American,"
1914.B5

"The Greed of the Landlord,"
1907.B1

"He Intends to Appoint Women,"
1895.B7

"Hear Riis Talk of Slums,"
1900.B20

"Hearing a Lecture by Jacob A.
Riis," 1893.B14

"Heredity and Poverty,"
1892.B9

"Home Named for Mr. Riis,"
1901.B4
"Home, School, Play,"
1898.B6
"Honored by the King of His
Fatherland," 1900.B21
"Honoring Jacob A. Riis,"
1901.B5
"Horrors of the Sweat Shop,"
1891.B12
"The Housing Problem Facing
Congress," 1904.B2
"How Criminals Are Made,"
1897.B10
"How Jacob A. Riis Became
Roosevelt's Ideal Citizen,"
1903.B10
"How the Other Half Live,"
Boston Herald, 1891.B13
"How the Other Half Lives,"
Asbury Park Spray,
1892.B10
"How the Other Half Lives,"
Boston Advertiser,
1891.B14
"How the Other Half Lives,"
Boston Post, 1890.B5
"How the Other Half Lives,"
Boston Post, 1891.B15
"How the Other Half Lives,"
Boston Times, 1890.B6
"How the Other Half Lives,"
*Chautauqua Assembly
Herald*, 1891.B16
"How the Other Half Lives,"
Christian Intelligencer,
1890.B7
"'How the Other Half Lives,'"
Coup D'Etat, 1893.B15
"How the Other Half Lives.
A Glimpse at Darkest New
York," 1890.B8
"How the Other Half Lives,"
illegible source, 1891.B20
"How the Other Half Lives,"
London *Morning Post*,
1891.B17
"How the Other Half Lives,"
Mail and Express, 1890.B9
"How the Other Half Lives,"
Nation, 1891.B18

"How the Other Half Lives,"
New Haven Journal-Courier,
1891.B19
"How the Other Half Lives,"
New York *Evening Sun*,
1890.B10
"How the Other Half Lives,"
New York *Evening Sun*,
1890.B11
"How the Other Half Lives,"
no journal given, 1893.B16
"How the Other Half Lives,"
Rockford Morning Republican,
1893.B17
"How the Other Half Lives,"
San Francisco Chronicle,
1890.B12
"How the Other Half Lives,"
War-Cry, 1891.B21
"How the Other Half Lives,"
Waterbury Daily Republican
1889.B2
"How the Other Half Lives,"
Zion's Herald, 1890.B13
Illegible title, illegible
source, 1900.B22
Illegible title, *St. George's
Chronicle*, 1894.B6
"Illustrated Lectures,"
1893.B18
"In Darkest Chicago," 1900.B23
"In Memory of Jacob Riis,"
1849.B1
"In Memory of Mr. Gilder,"
1910.B1
"In Memory of Waring,"
1898.B7
"In Slums of a Great City,"
1900.B24
"In the Footsteps of Jacob
Riis," 1949.B2
"In the Slums of New York,"
1892.B11
"In the World of Literature,"
1890.B14
"Interesting Indeed," 1893.B19
"International Convention of
the Brotherhood of St.
Andrew," 1897.B11
"Is There a Santa Claus?"
1904.B3

INDEX

"It Must and Shall Prevail,"
1898.B8

"Its Horrors Revealed,"
1891.B22

"J. A. Riis on Slum Life,"
1898.B9

"Jacob A. Riis," *Book Buyer*,
1891.B23

"Jacob A. Riis," Chicago
(illegible), 1900.B25

"Jacob A. Riis," *Literary
Digest*, 1914.B6

"Jacob A. Riis," *Outlook*,
1903.B11

"Jacob A. Riis," *Social
Service Review*, 1949.B3

Jacob A. Riis; A Sketch of
His Life and Work,
1904.B4

"Jacob A. Riis Before Holyoke
Audiences," 1898.B10

"Jacob A. Riis Before the
Church Club," 1893.B20

"Jacob A. Riis Buried,"
1914.B7

"Jacob A. Riis Collapses,"
1914.B8

"Jacob A. Riis Dissents,"
1906.B1

"Jacob A. Riis Dying," *New
York Times* (21 May),
1914.B9

"Jacob A. Riis Dying, *New
York Times* (26 May),
1914.B10

"Jacob A. Riis for Mayor?"
1905.B1

"Jacob A. Riis Honored,"
1901.B6

"The Jacob A. Riis House,"
1901.B7

"Jacob A. Riis Improves,"
1914.B11

"Jacob A. Riis in Detroit
Last Week," 1901.B8

"Jacob A. Riis Is Ill,"
1906.B2

"Jacob A. Riis Park," 1914.B12

"Jacob A. Riis, Reformer,
Dead," 1914.B13

"Jacob A. Riis, Roosevelt's
Ideal Citizen," 1914.B14

"Jacob A. Riis Speaks to
Large Audience," 1900.B26

"Jacob A. Riis Speaks to
Schoolboys," 1901.B9

"Jacob A. Riis Tells of the
Slums," 1900.B27

"Jacob A. Riis Was Anxious to
See the Fire," 1901.B10

"Jacob A. Riis Weaker," *New
York Times* (22 May),
1914.B15

"Jacob A. Riis Weaker," *New
York Times* (23 May),
1914.B16

"Jacob Riis an 'Easy Mark,'"
1899.B3

"Jacob Riis and His Compatriots," 1900.B28

"Jacob Riis and His Work,"
1914.B17

"Jacob Riis Doesn't Know
Passaic," 1896.B6

"Jacob Riis' Epic of the
Slums," 1900.B29

"Jacob Riis: Friend of the
American People," 1914.B18

"Jacob Riis His Text," 1903.B12

"Jacob Riis on New York Slums,"
1900.B30

"Jacob Riis on the Tramp
Nuisance," 1900.B31

"The Jacob Riis Park," 1914.B19

"Jacob Riis Seriously Ill,"
1914.B20

"Jacob Riis' Silver Wedding
in His Little White House,"
1901.B11

"Jacob Riis Still Improves,"
1914.B21

"Jacob Riis Talks of the Poor,"
1893.B21

"Jacob Riis Tells of His Early
Trials," 1906.B3

"Jacob Riis's Books," 1914.B22

"Jacob Riis's Health Improving," 1914.B23

"Jacob Riis's Lecture,"
1900.B32

"Jacob Riis's Will Gives All
   to Widow," 1914.B24
"Jewish Success," 1900.B33
"King's Daughters' Day,"
   1896.B7
"The King's Daughters in a
   Great City," 1892.B12
"King's Daughters' Settle-
   ment," *Charities*, 1899.B4
"The King's Daughters'
   Settlement," *Evangelist*,
   1901.B12
"Last Words," 1892.B13
"League to Promote American
   Ideals," 1918.B1
"Lecture at New Century
   Club," 1895.B8
"Lecture by Jacob A. Riis,"
   Literary News-Letter,
   1894.B7
"A Lecture by Jacob A. Riis,"
   New York Tribune, 1895.B9
"Letter," 1900.B34
"Life in the Slums," 1893.B22
"Lights and Shadows of Slum
   Life in New York," 1904.B5
"Literary Brevities,"
   1890.B15
"Literary Necrology,"
   1914.B25
"Literary Notes," 1909.B1
"Literature," *Critic*,
   1890.B16
"Literature," New York
   Evening Post, 1898.B11
"Literature Today," 1891.B24
"Live Among the Poor,"
   1895.B10
"Lose Hope for Jacob Riis,"
   1914.B26
"The Lounger," *Critic*
   (17 January), 1891.B25
"The Lounger," *Critic*
   (January), 1904.B6
"Low Life in London," 1893.B23
"Made Trouble for College
   Women," 1893.B24
"Magazine Articles," 1895.B11
"Making a Way Out of the
   Slum," 1901.B13
"The Making of an American,"
   1901.B14

"Making Thieves in the
   Metropolis," 1894.B8
"Matters We Ought to Know,"
   1891.B26
"Memorial of a Reporter's
   Service," 1901.B15
"Memorial Service for Riis,"
   New York Times (1 January),
   1915.B1
"Memorial Service for Riis,"
   New York Times (13 June),
   1914.B27
"Memorial Service to Jacob A.
   Riis," 1914.B28
"A Memorial to Jacob Riis,"
   1915.B2
"'A Message from the Slums,'"
   1895.B12
"Millions of Babies," 1896.B8
"A Miracle and a Miracle
   Worker," 1897.B12
"Miscellaneous," 1898.B12
"Misery in the Slums,"
   1892.B14
"Modern American Idealists,"
   1904.B7
"A Monument to Jacob A. Riis,"
   1914.B29
"Moss and Parker in a Row,"
   1897.B13
"Move for Slum Parks,"
   1899.B5
"Mr. Jacob A. Riis," 1901.B16
"Mr. Riis as an Advance Agent
   of the Portland Conference,"
   1905.B2
"Mr. Riis Injures His Eyes,"
   1895.B13
"Mr. Riis' Lecture," 1892.B15
"Mr. Riis Lectures at Harvard
   on New York Slums," 1900.B35
"Mr. Riis Tells the Other
   Half," 1891.B27
"Mr. Riis to Lecture on Tene-
   ments--Matinee at Abbey's
   Theatre," 1895.B14
"Mr. Riis's Autobiography,"
   1901.B17
"Mr. Riis's Complaint,"
   1895.B15
"Mr. Riis's Figures Were
   Close," 1895.B16

"Mr. Riis's Hen Roost,"
1896.B9
"Mr. Riis's Lay Sermon,"
1898.B13
"Mr. Riis's Lecture,"
1895.B17
"Mrs. Humphrey Ward on Play,"
1908.B2
"Mrs. Roosevelt Asks Toler-
ance of Views," 1949.B4
"Mulberry Bend's Park,"
1897.B14
"Named 'Jacob A. Riis House,'"
1901.B18
"Naming a New Settlement
House," 1901.B19
"The National Conference at
Washington," 1901.B20
"Need of More Schools,"
1895.B18
"The New Book," 1909.B2
"New Books," *New London
Telegraph*, 1892.B16
"The New Books," *Outlook*,
1910.B2
"New Literature," *Brooklyn
Times*, 1890.B17
"New Playgrounds for Cleve-
land," 1900.B36
"New Publications," New
Orleans *Times Democrat*,
1893.B25
"New Publications," *New York
Times*, 1893.B26
"New Site for the House of
Refuge," 1909.B3
"New York and London Con-
trasted," 1891.B28
"New York Slums," 1900.B37
"New York Slums Improved,"
1900.B38
"New York Tenements," *Brooklyn
Eagle*, 1897.B15
"New York Tenements," London
Saturday Review, 1891.B29
"New York's Criminals,"
1893.B27
"Nibsy's Christmas," *Boston
Times*, 1893.B28
"Nibsy's Christmas," *New York
Evangelist*," 1893.B29

No heading found, *Argonaut*,
1890.B18
No heading found, *Boston
Budget and Beacon*, 1890.B19
No heading found, *Boston Eve-
ning Record*, 1891.B30
No heading found, *Boston Eve-
ning Transcript*, 1891.B31
No heading found, *Boston Eve-
ning Transcript*, 1898.B14
No heading found, *Boston
Gazette*, 1890.B20
No heading found, *Boston
Gazette*, 1893.B30
No heading found, *Boston
Herald*, 1894.B9
No heading found, *Boston
Journal*, 1890.B21
No heading found, Boston
Literary World, 1892.B17
No heading found, *Boston
Times*, 1890.B15
No heading found, *Brooklyn
Times*, 1891.B32
No heading found, *Brooklyn
Times*, 1892.B18
No heading found, *Buffalo
Express*, 1890.B22
No heading found, *Cambridge
Tribune*, 1890.B23
No heading found, *Charities*,
1899.B6
No heading found, *Charities*,
1901.B21
No heading found, *Chicago
Herald*, 1893.B31
No heading found, Chicago
Inter-Ocean, 1890.B24
No heading found, *Chicago
Tribune*, 1891.B33
No heading found, *Christian
at Work*, 1890.B25
No heading found, *Christian
at Work*, 1891.B34
No heading found, *Christian
Inquirer*, 1890.B26
No heading found, *Churchman*,
1900.B39
No heading found, *Churchman*,
1901.B22
No heading found, *Cleveland
Leader*, 1890.B27

No heading found, *Detroit Free Press*, 1900.B40

No heading found, *Detroit Journal*, 1890.B28

No heading found, England *Mercury*, 1891.B35

No heading found, *Evangelist*, 1889.B3

No heading found, *Evangelist*, 1891.B36

No heading found, *Farm, Field, and Fireside*, 1892.B19

No heading found, *Harper's Weekly*, 1901.B23

No heading found, *Hartford Courant*, 1890.B29

No heading found, *Home Journal*, 1890.B30

No heading found, illegible source, 1895.B19

No heading found, *Independent*, 1892.B20

No heading found, *Indianapolis News*, 1890.B31

No heading found, *London Daily News*, 1891.B37

No heading found, London *Morning Advertiser*, 1889.B4

No heading found, London *Spectator*, 1893.B32

No heading found, *Mail and Express*, 1890.B32

No heading found, *Milwaukee Sentinel*, 1891.B38

No heading found, *Minneapolis Tribune*, 1891.B39

No heading found, *Morning News*, 1890.B33

No heading found, *New England Magazine*, 1891.B40

No heading found, New York *Commercial Advertiser*, 1891.B41

No heading found, *New York Critic*, 1891.B42

No heading found, *New York Evangelist*, 1893.B33

No heading found, New York *Evening Post*, 1889.B5

No heading found, New York *Evening Post*, 1891.B43

No heading found, New York *Evening Post*, 1892.B21

No heading found, New York *Evening Post*, 1899.B7

No heading found, New York *Evening Post*, 1901.B24

No heading found, New York *Evening Sun*, 1900.B41

No heading found, *New York Herald*, 1890.B34

No heading found, New York *Sun*, 1890.B35

No heading found, New York *Sun*, 1892.B22

No heading found, New York *Sun*, 1892.B23

No heading found, New York *Sun*, 1894.B9

No heading found, New York *Sun*, 1895.B20

No heading found, New York *Sun*, 1897.B16

No heading found, New York *Sun*, 1904.B8

No heading found, New York *Sun*, 1905.B3

No heading found, *New York Tribune*, 1895.B21

No heading found, New York *World*, 1891.B44

No heading found, New York *World*, 1895.B22

No heading found, New York *World*, 1901.B25

No heading found, *Newark Daily Advertiser*, 1890.B36

No heading found, no journal given, 1903.B13

No heading found, no journal given, 1904.B9

No heading found, *Normal School Echo*, 1893.B34

No heading found, *People's Monthly*, 1900.B42

No heading found, *Pittsburgh Chronicle Telegraph*, 1890.B37

No heading found, *Pittsburgh Times*, 1890.B38

INDEX

No heading found, *Portland Advertiser*, 1890.B39

No heading found, *Presbyterian*, 1890.B40

No heading found, *Public Opinion*, 1890.B41

No heading found, *Richmond Hill Record*, 1900.B43

No heading found, *Silver Cross*, 1890.B42

No heading found, *Silver Cross*, 1891.B45

No heading found, *Silver Cross*, 1891.B46

No heading found, *Silver Cross*, 1891.B47

No heading found, *Spirit*, 1891.B48

No heading found, *Springfield Daily Union*, 1890.B43

No heading found, *St. Louis Globe-Democrat*, 1900.B44

No heading found, *St. Louis Republic*, 1890.B44

No heading found, *Sunday School Times*, 1891.B49

No heading found, *Time Nationalist*, 1890.B45

No heading found, *Times-Democrat*, 1891.B50

No heading found, *Union Signal*, 1894.B10

No heading found, *University Review*, 1893.B35

No heading found, *Wellesley Magazine*, 1893.B36

No heading found, *Working Woman*, 1891.B51

"A Notable Silver Wedding," 1901.B26

"Notes," *Nation*, 1894.B11

"Notes," *Nation*, 1901.B27

"Offers Brighton for Park," 1911.B2

"On Tenement-House Life," 1893.B37

"One Minute Biographies," 1930.B1

"The Other Half," Baltimore *Sun*, 1892.B24

"The Other Half," no journal given, 1893.B38

"The 'Other Half's' Champion," 1891.B52

"Our Boys and Girls," 1893.B39

"Our Filthy Thoroughfares," 1893.B40

"Ousted the Trustees," 1892.B25

"The Overcrowded Poor," 1900.B45

"Parks and Play-Grounds," 1897.B17

"Phases of Modern Life," 1892.B26

"Play as Part of an Education," 1897.B18

"Playground for City Children," 1897.B19

"Playgrounds As a Cure for City Crime," 1900.B46

"Playgrounds for City Poor," 1895.B23

"Plenty of Work Ahead," 1896.B10

"The Poor and Their Homes," 1890.B46

"Poor Children," 1894.B12

"Poverty in New York," 1892.B27

"President at Richmond Hill," 1903.B14

"President at Riis's Home," 1903.B15

"President Roosevelt," 1904.B10

Picture entitled "President Roosevelt at Chautauqua," 1904.B11

"President Roosevelt Stops at Richmond Hill," 1903.B16

"President Roosevelt's Ideal Citizen Described by the Citizen Himself in His Remarkable Book 'The Making of an American,'" 1903.B17

"The Press in Social Work," 1912.B2

"The Problem of Destitution," 1890.B47

"The Question of Ready-Made Farms," 1910.B3

"Reform of New York's Morals," 1900.B47

"Regeneration of Our
'Tony,'" 1898.B15
"Remedies for 'Sweating,'"
1891.B53
"Reporter in Slums,"
1900.B48
"Reporter J. A. Riis,"
1891.B54
"A Reporter's Experience,"
1891.B55
"Result of Mr. Riis'
Lecture," 1896.B11
"Rewards of Study Given to
Graduates," 1899.B8
"The Rights of Children,"
1901.B28
"Riis Comes Tonight,"
1900.B49
"Riis' Conquest of the
Slums," 1901.B29
"Riis Gymnasium Opens on
Roosevelt Birthday,"
1906.B4
"Riis Is Called 'My Ideal
Man' by Roosevelt,"
1903.B18
"Riis, Jacob August,"
Harper's Encyclopedia of
United States History from
458 A.D. to 1902, 1902.B2
"Riis, Jacob August,"
National Cyclopaedia of
American Biography,
1906.B5
"Riis, Jacob August," New
Encyclopedia of Social
Reform, 1908.B3
"Riis, Jacob August,"
Twentieth Century Bio-
graphical Dictionary of
Notable Americans, 1904.B12
"Riis, Jacob August," Who
Was Who in America; 1897-
1942, 1943.B2
"Riis, Jacob August," Who's
Who in America; 1899-1900,
1899.B9
"Riis, Jacob August," Who's
Who in America; 1900-1902,
1901.B30

"Riis, Jacob August," Who's
Who in America; 1903-1905,
1903.B19
"Riis, Jacob August," Who's
Who in America; 1906-1907,
1906.B6
"Riis, Jacob August," Who's
Who in America; 1908-1909,
1908.B4
"Riis, Jacob August," Who's
Who in America; 1910-1911,
1910.B4
"Riis, Jacob August," Who's
Who in America; 1912-1913,
1912.B3
"Riis, Jacob August," Who's
Who in America; 1914-1915,
1914.B31
"The Riis Lecture," 1894.B13
"Riis on Play and Playgrounds,"
1908.B5
"Riis on Slums," 1900.B50
"Riis on the Tenement
Problem," 1900.B51
"Riis on Tramp Problem"
1900.B52
"Riis; One of 'Other Half,'"
1900.B53
"Riis Photos Show City's Old
Slums," 1947.B3
"Riis Praises the President,"
1904.B13
"The Riis Silver Wedding,"
1901.B31
"Riis Visits the Slums,"
1900.B54
"Riis Week Proclaimed,"
1949.B5
"Riis's Condition Grave,"
1914.B31
"Riis's Condition Unchanged,"
1914.B32
"Roosevelt Back," 1903.B20
"Roosevelt for Mayor,"
1906.B7
"Roosevelt in 1916," 1914.B33
"Roosevelt Likes Fighting
Men," 1903.B21
"Roosevelt Mourns for Riis,"
1914.B34
"Roosevelt the Man--Roosevelt
the Citizen," 1904.B14

Index

"A Sad Exhibit," 1893.B41

"Saviors of Society,"
1900.B55

"Says the Streets Need
Cleaning," 1893.B42

"Scenes in the Big Tene-
ments," 1897.B20

"School Reform Discussed,"
1894.B14

"Schoolrooms for Clubs,"
1897.B21

"The Seamy Side," 1890.B48

"A Seer," 1914.B35

"Shadows of a Great City,"
1891.B56

"Short Interviews," 1901.B32

"Silver Lake Assembly,"
1892.B28

"Sketches by Riis," 1903.B22

"Slum Battle," 1901.B33

"Slum Boys of New York,"
1898.B16

"Slumming with Mr. Riis,"
1900.B56

"Slums of a Great City,"
1891.B57

"The Slums of New York,"
Churchman, 1893.B43

"Slums of New York,"
Muskegan Morning News,
1901.B34

"The Slums of New York,"
Tribune Republican,
1899.B10

"Small Parks for the Poor,"
1891.B58

"Smashing the Frying-Pan and
'Ice-Water Coolers,'"
1901.B35

"Social Leaders Arrange
Benefits for Several Worthy
Institutions," 1895.B24

"Sociological Work," 1900.B57

"Sociologist at a Dance,"
1901.B36

"Some Tenement Problems,"
1900.B58

"Something to Think About,"
1891.B59

"Songs to Keep Jacob Riis'
Memory Green," 1915.B3

"Spoke of the Slums," 1893.B44

"Squalid Abodes," 1891.B60

"Stories of Slum Life,"
1901.B37

"The Struggle with the Tenement," 1900.B59

"Study Hours by the Lake,"
1891.B61

"A Study of Darkest New York,"
1892.B29

"A Study of Immigrant
Children," 1893.B45

"Sunday at Lakeside," 1892.B30

"The Sweating System,"
1891.B62

"Talk about New Books,"
1891.B63

"Talked on the Tenement House
Problem," 1896.B12

"Talks of the Tenement House,"
1900.B60

"Tammany Versus Decency,"
1901.B38

"Tammany Versus the People,"
1913.B1

"Ten Years' War," *Boston
Daily Advertiser*, 1900.B61

"A Ten Years' War,"
Charities, 1900.B62

"A Ten Years' War," *Holyoke
Transcript*, 1900.B63

"A Ten Years' War," *Literary
Digest*, 1900.B64

"The Tenement Children,"
1895.B25

"Tenement House Boy," 1900.B65

"Tenement-House Children,"
1895.B26

"Tenement House Evil,"
1893.B46

"Tenement House Laror,"
1891.B64

"Tenement House Reform in
New York, 1834-1900,"
1900.B66

"Thanks from Riis Family,"
1914.B36

"That Wretched Other Half,"
1892.B31

"Their Salvation," 1898.B17

"Theodore Roosevelt the Citizen," 1904.B15

"Theodore Roosevelt: the
Man and the Citizen,"
1904.B16
"They Cheered Roosevelt,"
1898.B18
"They Work in the Tenements,"
1896.B13
"To Have a New Party,"
1896.B14
"To Name a Park for Jacob
Riis," 1914.B37
"Tony's Hardships," 1898.B19
"Tour of the Sweatshops,"
1900.B67
"Training of the Youth,"
1900.B68
"Treason," 1891.B65
"Tributes to Riis by Social
Workers," 1914.B38
"Truant Schools Discussed,"
1896.B15
"'Twas Woman's Club Day,"
1895.B27
"Twenty-Five Years and
After," 1907.B2
"The Two Halves of Society,"
1890.B49
"$231,698.81 for the
Neediest," 1925.B1
"Two National Boys' Club
Organizations," 1907.B3
"The Unitarian Club,"
1891.B66
"An Unpleasant Discovery,"
1900.B69
"Useful Mission Work,"
1895.B28
"Want Riis Honored,"
1914.B39
"Want Sunlight in Slums,"
1899.B11
"What if Tony Does Play
Hookey," 1894.B15
"What to Do With the Slums,"
1900.B70
"Why Their Names Are in the
Town Hall," 1923.B1
"A Wicked Four Hundred,"
1890.B50
"Widow Seeks Riis Will,"
1914.B40

"Will It Bear Good Fruit,"
1897.B22
"Wiping Out the New York
Slums," 1898.B20
"Woes of the Poor," 1893.B47
"Women Denounce Vice,"
1901.B39
"Work Among the Poor,"
1895.B29
"Work for Athletes," 1897.B23
"World Has Killed the
Sweatshops," 1898.B21
"'World Is Good, Not Bad'
Says Jacob A. Riis,"
1901.B40
"The Writer of the Poor,"
1893.B48
Arland, Wirt, "Little Children
of the Poor," 1892.B32
Astor, Gerald, The New York Cops;
An Informal History, 1971.B1
Atkins, Gordon, "Health, Housing
and Poverty in New York City,
1865-1898," 1947.B4
Ayres, Phillip W., "The Summer
School in Philanthropic Work,"
1900.B71; "Summer School in
Philanthropy," 1898.B22

Bannister, Robert C., Ray Stannard
Baker; The Mind and Thought of
a Progressive, 1966.B1
Bay, J. Christian, ed., Denmark
in English and American Lit-
erature: A Bibliography
Edited for the Danish Amer-
ican Association, 1915.B4
Bellamy, David G., "Riis, Jacob
August (1849-1914)," 1965.B1
Bigelow, Donald N., "Introduction"
in How the Other Half Lives;
Studies Among the Tenements
of New York, 1957.B1
Bishop, Joseph Bucklin, Theodore
Roosevelt and His Time,
1920.B1
Blue Network Co., "The Making
of an American," 1942.B1
Blumberg, Dorothy Rose, Florence
Kelley; The Making of a
Social Pioneer, 1966.B2

INDEX

Brandes, Joseph and Martin
Douglas, Immigrants to Freedom; Jewish Communities in
Rural New Jersey since 1882,
1971.B2

Bremner, Robert H., "The Big
Flat: History of a New York
Tenement House," 1958.B2;
From the Depths; The Dis-
covery of Poverty in the
United States, 1956.B1

Brisbane, Arthur, "Some Good
Accomplished," 1895.B30

Brooks, Van Wyck, The Confident
Years: 1885-1915, 1952.B1

Brown, Francis J. and Joseph S.
Roucek, eds., One America,
1952.B2

Bruno, Frank, Trends in Social
Work as Reflected in the Proceedings of the National Conference of Social Work, 1874-
1946, 1948.B2

Bruno, Frank J. and Louis Towley,
Trends in Social Work 1874-
1956; A History Based on the
Proceedings of the National
Conference of Social Work,
1957.B2

Buell, George C., "A Man in
Mulberry Street: Jacob A.
Riis and the Awakening of
Social Consciousness in
America (1870-1914)," 1952.B3

Burgess, Charles O., "The Newspaper as Charity Worker: Poor
Relief in New York City, 1893-
1894." 1962.B1

Burton, Margaret E., "A Servant
of the City," 1915.B5

Buttenheim, Harold S., "Jacob
Riis Valiant Foe of the Slum,"
1949.B6

Cady, Joseph Lawrence, "The Containment of Chaos; The Representation of Poverty in
Fiction by Authors Associated
with the Dominant Literary
Culture in Late Nineteenth
Century America," 1968.B1

Caine, Stanley P., "The Origins
of Progressivism," 1974.B2

Calkins, Raymond, Substitutes
for the Saloon, 1919.B1

Campbell, Helen, Knox, Thomas W.,
and Byrnes, Thomas, Darkness
and Daylight; or, Lights and
Shadows of New York Life,
1891.B67

Carlson, Robert A., "Americaniza-
tion as an Early Twentieth-
Century Adult Education
Movement," 1970.B1

Carter, Richard, The Gentle
Legions, 1961.B1

Cary, H. M., "A Modern Book of
Acts II. A Knight in the
Slums--Jacob August Riis,"
1917.B1

Cerillo, Augustus, Jr., "Reform
in New York City: A Study
of Urban Progressivism,"
1969.B1

Charnwood, Lord, Theodore
Roosevelt, 1923.B2

Chessman, G. Wallace, Governor
Theodore Roosevelt; The Albany
Apprenticeship, 1898-1900,
1965.B2; Theodore Roosevelt
and the Politics of Power,
1969.B2

Churchill, Allen, The Roosevelts;
American Aristocrats, 1965.B3

Citizens' Housing and Planning
Council of New York, "The
Story of Jacob A. Riis: A
Dramatic Narration for Radio,"
1949.B7

Cockerell, T. D. A., "Battle with
the Slums," 1903.B23

Community Service Society of New
York, Frontiers in Human Welfare; The Story of a Hundred
Years Service to the Community
of New York, 1848-1948,
1948.B3

Cordasco, Francesco, "Introduction,"
in The Children of the Poor,
1970.B2

Cordasco, Francesco and Salvatore LaGumina, _Italians in the United States: A Bibliography of Reports, Texts, Critical Studies and Related Material_, 1972.B1

Cordasco, Francesco, ed., _Jacob Riis Revisited; Poverty and the Slum in Another Era_, 1968.B2

Craig, Oscar, "Agencies for the Prevention of Pauperism," 1895.B31

Crane, Stephen, "On the Jersey Coast," 1892.B33

Cremin, Lawrence A., _The Transformation of the School; Progressivism in American Education, 1876-1957_, 1961.B2

Curti, Merle, _The Growth of American Thought_, 1943.B3

Cutting, R. Fulton, "President's Report," 1906.B8

Daniels, Jonathan, _They Will Be Heard; America's Crusading Newspaper Editors_, 1965.B4

David, Henry, "Notices and Reviews of Books," 1939.B1

Davis, Allen F., _Spearheads for Reform; The Social Settlements and the Progressive Movement_, 1967.B1

DeForest, Robert W. and Lawrence Vieller, eds., _The Tenement House Problem_, 1903.B24

Destler, Chester McArthur, _Henry Demarest Lloyd and the Empire of Reform_, 1963.B1

Devine, Edward T., "The Making of an American," 1902.B3; "The Shiftless and Floating City Population," 1897.B24; _Social Work_, 1922.B1; _When Social Work Was Young_, 1939.B2

Devins, Rev. John B., "The Children of the Poor," 1893.B49

Dillard Irving, "Six Decades Later," 1973.B1

Doctorow, E. L., _Ragtime_, 1975.B2

Dorf, A. T., "Danish Americans," 1937.B2

Dorn, Jacob Henry, _Washington Gladden; Prophet of the Social Gospel_, 1966.B3

Duffus, R. L., _Lillian Wald, Neighbor and Crusader_, 1938.B1

Dumond, Dwight Lowell, _America in Our Time; 1896-1946_, 1947.B5

Dutton, Edith Kellog, "The Making of an American," 1902.B4

Editors of _Fortune_, _Housing America_, 1932.B1

Editors of _Outlook_, "Preface" to "A Gift of Health," 1906.B9

Einstein, Lewis, _Roosevelt, His Mind in Action_, 1930.B2

Ellis, David M., Frost, James A., Syrett, Harold C., and Carmen, Henry J., _A History of New York State_, 1967.B2

Ellis, Edward Roth, _The Epic of New York City_, 1966.B4

Elsing, William T., "The Autobiography of New York's Most Useful Citizen," 1901.B41

Emery, Edwin and Henry Ladd Smith, _The Press and America_, 1954.B1

F., H., "Talk and Alarm in Europe," 1891.B68

F., J., "Darkest New York," 1890.B51

Faris, John T., "From Carpenter's Apprentice to Philanthropist," 1922.B2

Faulkner, Harold U., _Politics, Reform, and Expansion, 1890-1900_, 1959.B1; _The Quest for Social Justice, 1898-1914_, 1931.B1

Felt, Jeremy P., _Hostages of Fortune; Child Labor Reform in New York State_, 1965.B5

Index

Field, Clara, "Correspondence," 1905.B4

Filler, Louis, Crusaders for American Liberalism; The Story of the Muckrakers, 1939.B3; "Riis, Jacob A.," 1963.B2

Fine, David Martin, "The Immigrant Ghetto in Fiction, 1885-1917," 1969.B3

Fitch, illegible, No heading found, San Francisco Chronicle, 1899.B12

Flower, B. O., Civilization's Inferno; or, Studies in the Social Cellar, 1893.B50; "Some Sidelights of the Tenement House Evil," 1894.B16

Flynn, Clarence, "Jacob A. Riis," 1937.B3

Furer, Howard B., ed. and comp., The Scandinavians in America 986-1970; A Chronology and Fact Book, 1972.B2

Gabriel, Ralph, The Course of American Democratic Thought; An Intellectual History Since 1815, 1940.B1

Gardener, Joseph L., Theodore Roosevelt as ex-President, 1973.B2

Garraty, John A., The New Commonwealth, 1877-1890, 1968.B3

Gartner, Carol Blicker, "A New Mirror for America: The Fiction of the Immigrant of the Ghetto, 1890-1930," 1970.B3

Gernsheim, Helmut with Alison Gernsheim, A Concise History of Photography, 1965.B6; The History of Photography from the Camera Obscura to the Beginning of the Modern Era, 1969.B4

Gilder, Joseph B., "The Making of Jacob A. Riis," 1902.B5

Gilder, Rosamond, ed., Letters of Richard Watson Gilder, 1916.B1

Gillin, John Lewis, Poverty and Dependency; Their Relief and Prevention, 1921.B1

Gilman, Bradley, Roosevelt, the Happy Warrior, 1921.B2

Glaab, Charles N. and A. Theodore Brown, A History of Urban America, 1967.B3

Gladden, George, "Theodore Roosevelt. Two New Books," 1904.B17

Gladden, Washington, Recollections, 1909.B4

Gompers, Samuel, Seventy Years of Life and Labor, 1925.B2

Green, Constance McLaughlin, Washington; Capital City, 1879-1950, 1963.B3

Greer, Rev. Dr., "Sermons of the Day," 1891.B69

Groszmann, Maximilian P. E., "Criminality in Children. II. As to Cures," 1899.B13

Gullason, Thomas Arthur, "The Sources of Stephen Crane's Maggie," 1959.B2

Hagedorn, Hermann, ed., The Americanism of Theodore Roosevelt; Selections from His Writings and Speeches, 1923.B3

Hapgood, Hutchins, "Jacob A. Riis's 'The Making of an American,'" 1902.B6

Harbaugh, William Henry, Power and Responsibility; The Life and Times of Theodore Roosevelt, 1961.B3

Harap, Louis, The Image of the Jew in American Literature; from Early Republic to Mass Immigration, 1974.B3

Harrison, Shelby M., The Social Survey; The Idea Defined and Its Development Traced, 1931.B2

Hartmann, Edward George, The Movement to Americanize the Immigrant, 1948.B4

Henderson, C. R., "The New Books," 1899.B14

Herriot, Frank I., "The Poor in Great Cities," 1896.B15

Higham, John, "Origins of Immigration Restrictions, 1882-1897: A Social Analysis," 1952.B4; Strangers in the Land; Patterns of American Nativism, 1860-1925, 1955.B1

Hodges, Leigh Mitchell, "The Optimist: A Little Look at the Brighter, Better Side," 1903.B25; "Story by Jacob Riis Recalled," 1949.B8

Holden, Arthur C., The Settlement Idea; A Vision of Social Justice, 1922.B3

Holl, Jack M., "The George Junior Republic and the Varieties of Progressive Reform," 1969.B5; Juvenile Reform in the Progressive Era; William R. George and the Junior Republic Movement, 1971.B3

Holmes, John Hayes, "Riis, Jacob August," 1935.B1

Huebner, Grover D., "The Americanization of the Immigrant," 1906.B10

Hughes, Rev. Hugh Price, "Evangelization of Great Cities," 1891.B70

Hull, William I., "The Children of the Other Half," 1897.B25

Hunter, Robert, Poverty, 1904.B18

Huntington, J. O. S., "In Memoriam, Mrs. Jacob A. Riis," 1905.B5; "Jacob Riis Revivalist," 1910.B5

Hurwitz, Howard Lawrence, Theodore Roosevelt and Labor in New York State, 1880-1900, 1943.B4

Husband, Joseph, "Jacob A. Riis," 1920.B2

Jensen, Oskar, Dansk-Amerikaneren Jacob A. Riis, 1924.B1

Johnson, Robert Underwood, Remembered Yesterdays, 1923.B4

Joseph, Samuel, History of the Baron De Hirsch Fund; The Americanization of the Jewish Immigrant, 1935.B2

Josephson, Matthew, The President Makers; The Culture of Politics and Leadership in an Age of Enlightenment, 1896-1916, 1940.B2

Kaplan, Justin, Lincoln Steffens, A Biography, 1974.B3

Kay, Jane Holtz, "Recording the Innocent," 1975.B3

Keefer, Truman Frederick, Ernest Poole, 1966.B5

Kellogg, Paul U., "What Jacob Riis and a Thousand Boys Are Up To: The Opening of the Roosevelt Gymnasium on Henry Street This Week," 1907.B4

Kingsdale, Jon M., "The 'Poor Man's Club': Social Functions of the Urban Working-Class Saloon," 1973.B3

Kinkead, Alexander L., No heading found, Epoch, 1891.B71

Klein, Woody, Let in the Sun, 1964.B1

Kobre, Sidney, Development of American Journalism, 1969.B6

Kouwenhoven, John Atlee, The Columbia Historical Portrait of New York; An Essay in Graphic History in Honor of the Tricentennial of New York City and the Bicentennial of Columbia University, 1953.B1

Landesman, Alter F., Brownsville; The Birth, Development and Passing of a Jewish Community in New York, 1969.B7

Lane, James B., "Bridge to the Other Half: The Life and Urban Reform Work of Jacob A. Riis," 1970.A1; "Jacob A. Riis and Scientific

Philanthropy During the Progressive Era," 1973.B4; Jacob A. Riis and the American City, 1974.A2; "Unmasking Poverty: Jacob A. Riis and How the Other Half Lives," 1971.B4

Lee, Joseph, Constructive and Preventive Philanthropy, 1902.B7

Lens, Sidney, Poverty; America's Enduring Paradox, 1934.B1

Leonard, Priscilla, "The Christmas Stamp in America," 1908.B6

Levine, Daniel, Jane Addams and the Liberal Tradition, 1971.B5

Levine, Jerald Elliot, "Police, Parties, and Polity: The Bureaucratization, Unionization and Professionalization of the New York City Police, 1870-1917," 1971.B6

Lodge, Henry Cabot, "The Restriction of Immigration," 1891.B72; ed., Selections from the Correspondence of Theodore Roosevelt and Henry Cabot Lodge, 1884-1912, 1925.B3

Longworth, Alice Roosevelt, Crowded Hours, 1933.B2

Lorant, Stefan, The Life and Times of Theodore Roosevelt, 1959.B3

Lotz, Charles J., "Jacob Riis--Journalist," 1940.B3

Lubove, Roy, "Introduction," in The Making of an American, 1966.B6; "Lawrence Veiller and the New York State Tenement House Commission," 1961B4; The Progressives and the Slums; Tenement House Reform in New York City, 1890-1917, 1962.B2

McKelvey, Blake, The Urbanization of America, 1860-1915, 1963.B4

McLoughlin, William P., "Evictions in New York's Tenement Houses," 1892.B34

McNutt, George, "Riis's Fight on Slums," 1900.B72

Madison, Charles A., "Preface," in How the Other Half Lives; Studies Among the Tenements of New York, 1971.B7

Mann, Arthur, Yankee Reformers in the Urban Age, 1954.B2

Marcuse, Maxwell F., This Was New York!; A Nostalgic Picture of Gotham in the Gaslight Era, 1965.B7

Marshall, Dexter, "Our New York Letter," 1900.B73

Martin, Jay, Harvests of Change; American Literature, 1865-1914, 1967.B5

Meyer, Edith Patterson, "Not Charity but Justice"; The Story of Jacob A. Riis, 1974.A3

Meyer, Grace M., Once Upon a City: New York from 1890-1910 as Photographed by Byron and Described by Grace M. Meyer, 1958.B3

Meyer, Isidore S., "Book Reviews," 1970.B4

Morris, Lloyd, Incredible New York; High Life and Low Life of the Last Hundred Years, 1951.B1

Morris, Richard B., "The Metropolis of the State," 1937.B4

Moses, Robert, "The Living Heritage of Jacob Riis," 1949.B9

Mott, Frank Luther, A History of American Magazines, 1938.B2

Neidle, Cecyle S., The New Americans, 1967.B4

Nevins, Allan, Abram S. Hewitt: with Some Account of Peter Cooper, 1934.B2; "Introduction," in Jacob A. Riis; Police Reporter, Reformer, Useful Citizen, 1893.B3; "Past, Present and Future," 1948.B5

Newhall, Beaumont, The History
of Photography, from 1839
to the Present Day, 1964.B2
Noble, David, W., The Progressive
Mind, 1890-1917, 1970.B5
Novotny, Ann, Strangers at the
Door; Ellis Island, Castle
Garden, and the Great Migra-
tion to America, 1971.B8

Oakley, Amy, Scandinavia
Beckons, 1938.B4
O'Brien, Frank M., The Story
of the Sun, 1918.B2
Owre, J. Riis, "Genealogy of
the Riis Family," 1939.B4;
"Preface" and "Epilogue,"
in The Making of an American,
1970.B6

P., H. O., No heading found,
Twentieth Century, 1891.B73
Parkman, Mary R., "A Modern
Viking: Jacob Riis,"
1917.B2
Paulding, J. K., "The Public
School as a Center of Com-
munity Life," 1898.B23
Peck, Harry Thurston, "Two Books
about President Roosevelt,"
1904.B19
Perry, Arthur, "Wider Use of the
School Plant," 1911.B3
Phillips, Harlan B., "Walter
Vrooman: Agitator for Parks
and Playgrounds," 1952.B5
Pollack, Peter, The Picture His-
tory of Photography, from
the Earliest Beginnings to
the Present Day, 1958.B4
Poole, Ernest, The Bridge; My
Own Story, 1940.B4
Pryor, James W., "Notes on
Municipal Government,"
1896.B16

Rainsford, W. S., The Story of a
Varied Life; An Autobiography,
1922.B4
Rainwater, Clarence E., The Play
Movement in the United States;

A Study of Community
Recreation, 1921.B3
Ravitch, Diane, The Great School
Wars: New York City, 1805-
1973; A History of the Pub-
lic Schools as Battlefield of
Social Change, 1974.B5
Reviews:
The Battle with the Slum
    Allen, William H., "The
      Battle with the Slum,"
      Annals of the American
      Academy of Political and
      Social Science, 1903.B1
    Anon., "The Battle with the
      Slum," Nation, 1903.B2
    "Battle with the Slum (The),"
      Outlook, 1903.B3
    "Battles with Slums," 1900.B7
    "Books of the Week," 1903.B5
    Cockerell, T. D. A., "Battle
      with the Slums," Dial,
      1903.B23
"The Battle with the Slums"
    Anon., No heading found,
      Charities, 1901.B21
The Children of the Poor
    Anon., "Book of Today,"
      1893.B5
    "The Children of the Poor,"
      Buffalo Christian Advocate,
      1892.B1
    "The Children of the Poor,"
      Christian Register, 1892.B2
    "The Children of the Poor,"
      Christian Union, 1892.B3
    "'The Children of the Poor,"
      Critic, 1892.B4
    "'The Children of the Poor,'"
      Five Points House of
      Industry Report, 1893.B6
    "'The Children of the Poor,'"
      Humanity and Health,
      1893.B7
    "Children of the Poor,"
      London Public Opinion,
      1893.B8
    "The Children of the Poor,"
      Monthly Bulletin of St.
      John's Guild, 1892.B5
    "Children of the Poor," New
      York Evening Sun, 1892.B6

INDEX

"Children of the Poor,"
  San Francisco Chronicle,
  1892.B7
"'The Children of the Poor,'"
  Zion's Herald, 1892.B8
"Citizenship in the Tene-
  ments," 1897.B2
"Heredity and Poverty,"
  1892.B9
"New Books," 1892.B16
"New Publications," 1893.B25
No heading found, *Brooklyn
  Daily Times*, 1892.B18
No heading found, *Farm,
  Field, and Fireside*,
  1892.B19
No heading found, *Indepen-
  dent*, 1892.B20
No heading found, London
  Spectator, 1893.B32
No heading found, New York
  Evening Post, 1892.B21
No heading found, New York
  Sun, 1892.B22
No heading found, *University
  Review*, 1893.B35
"A Study of Immigrant Chil-
  dren," 1893.B45
Devins, Rev. John B., "The
  Children of the Poor,"
  1893.B49
Children of the Tenements
  Anon., "Sketches by Riis,"
  1903.B22
Hero Tales of the Far North
  Anon., "The New Books,"
  1910.B2
"How the Other Half Lives"
  Anon., "How the Other Half
  Lives," 1889.B2
No heading found, *Evangelist*,
  1889.B3
No heading found, London
  Morning Advertiser, 1889.B4
How the Other Half Lives
  Anon., "Book Notices,"
  Silver Cross, 1891.B1
"Book Notices," *Silver Cross*,
  1891.B2
"Books about Four Great
  Cities," 1891.B3

"Booth and Riis," 1890.B2
"Charles Scribner's Son's
  New Books," 1891.B4
"Citizenship in the Tenements,"
  1897.B2
"Darkest New York," 1890.B3
"Editorial Notes," 1891.B8
"How the Other Half Lives,"
  Boston Post, 1890.B5
"How the Other Half Lives,"
  Boston Times, 1890.B6
"How the Other Half Lives,"
  Christian Intelligencer,
  1890.B7
"How the Other Half Lives.
  A Glimpse at Darkest New
  York," 1890.B8
"How the Other Half Lives,"
  illegible source, 1891.B20
"How the Other Half Lives,"
  London *Morning Post*,
  1891.B17
"How the Other Half Lives,"
  Nation, 1891.B18
"How the Other Half Lives,"
  New York *Evening Sun*,
  1890.B10
"How the Other Half Lives,"
  San Francisco Chronicle,
  1890.B12
"How the Other Half Lives,"
  Zion's Herald, 1890.B13
"In the Slums of New York,"
  1892.B11
"In the World of Literature,"
  1890.B14
"Literary Brevities," 1890.B15
"Literature," 1890.B16
"Literature Today," 1891.B24
"Matters We Ought to Know,"
  1891.B26
"New Literature," 1890.B17
"New York and London Con-
  trasted," 1891.B28
"New York Tenements,"
  1891.B29
No heading found, *Argonaut*,
  1890.B18
No heading found, *Boston
  Gazette*, 1890.B20
No heading found, *Boston
  Journal*, 1890.B21

No heading found, *Boston Times*, 1890.B6

No heading found, *Buffalo Express*, 1890.B22

No heading found, *Cambridge Tribune*, 1890.B23

No heading found, Chicago *Inter-Ocean*, 1890.B24

No heading found, *Christian at Work*, 1890.B25

No heading found, *Christian at Work*, 1891.B34

No heading found, *Christian Inquirer*, 1890.B26

No heading found, *Cleveland Leader*, 1890.B27

No heading found, Coventry, England *Mercury*, 1891.B35

No heading found, *Detroit Journal*, 1890.B28

No heading found, *Evangelist*, 1891.B36

No heading found, *Hartford Courant*, 1890.B29

No heading found, *Home Journal*, 1890.B30

No heading found, *Indianapolis News*, 1890.B31

No heading found, *Mail and Express*, 1890.B32

No heading found, *Milwaukee Sentinel*, 1891.B38

No heading found, *Minneapolis Tribune*, 1891.B39

No heading found, *Morning News*, 1890.B33

No heading found, *New England Magazine*, 1891.B40

No heading found, *New York Critic*, 1891.B42

No heading found, New York *Evening Post*, 1891.B43

No heading found, *New York Herald*, 1890.B34

No heading found, New York *Sun*, 1890.B35

No heading found, New York *World*, 1891.B44

No heading found, *Newark Daily Advertiser*, 1890.B36

No heading found, *Pittsburgh Chronicle Telegraph*, 1890.B37

No heading found, *Pittsburgh Times*, 1890.B38

No heading found, *Portland Advertiser*, 1890.B39

No heading found, *Presbyterian*, 1890.B40

No heading found, *Public Opinion*, 1890.B41

No heading found, *Silver Cross*, 1891.B42

No heading found, *Spirit*, 1891.B48

No heading found, *Springfield Daily Union*, 1890.B43

No heading found, *St. Louis Republic*, 1890.B44

No heading found, *Sunday School Times*, 1891.B49

No heading found, *Time Nationalist*, 1890.B45

No heading found, *Working Woman*, 1891.B51

"The 'Other Half's' Champion," 1891.B42

"The Poor and Their Homes," 1890.B46

"The Seamy Side," 1890.B48

"Talk about New Books," 1891.B63

"The Two Halves of Society," 1890.B49

"A Wicked Four Hundred," 1890.B50

Bigelow, Donald N., "Introduction," in How the Other Half Lives; Studies Among the Tenements of New York, 1957.B1

Cady, Joseph Lawrence, "The Containment of Chaos; The Representation of Poverty in Fiction by Authors Associated with the Dominant Literary Culture in Late Nineteenth Century America," 1968.B1

F., H., "Talk and Alarm in Europe," 1891.B68

F., J., "Darkest New York," 1890.B51

Index

Kinkead, Alexander L., No heading found, *Epoch*, 1891.B71

Madison, Charles A., "Preface," in How the Other Half Lives; Studies Among the Tenements of New York, 1971.B7

P., H. O., No heading found, *Twentieth Century*, 1891.B73

Warner, Sam Bass, Jr., "Editor's Introduction," in How the Other Half Lives; Studies Among the Tenements of New York, 1970.B11

"How to Bring Work and Workers Together"

Anon., No heading found, *Boston Herald*, 1894.B9

No heading found, *Union Signal*, 1894.B11

Is There a Santa Claus?

Anon., "Is There a Santa Claus?," 1904.B3

The Making of an American

Anon., "Autobiography of an Immigrant," 1902.B1

"Casual Comment," 1914.B2

"Jacob Riis His Text," 1903.B12

"The Making of an American," 1901.B14

"Mr. Riis's Autobiography," 1901.B17

"Notes," 1901.B27

"President Roosevelt's Ideal Citizen Described by the Citizen Himself in His Remarkable Book 'The Making of an American,'" 1903.B17

Devine, Edward T., "The Making of an American," 1902.B3

Dutton, Edith Kellog, "The Making of an American," 1902.B4

Gilder, Joseph B., "The Making of Jacob A. Riis," 1902.B5

Hapgood, Hutchins, "Jacob A. Riis's 'The Making of an American,'" 1902.B6

"The Making of Thieves in New York"

Anon., "Notes," 1894.B8

"Making a Way Out of the Slum"

Anon., "Lights and Shadows of Slum Life in New York," 1904.B5

"Making a Way Out of the Slum," 1901.B13

"Midwinter in New York"

Anon., "Lights and Shadows of Slum Life in New York," 1904.B5

Nibsy's Christmas

Anon., "Book Notices," 1893.B4

"New Publications," 1893.B26

"Nibsy's Christmas," *Boston Times*, 1893.B28

"Nibsy's Christmas," *New York Evangelist*, 1893.B29

No heading found, *Boston Gazette*, 1893.B30

"Our Boys and Girls," 1893.B39

The Old Town

Anon., "The New Book," 1909.B2

"Literary Notes," 1909.B3

Out of Mulberry Street

Anon., "Miscellaneous," 1898.B12

Fitch, illegible, No heading found, *San Francisco Chronicle*, 1899.B12

Henderson, C. R., "The New Books," 1899.B14

A Ten Years' War

Anon., "Among the New Books," 1900.B1

"Chronicle and Comment," 1900.B11

Illegible title, illegible source, 1900.B22

"Jacob Riis' Epic of the Slums," 1900.B27

No heading found, *Churchman*, 1900.B39

No heading found, *Detroit Free Press*, 1900.B40
No heading found, New York *Evening Sun*, 1900.B41
No heading found, *People's Monthly*, 1900.B42
No heading found, *St. Louis Globe-Democrat*, 1900.B44
"Ten Years' War," *Boston Daily Advertiser*, 1900.B61
"A Ten Years' War," *Charities*, 1900.B62
"A Ten Years' War," *Holyoke Transcript*, 1900.B63
"A Ten Years' War," *Literary Digest*, 1900.B64
Sill, Henry A., "A Ten Years' War," 1901.B43
Stoddard, Richard Henry, "Literature," 1900.B74
Theodore Roosevelt the Citizen
  Anon., "President Roosevelt," 1904.B10
  "Roosevelt the Man--Roosevelt the Citizen," 1904.B14
  "Theodore Roosevelt the Citizen," 1904.B15
  "Theodore Roosevelt: the Man and the Citizen," 1904.B16
  Gladden, George, "Theodore Roosevelt. Two New Books," 1904.B17
  Peck, Harry Thurston, "Two Books about President Roosevelt," 1904.B19
  Rice, Wallace, "President Roosevelt as a Hero," 1904.B20
Reynolds, Marcus T., The Housing of the Poor in American Cities, 1893.B51
Rezneck, Samuel, "Unemployment, Unrest, and Relief in the United States during the Depression of 1893-97," 1953.B2
Rice, Wallace, "President Roosevelt as a Hero," 1904.B20

Riis, Roger William, "Foreword" in Jacob A. Riis; Police Reporter, Reformer, Useful Citizen, 1938.B5; "The Most Unforgettable Character I've Met," 1942B2; "My Father," 1938.B6; "Worms for Bait," 1927.B1
Rischin, Moses, The Promised City; New York's Jews, 1870-1914, 1962.B3
Robbins, Jane E., "A Maker of Americans," 1914.B41
Rogers, "A 'Jacob A. Riis Park,'" 1914.B42
Rogers, James Edward, The Child and Play, 1932.B2
Roosevelt, Theodore, "Administering the New York Police Force," 1897.B26; An Autobiography, 1913.B2; "Introduction," in The Making of an American, 1919.B2; "Jacob Riis," 1914.B43; Letters from Theodore Roosevelt to Anna Roosevelt Cowles, 1870-1918, 1924.B2; The Letters of Theodore Roosevelt; The Big Stick, 1905-1907, 1952.B6; The Letters of Theodore Roosevelt; The Big Stick, 1907-1909, 1952.B7; The Letters of Theodore Roosevelt; The Days of Armageddon, 1914-1919, 1954.B3; The Letters of Theodore Roosevelt; The Days of Armageddon, 1909-1914, 1954.B4; The Letters of Theodore Roosevelt; The Square Deal, 1901-1903, 1951.B2; The Letters of Theodore Roosevelt; The Square Deal, 1903-1905, 1951.B3; The Letters of Theodore Roosevelt; The Years of Preparation, 1898-1900, 1951.B4; The Letters of Theodore Roosevelt; The Years of Preparation, 1868-1898, 1951.B5; Letters to Kermit from Theodore Roosevelt, 1902-1908, 1946.B1;

INDEX

"Municipal Administration:
The New York Police Force,"
1897.B27; "The New York
Police," 1913.B3; "Police
Department," 1896.B17;
"Reform through Social Work.
Some Forces that Tell for
Decency in New York City,"
1901.B42

Scheiner, Seth M., "The New York
City Negro and the Tenement,"
1964.B3
Schlesinger, Arthur M., The
American as Reformer,
1950.B1; The Rise of the
City, 1878-1898, 1933.B3
Sill, Henry A., "A Ten Years'
War," 1901.B43
Simkovitch, Mary Kingsbury,
Here is God's Plenty; Reflec-
tions on American Social Ad-
vance, 1949.B10; Neighborhood;
My Story of Greenwich House,
1938.B7
Skardal, Dorothy Burton, The
Divided Heart, 1974.B6
Skolnik, Richard, "Civic Group
Progressivism in New York
City," 1970.B7
Smith, William Carlson, Americans
in the Making; The Natural
History of the Assimilation
of Immigrant, 1939.B5
Steffens, Lincoln, The Autobiog-
raphy of Lincoln Steffens,
1931.B3; "Jacob A. Riis:
Reporter, Reformer, American
Citizen," 1903.B26
Still, Bayrd, Mirror for Gotham;
New York as Seen by Contem-
poraries from Dutch Days to
the Present, 1956.B2
Stinson, John D., "The Papers of
Jacob A. Riis and of the
Jacob A. Riis Neighborhood
Settlement in the New York
Public Library," 1970.B8
Stoddard, Richard Henry,
"Literature," 1900.B74

Stoy, Elinor H., "Child-Labor,"
1906.B11
Sullivan, Mark, Our Times; The
Turn of the Century, 1926.B1
Swett, Steven C., "The Test of a
Reformer: A Study of Seth
Low, New York City's Mayor,
1902-1903," 1960.B1

Tenement-House Committee of 1894,
Report of the Tenement-House
Committee of 1894, 1895.B32
Thayer, William Roscoe, Theodore
Roosevelt; An Intimate
Biography, 1919.B3
Thomas, Lately, The Mayor Who
Mastered New York; The Life
& Opinions of William J.
Gaynor, 1969.B8
Tolman, William Howe and
William I. Hull. Handbook of
Sociological Information with
Especial Reference to New
York City, 1894.B17
Trattner, Walter I., Crusade for
the Children; A History of
the National Child Labor
Committee and Child Labor
Reform in America, 1970.B9;
Homer Folks; Pioneer in Social
Welfare, 1968.B4
Trenor, J. D., "Proposals Affect-
ing Immigration," 1904.B21
Tripp, Wendell, "Recent Publica-
tions," 1973.B5

Vecoli, Rudolph, "Introduction,"
in The Children of the Poor,
1970.B10

Wade, Mary, "Jacob Riis," 1916.B2
Wagenknecht, Edward, The Seven
Worlds of Theodore Roosevelt,
1958.B5
Wald, Lillian D., The House on
Henry Street, 1915.B6; Win-
dows on Henry Street, 1934.B3
Ware, Louise, Jacob A. Riis;
Police Reporter, Reformer,
Useful Citizen, 1938.A1

Warner, Sam Bass, Jr., "Editor's Introduction," in How the Other Half Lives; Studies Among the Tenements of New York, 1970.B11

Waterman, Mrs. John Barnett, " "The Poor White Boy of the South: The Mobile Boys' Club," 1907.B5

Watson, Frank Dekker, The Charity Organization Movement in the United States; A Study in American Philanthropy, 1922.B5

Weinstein, Gregory, Reminiscences of an Interesting Decade; The Ardent Eighties, 1928.B1

Weiss, Margret R., "The Formidable Frances B. Johnston," 1975.B4

Whisnant, David E., "Selling the Gospel News, or: The Strange Career of Jimmy Brown the Newsboy," 1972.B3

Wiebe, Robert H., Businessmen and Reform; A Study of the Progressive Movement, 1962.B4; The Search for Order, 1877-1920, 1967.B6

Winship, A. E., "Jacob Riis," 1914.B44; "Roxy and Timon of Hester St.," 1913.B4

Wise, William, The Story of Mulberry Bend, 1963.B5

Wittke, Carl, We Who Built America; The Saga of the Immigrant, 1946.B2

Workers of the Federal Writers' Union Project, Works Progress Administration in the City of New York, The Italians of New York; A Survey, 1938.B8

Ziff, Larzer, The American 1890s; Life and Times of a Lost Generation, 1966.B7